COMPARATIVE GOVERNMENT AND POLITICS

Published

Maura Adshead and Jonathan Tonge
Politics in Ireland

Rudy Andeweg and Galen A. Irwin
Governance and Politics of the Netherlands (3rd edition)

Tim Bale
European Politics: A Comparative Introduction (2nd ed

Nigel Bowles
Government and Politics of the United S

Paul Brooker
Non-Democratic Regimes (2nd edition)

Kris Deschouwer
The Politics of Belgium

Robert Elgie
Political Leadership in Liberal Democracies

Rod Hague and Martin Harrop
* Comparative Government and Politics: An Introduction (7th edition)

Paul Heywood
The Government and Politics of Spain

Xiaoming Huang
Politics in Pacific Asia

B. Guy Peters
Comparative Politics: Theories and Methods
(Rights: World excluding North America)

Tony Saich
Governance and Politics of China (2nd edition)

Anne Stevens
Government and Politics of France (3rd edition)

Ramesh Thakur
The Government and Politics of India

Forthcoming

Tim Haughton and Datina Malová
Government and Politics of Central and Eastern Europe

Robert Leonardi
Government and Politics in Italy

* Published in North America as **Political Science: A Comparative Intoduction (5th edition)**

Comparative Government and Politics
Series Standing Order
ISBN 0–333–71693–0 hardback
ISBN 0–333–69335–3 paperback
(outside North America only)

You can receive future titles in this series as they are published by placing a standing order. Please contact your bookseller or, in the case of difficulty, write to us at the address below with your name and address, the title of the series and one of the ISBNs quoted above.

Customer Services Department, Macmillan Distribution Ltd
Houndmills, Basingstoke, Hampshire RG21 6XS, England

The Politics of Belgium

Governing a Divided Society

Kris Deschouwer

First published 2009 by
PALGRAVE MACMILLAN

Palgrave Macmillan in the UK is an imprint of Macmillan Publishers Limited, registered in England, company number 785998, of Houndmills, Basingstoke, Hampshire RG21 6XS.

Palgrave Macmillan in the US is a division of St Martin's Press LLC, 175 Fifth Avenue, New York, NY 10010.

Palgrave Macmillan is the global academic imprint of the above companies and has companies and representatives throughout the world.

Palgrave® and Macmillan® are registered trademarks in the United States, the United Kingdom, Europe and other countries.

ISBN-13: 978–0–230–21814–7   hardback
ISBN-13: 978–0–230–21815–4   paperback

This book is printed on paper suitable for recycling and made from fully managed and sustained forest sources. Logging, pulping and manufacturing processes are expected to conform to the environmental regulations of the country of origin.

A catalogue record for this book is available from the British Library.

A catalog record for this book is available from the Library of Congress.

10 9 8 7 6 5 4 3 2 1
18 17 16 15 14 13 12 11 10 09

Printed and bound in Great Britain by
CPI Antony Rowe, Chippenham and Eastbourne

Contents

List of Figures and Tables

Figures

Tables

Chapter 1

Why Belgium?

Who needs Belgium?

After a period of relative stability, during which four consecutive governments between 1991 and 2007 went to the very end of their four-year mandate, 2007 marked the beginning of a new period of instability and gridlock. The formation of a federal coalition after the elections of June 2007 appeared to be a difficult and painful enterprise. Only half a year later a new government took the oath, but that was only a transition government which was replaced three months later. And that new government was gone after nine months.

These events of 2007 and 2008 fuelled quite radical thoughts about Belgium and about its political future. Comments in the international press suggested that it was time for Belgium to call it a day, to end the suffering and to split the country up between the Dutch-speakers of the north (Flanders) and the French-speakers of the south (Wallonia). 'Who needs Belgium?' asked *The Economist*.

And in Belgium too the newspapers and discussion programmes on radio and television had been voicing strong opinions about the future of Belgium ranging from splitting it up between France and the Netherlands over the creation of an independent Flanders and a smaller Belgium composed of Wallonia and Brussels to the fierce and emotional defence of the survival of the country. Voices defending a final post-Belgium solution were stronger in Flanders. Voices defending Belgium were stronger in the south and in Brussels, where surprisingly large numbers of inhabitants appeared to have a Belgian flag to hang out of their window.

The flags have long gone back to the cupboards. And Belgium has not called it a day. Some hope and some fear that it may happen sooner or later. Others believe that the country has grown far too old to be torn apart into bits and pieces that only make sense as long as they belong together.

1

The question whether someone needs Belgium and why one would need it is not easy to answer. But that is probably the case for most countries in the world. They happen to be on the map as a result of events and decisions that might possibly have been different but that define and mark the very existence and meaning of a country. In this chapter and further in this book we will show and explain how and why Belgium is quite an interesting country.

Obviously it is not its size that makes it remarkable. Belgium is indeed a small country. It covers only 32,500 square kilometres and has 10.5 million inhabitants. That is hardly more than in metropolitan Paris or Greater London. It holds 22 of the 785 seats in the European Parliament, or less than 3 per cent of the total number. Yet in the context of the European Union Belgium is more than just a small country. One could almost say that Belgium's capital city Brussels simply is the European Union. Brussels is where the important political meetings are organized. Brussels is where the Commission has its headquarters. And Belgian politicians are quite visible in the European Union, although they have also sometimes missed a few opportunities to become really big in Europe.

Former Prime Minister Dehaene had strongly impressed his colleagues with the way in which he had chaired the Union in 1993. He was a man who could succeed to Jacques Delors as the president of the Commission. His very outspoken pro-European position did, however, not please British Prime Minister John Major who vetoed Dehaene's candidacy in 1994.

Former Prime Minister Guy Verhofstadt is another famous warrior for a stronger and more integrated Europe. During the Belgian presidency in 2001 he convinced the European leaders to issue the 'Declaration of Laeken' (location of the royal palace in Brussels), calling for a convention to make the European institutions better performing and more transparent and democratic. French former president Valery Giscard-D'Estaing formally chaired the convention, with the more than active assistance of former Italian Prime Minister Giuliano Amato and, again, the Belgian Jean-Luc Dehaene. The Constitutional Treaty that resulted from the convention was never ratified, but that did not temper Verhofstadt's ambitions. He tried to become president of the Commission in 2004, but failed. He published a few years later a rather provocative booklet entitled *The United States of Europe* (Verhofstadt, 2006). It defends a truly federal Europe, and goes far beyond what is acceptable to many other European leaders.

Belgium's colonial past in central Africa is another element that makes it more visible once in a while. It gives it the ambition to be an active player in the difficult and painful processes of state building and peace building in Congo, Rwanda and Burundi. Its colonial past in that area does give it the experience and expertise to play a meaningful role, but that same colonial past sometimes turns Belgium into a disturbing and not fully accepted partner in the former colony. Belgian UN troops were in Rwanda when the genocide started in 1994 and they were immediately caught in the action. Ten of them were killed, which led to the decision not to participate in military peacekeeping operations in the old colonies any more.

It is thus not primarily its relevance on the international, the European or the African scene that makes Belgium an interesting country to look at. It deserves attention though for its domestic politics. Belgium does not feature in many political science handbooks or in handbooks of comparative politics. Here also the larger countries and important world powers seem at first sight more interesting to look at. And yet there is much to be said about what is going on inside that little country. It is an interesting example of a number of political developments and choices that deserve closer attention. If one wants to understand the origins and working principles of a consociational democracy, Belgium is a good place to start. It is therefore also an interesting example of a segmented society, of pillarization and of strongly developed neo-corporatist interest mediation. It is a real 'partitocracy', a system with a strong and central position for the political parties that are present in and control almost all aspects of policymaking. If one wants to unravel the logic of a federal state that came into being after a process of decentralization and devolution, Belgium is a good choice. If one wants to witness the impact of the world economy on a small country and the way in which a small country deals with increasing economic globalization, Belgium is the right place to be. If one wants to understand how a deeply divided country can survive but also constantly put itself into question, Belgium is good destination.

Consociational democracy

What is remarkable about Belgium is not that it is a culturally divided society – most of the countries in the contemporary worlds are divided into separate and distinct cultural, religious, or ethnic communities – but that its cultural communities coexist peacefully and democratically. What is more, Belgium can legitimately claim to be the most thorough example of consociational democracy, the type of democracy that is most suitable for deeply divided societies. (Lijphart, 1981b: 1)

The most thorough example is – according to Lijphart – also a very young example, only in place since 1970. He refers then clearly to the way in which the relations between the language groups have been pacified. The first publications on the working principles and the conditions of consociational democracy in a number of countries – including Belgium – did however look back at a much older practice (Lijphart, 1969; Huyse, 1971; Andeweg, 2000). The reason for including Belgium in the category of consociational democracies was then not the way in which relations between the language groups were organized but the way in which Belgian democracy could survive despite deep religious and economic divisions. Belgium was seen as a *segmented society* (Lorwin, 1966; 1974a; 1974b). This segmentation refers to the existence of a dense network of organizations belonging to the same subculture and almost fully encapsulating its members. Memberships of organizations belonging to the same network are thus overlapping. The population is neatly divided into separate worlds. The segments or 'pillars' of society (Rokkan, 1977; Billiet, 1982; Hellemans, 1990; Andeweg & Urwin, 2005) provide their members with a variety of services, from the cradle to the grave.

Societies displaying these deep and institutionalized division lines have a more vulnerable democracy. The deep divisions create a strong centrifugal logic because parties representing the segments in the electoral arena mobilize and support demands for which a common response is difficult to find. Consociational democracy is then a set of practices that allow divided and segmented societies to survive. The basic practices are *power sharing* between the elites of the segments and *segmental autonomy*. The latter allows each segment to organize its life and world according to its own principles, and it takes away the need for a common policy that fits all subcultures. Granting and organizing segmental autonomy further reinforces the segmentation, by giving organizations of the pillar network the means to offer state-sponsored services – like education or healthcare – to their members.

Belgium does indeed fit nicely into this crude description of a typical consociational democracy. Its origins can be traced back to the end of the First World War. At that time it had become quite clear that a number of pressing problems were lying on the table. Disagreements between the Catholic Church and its organizations on the one hand and defenders of a lay society on the other hand had already led to harsh conflicts about the way in which the Belgian school system could be organized. The growing labour movement had also claimed better wages and work conditions and especially the right to vote. The latter had been granted in a limited way in 1893, and that was enough to bring to the fore a strong Workers' party built on the network of organizations of the labour movement. The introduction of proportional representation in 1900 made it even stronger.

In 1918 King Albert I decided to bring together the leaders of the three political parties – Catholics, socialists and liberals – to discuss the way in which the country would deal with these deep and organized divisions. One of the important decisions was to introduce universal male suffrage immediately for the first postwar elections, even if the constitution did not allow for it. This 'Pact of Loppem' (referring to the location of the castle where the King had invited the party elites) can be considered as the starting point of Belgian consociationalism. It introduced the practice that whenever really important matters have to be decided upon, the party leaders of the major societal movements try to find a common agreement. And that agreement comprises a mix of subtle compromising for common policies and further granting of autonomy to the segments for policies and services.

Giving the societal segments the right to organize their own services with state subsidies was already a common practice towards the turn of the century and was very much the result of the large impact of the Catholic party at that time. Rather than opting for a direct role of the state, it encouraged a free initiative in the social sector. Health insurance and pensions were offered by private companies who received subsidies from the state. When the Workers' party became stronger it did not deviate from that logic and organized, for instance, state subsidies for trade unions paying unemployment money to their members (Luyten, 2006). The development of the welfare state with its system of social security after the Second World War has then further contributed to the strengthening and survival of the pillar organizations.

The Catholics and the socialists thus created and incorporated a whole range of auxiliary organizations that formed two solid pillars. The Catholic pillar has always had the Church at its centre. It contains a wide variety of organizations that label themselves Catholic or Christian. The Catholic schools are an important part of it and the defence of the Catholic schools in the late 19th century was one of the important catalysts for the building of a solid Catholic network of organizations. It further includes hospitals, homes for the elderly, youth and sports organizations, banks and insurance companies and a wide range of professional organizations for farmers, industrial workers, civil servants and employers, with many of them also having their own women's organization.

The socialist pillar is, from its very beginnings, much more a party-related pillar. It has no school system, but defends the public state-funded schools together with the Liberal party and pillar. The socialist pillar is simply the network of organizations linked to the socialist labour movement and held together by the Socialist party.

There is also a much smaller liberal pillar. The Liberal party is indeed not built on a mass movement. There was never the need to unite the movement in strong and mutually linked organizations in order to gain or retain power. The party however did build links with a number of liberal auxiliary organizations including a (smaller) liberal trade union, a liberal health insurance organization and many liberal cultural and philosophical organizations.

The segmentation and pillarization of Belgium is thus built on both religious and social and economic cleavages. Yet the third Belgian cleavage – the division into two language groups – plays a crucial role in the way in which the pillars can function. The Pact of Loppem also had to discuss the demands voiced in the north of the country to have the Dutch language fully recognized as a second official language of the country. Indeed, in 1830 Belgium had, de facto, opted for French only as the official language. Actually the constitution simply states that the use of language is free. At that time, however, that meant that French would be used, since that was the language spoken by the Belgian elite. And while the principle of freedom of the use of language remains in the constitution, the practice is thus different. From 1918 on a territorial solution for the use of language was gradually put into place, and the granting of universal male suffrage after the First World War also gave the demographic majority of the Dutch-speakers more of a say. From 1918 on the problem of the use of language was here to stay.

Yet the differences between north and south are not limited to the use of language. And these further differences are translated very clearly in the organization of the pillars. The Catholic pillar was very strong in Flanders, where indeed the vast majority of the population was Catholic and voted for the party political exponent of the pillar. The Socialist party was very strong in the industrial areas of Wallonia, where it rapidly became the overwhelmingly dominant political force. The socialist pillar was thus very strong in Wallonia and quite weak in Flanders. The liberal pillar was weak in both regions. Today these pillars are less important and less integrated than in the early 20th century, but the pillar organizations are still very visible and do play a role in political decision-making (see Chapter 8 for more details).

The first experience with consociational logic in 1918 did, however, not mean that power sharing between the three parties and their pillars became the normal and daily practice. The Socialist party remained for a few more decades a less 'traditional' government partner. The full entrance of the Socialist party was realized during and immediately after the Second World War. The development of the welfare state and of its social security system gave the socialist pillar – especially its trade unions – a secured place in the management of social and economic policies.

The consociational techniques were again used in the 1950s, but only after a number of deep crises where attempts were made by the Catholic movement and then by a coalition of liberals and socialists to really 'win' the battle in a purely majoritarian way. The awareness that the majoritarian strategy would be very disruptive for the country in the end brought the elites of the three parties and movements back to the negotiating table for a consociational compromise. The 1950s in Belgium are a nice illustration of the 'self-denying prophecy' identified by Lijphart as one of the mechanisms through which divided societies learn that majoritarian devices should be replaced by consociational techniques (Lijphart, 1969; 1977). Confrontation with the devastating effects of a majoritarian strategy convinced the political elite to change the rules of the game.

The first crisis occurred in 1950, when a referendum was organized to decide whether King Leopold III – who was not in the country when it was liberated from German occupation – could come back to the country and to the throne. The issue had been poisoning political debate since the end of the war and divided the political landscape into two camps. On the one side there were the Christian democrats who wanted the King to come back. On the other were the socialists and the liberals (and the communists) who believed that the decisions taken by the King under the German occupation did not allow him to return to the throne. The referendum – a purely majoritarian technique – produced a 'yes' vote of 57 per cent. But the unequal territorial strength of the two camps meant that the majority had been produced in the north of the country, while Brussels and (most places in) Wallonia had voted against the return of the King. The King did come back but after violent riots, with three people killed, the elites of the three large political movements got together and convinced King Leopold III to leave the throne for his son Beaudoin. The winning of the referendum by the Catholic movement had proved to be only an illustration of the fact that majority is not the best decision-making device in a divided country (Stengers, 1980; Luyckx, 1985; Mabille, 1986; Dumoulin et al., 2006; 2007).

Between 1950 and 1958 first the Christian democrats governed alone and when they lost power, an anti-Catholic coalition of socialists and liberals was formed. It tried to promote the state-sponsored secondary schools to the detriment of the Catholic school network. Massive protest by the Catholic pillar did however put an end to yet another attempt to play a majoritarian game. A 'School Pact' was concluded in 1958, accepting once and for all the presence of both private (that is, Catholic) schools and of schools organized by the public authorities (Tyssens, 1997). This is again a copybook example of the granting of segmental autonomy – let both have the schools of their choice – as a device that avoids the need for one policy for all.

The working and evolution of consociational democracy in a country that fits very nicely the patterns described (and prescribed) by consociational theory makes the study of Belgian politics worthwhile. The relevance is not only in the historical developments, but also and even more in the consequences of them for the current functioning of the political system. The cleavages on which the pillarized organization of Belgian society was built have now been deeply eroded. Yet the weight of the three old political parties – even if they are today all split up along the language divide – is still considerable. Their grip on government, parliament and public administration is deep and solid. Social and economic policies and the management of the welfare state and the social security system are largely devolved to Christian, social-ist and liberal pillar organizations. The consociational responses to the old societal divisions have been deeply institutionalized. The old pillar organizations have become part of the state and remain strong and rich thanks to the state. The consociational democracy has been transformed into a 'depoliticized' or 'cartel' democracy, where the practices of consociational democracy are continued in a society that no longer needs these pacifying and protecting devices (Lijphart, 1977). A depoliticized democracy is likely to be challenged, to be questioned for its lack of debate and flexibility, for its lack of performance. Political movements criti-cizing the principle of consociational power sharing, with its blatant lack of alternation in power, might find fertile ground in old consociational democracies. In Austria the grand coalition between the socialist SPÖ and the Christian-democratic ÖVP was one of the targets of the populist movement FPÖ led by Jorg Haider. Forming that coalition time after time even if both parties lost at the polls made it quite easy to question the true demo-cratic nature of consociational Austria (Luther & Müller, 1992). In the Netherlands the elitist and closed nature of the system was one of the central criticisms of D66 in the 1960s and even more fiercely so of the Lijst (List) Pim Fortuyn in 2002 (Pennings & Keman, 2003). Belgium is – like Austria and the Netherlands – another place for watching this type of challenge to the very heart of the system.

Some kind of federal state

In 1993 Belgium wrote into its constitution that it was now a federal state. By entering the family of federal states Belgium has further stretched the meaning of the concept. Its political institu-tions do indeed display a combination of self-rule and shared rule, but the way in which this is organized differs markedly from the classic federations like the United States, Canada or Australia (Watts, 1999).

Belgium is typically a 'holding together' federation (Stepan, 1999), a federal-type system that came into being after a process of devolution and not of 'bringing together' existing entities. The enti-ties that together form the Belgian federation have not even a history of their own. They have no history that is older than

Belgium. It is the creation of Belgium and the choice of French as the official working language that have created a Dutch or Flemish linguistic identity and francophone responses to it. That debate about the use and the place of language has been settled in a more or less territorial way, which resulted after many piecemeal changes and adaptations in something that can be labelled a federation.

Like several other European countries, the Belgian state has been territorially reorganized to respond to societal demands for more autonomy. Similar changes have occurred in Spain, the UK, Italy and, to a lesser extent, France. Each of these countries has put into place its own particular response to the demands for autonomy. Like the consociational democracy that preceded it, the federal solution for Belgium is an attempt to deal with societal conflicts, to deal with diverging definitions of the country and with diverging demands for the way in which it could be reorganized. The federal solution is not the result of a blueprint. It is not the result of a deliberate choice. It is – as was consociational democracy – just the result of attempts to deal with divisions that might be or become disruptive.

Analysing the consequences of the newly installed federation is therefore very relevant. Since 1995 the political actors in Belgium have been looking for a way to adapt to the new institutional context. They have to organize the process of party political representation at two levels: this involves learning to deal with different electoral cycles and with the impact of election results and coalition formation at one level, and on the functioning of the coalition at the other level. The Belgian political actors – the parties in the first place – have been forced to adapt to this new multi-layered political environment in the absence of statewide parties, with parties mobilizing only on their own side of the language divide. That has so far not produced a very transparent or elegant picture.

The overall performance of the new federal system also shows quite mixed results. The state reform has increased government stability, but the discussions about the further functioning of the federal state have revealed views that are certainly not easier to deal with or to respond to. Interestingly, the federal state has built in a number of very strong consociational devices. Along with the neat separation of the two linguistic segments of society, the constitution requires the elites of both language groups to share power at the central level. The Belgian federation can only function if a minimal level of consensus is found between the two language groups. This puts pressure on their elites to find common solutions, but also builds in strong veto powers that can easily block all processes of decision-making. The very response to societal demands for autonomy – a federal state – seems to have created new difficulties in dealing with societal divisions.

Demands for further autonomy are voiced in Flanders, the now more prosperous region of federal Belgium. That is another quite striking and interesting feature. Like in Catalonia, the Basque country or Scotland, regions with a strong identity that have received far-reaching autonomy keep asking for more. It raises the very general question of whether territorial autonomy and federal-type solutions are an adequate way to ease the tensions in societies divided along identity lines. A deeper understanding of the way in which this functions in Belgium can be useful for a deeper understanding of that more general problem of democratic governance (Gagnon et al., 2003; O'Flynn & Russell, 2005; Norris, 2008).

Trust and support

Declining trust in politics is a theme that has been around for a few decades (see, for example, Pharr & Putnam, 2000). Mature democracies are confronted with feelings of disenchantment and acts of disengagement. Declining voter turnout, declining membership numbers of parties and the rise and success of anti-establishment parties can all be used and are all used as indicators of a crisis of representative democracy.

This is a universal debate that can also be witnessed in Belgium. Interestingly, the alleged problems of trust and the suggestions to remedy them are a good way to explore the core characteristics of the Belgian political system. These are indeed identified as the sources of malfunctioning that need to be removed to recreate the necessary support for the political system.

In 1990 the leader of the Flemish liberals and later prime minister Guy Verhofstadt published a pamphlet entitled *The citizen's manifesto* (Burgermanifest). It started with the simple statement that there was a deep and dangerous gap between politics and politicians and the citizens. He defended more possibilities for direct citizen participation. His analysis of the Belgian system was devastating. He saw it as closed and largely controlled by the

Catholic and socialist pillar organizations dividing it up between them. A leaner state, a true market-oriented management of the public administration, the removal of privileges for the pillar organizations and the introduction of forms of direct democracy were his basic ingredients for the recovery of the seriously ill patient called Belgium.

At the elections following the publication of this manifesto, it was not the Liberal party but a populist radical-right party, Vlaams Blok, that emerged as the surprising winner. It had already scored well at the local elections in Antwerp, challenging a coalition between Christian democrats and socialists that had been in power since 1921. At the federal level the outgoing coalition was the same, and it was formed again – be it not easily – after the 1991 elections and once more after the 1995 elections.

But the 1991 elections clearly marked the beginning of the debates about what was wrong with democracy in Belgium. The next two decades show a mix of a number of scandals and clear examples of the malfunctioning of the public authorities and a number of attempts at reforming the functioning of the state. In 1991, when the former Socialist party president and former minister André Cools was murdered, the investigation of the murder revealed, among other things, illicit party finance and deep encroachment of the Parti Socialiste into the state apparatus. In other parties too suspicious flows of money were discovered. And 1996 saw the failure to arrest Marc Dutroux who had kidnapped young girls and kept them imprisoned in his cellar. This brought into the open the poor functioning of the police forces and of the judicial administration and also triggered the largest protest march that Brussels has ever seen. Some 300,000 citizens participated in this 'White March'. The fact that stories about cover-up activities and involvement of 'high placed persons' were easily spread and believed also illustrated the thin level of trust for the Belgian system.

There were also many attempts to change the system, but many of these failed or did in the end not change anything fundamental. An ambitious plan for the reform of the administration was launched in 2000, with one of its aims being to reduce party-political control over the administration and power of 'ministerial cabinets' where parties and ministers can freely appoint collaborators. These cabinets did however survive at all levels of government.

There has been a major reform of the party finance system to reduce the chances of bribery and corruption. The results of this are very large amounts of money flowing towards the parties and a further strengthening of their power and presence. There have been attempts to give the state a more direct grip on policies related to wages and prices, but in the end the presence and power of the pillar organizations – trade unions in the first place – have remained intact.

The electoral system has been reformed in an attempt to give the voters more say in who can represent them. Yet the enlargement of the districts and the use of successor lists have increased the power of parties and not of the citizens in deciding who will have a seat. The newly introduced habit of standing for elections without accepting the seat when elected (because the candidate already has a seat in another parliament) has further reduced the transparency of selection and election.

In 1999 a brand new coalition formula was tried out – liberals, socialists and greens – which broke the old logic of having Flemish Christian democrats and francophone socialists as the core governing parties. Yet the francophone socialists remained in power and the Christian democrats were already back in power in Flanders in 2004 and at the federal level in 2007.

In 1993 and again in 2001 further reforms of the state towards a true federal system were accepted and implemented. The stability of the federal government was restored after a period of high instability in the 1970s and 1980s. But in 2004 the tensions started building up again, pitting Flemish and francophone parties against each other in another version of the old debates about the territorial boundaries between the language groups and about the very meaning of these boundaries. And the stability of the federal government was gone again. Demands for full independence of Flanders are voiced more than ever before, mainly with the argument that the Belgian state is not able to function properly. Since it cannot really be changed, it must disappear.

The debate about trust and legitimacy of representative democracy thus takes a quite interesting form. The Belgian state is deeply marked by first its long history of consociational democracy allowing for a deep encroachment of the traditional parties and their pillar organizations into the state apparatus. That was the answer to the development of the religious and economic cleavages. The Belgian state is further marked by its more recent history of federalism to deal with the territorial cleavage that partially coincides with the two other cleavages. These have been Belgium's institutional answers to societal divisions and diversity. And it is these institutional answers that are criticized when the effective functioning of democracy is on the agenda. Belgium is indeed a fascinating and interesting case (see also Linder, 1994).

Plan of the book

In Chapter 2 we present the history of Belgium. The process of state formation in 1830 deserves attention because the choices made at that time strongly define what Belgium has become and make clear which kind of political conflicts are likely to occur. The development of three conflict lines – religion, class and language – and the gradual expansion of voting rights had, by 1900, put in place a party landscape with three major parties. The chapter also describes the way in which Belgium became a colonial power as a result of the ambitious plans of King Leopold II. The fate of the country during the two World Wars and the gradual development of a new territorial organization of Belgium are also discussed.

Chapter 3 then fully focuses on this territorial reorganization of the country. It describes the long road towards the creation of a complex and hybrid federal state. The Belgian federation is indeed a very peculiar federation, with its double structure of regions and language communities, with its strong consociational logic and especially with its lack of agreement on a number of basic choices about the way in which the state should function and further evolve.

Chapter 4 deals with the political parties. It presents the rich party landscape of the country, with first its three traditional parties that are now split into six unilingual parties. It discusses the rise and fall of the regionalist parties and the development of the green party family and of a strong populist radical-right party in Flanders. The chapter takes a closer look at party organization and at the role of the party president, at the evolution of party membership and at the way in which political parties are financed.

Chapter 5 presents the electoral system that is used for federal and regional elections. The size of the electoral districts and the proportional electoral formula are presented. Next it discusses a few remarkable elements of elections in Belgium, such as the high degree of fragmentation, the increasing volatility and the degree to which north and south produce very different electoral results. It also presents some information on elections at the provincial and the local level.

Chapter 6 deals with the government. This is primarily a story about difficult processes of coalition formation. Governments in Belgium – both at the federal and at the regional level – are indeed always coalitions. That has direct consequences for the internal functioning and survival chances of the governments. The chapter also gives some information about governing at the local level.

Chapter 7 presents the parliament. It explains how and why the parliament is composed of two houses. It describes the way in which the legislative function is carried out and the way in which the members of parliament can control the government. It also discusses the changes in the composition of the parliament and concludes with a discussion of the very docile way in which Belgium MPs are supposed to fulfil their duty.

Chapter 8 looks at policymaking and at economic and social policy in particular. It stresses the strong grip of political parties and of their auxiliary organizations in both the preparation and implementation of the policies. It presents the system of social security and its vulnerability caused – among other reasons – by a problematic employment rate. It discusses the strong and weak points of the Belgian economy, the problem of the very high levels of public debt and the tensions caused by a very different economic outlook in Flanders and Wallonia.

Chapter 9 looks at Belgium from the perspective of world politics. It explains how Belgium is obviously a small and minor player on the international scene, but how it is able to play some role in the region of the Great Lakes in Africa. It shows how Belgium is a very good pupil in the European Union class, with its consistent and full commitment to a highly integrated and even truly federal Europe. The chapter also presents the way in which the substate level is developing a foreign (trade) policy of its own.

The final chapter looks at the future of Belgium, and especially at the territorial divide and how the way in which the political elite tries to or has to govern the country against the background of complex political institutions raises questions about governing capacity. Is it possible after all to govern a divided society?

Chapter 2

A Short Political History

More than 20 centuries ago Julius Caesar explicitly mentioned the Belgians in his account of the wars in Gaul: 'Of all these the Belgians are the bravest, because they live far away from culture and civilization, because they seldom see merchants who import things that weaken the soul, and because they are close to the Germans, who live over the Rhine and with whom they are constantly at war.' The 'Belgians' to whom Julius Caesar is referring here are one of the many tribes that had been like the rest of Gaul conquered by Caesar and made part of the Roman Empire. This mention of 'Belgians' in events that occurred more than 20 centuries ago does not, however, mean that the history of Belgium can really be traced back to these old times. For Caesar, Belgium and the Belgae only vaguely refers to the northern part of Gaul, north of Seine and Marne, an area which had then no fixed boundaries and which coincides only partially with what is today the Belgian state.

In this chapter we sketch the formation of the Belgian state and especially the way in which that happened. We show how and why the choices made in 1830 already lock in many features of the future of Belgium. We go through the 19th and the 20th centuries to see the political conflicts and divisions develop.

Union and separation of the Low Countries

Belgium claimed its independence after secession from the Kingdom of the Netherlands in 1830. The Belgium that was formed in 1830 had however never existed before. There is thus no history of the Belgian state that goes further back than 1830.

There is however a complex common history with what is today the Benelux – that is, Belgium, the Netherlands and Luxembourg. Until the Treaty of Münster in Westphalia created the Netherlands in 1648 a 'Union of Seventeen Provinces' had existed, composed more or less of the territories of the Benelux today (the most important unit not present in the Seventeen Provinces is the Princebishopric of Liège). This Union of Seventeen Provinces was not at all an independent country in the modern sense. It belonged to the Habsburg territories ruled by Emperor Charles V (himself born in Ghent in the County of Flanders), but it had indeed some common institutions among which was the Estates General (Staten-Generaal) with representatives from each of the provinces. The abdication of Charles V in 1555 and the spread of Protestantism broke the union apart after hostilities that lasted more than 80 years. The Treaty of Münster took the current Netherlands out of the Union and left the southern and Catholic Low Countries under the Habsburg rule until the French Revolution.

There had been an attempt though to create a new political unit as a breakaway from the Habsburg empire in 1790. Partly as an echo of the revolutionary spirit that reigned in France, the policies of the Habsburg emperor Joseph II were criticized by elites in several provinces of the southern Low Countries and especially in Brabant (with Brussels as its capital city). This short-lived attempt to claim independence is called the 'Brabant Revolution' and eventually gave the future Belgium its flag – black, red and yellow – and its national anthem, the *Brabançonne*. Internal divisions and the Austrian army quickly put an end to the new entity that had called itself the 'United Netherlands States' (Verenigde Nederlandse Staten) in Dutch and the 'United Belgian States' (Etats Belgiques Unis) in French. It had brought together ten entities that covered to a large extent the current territory of Belgium, with the exception (still) of the Princebishopric of Liège and the Duchy of Luxembourg.

The Habsburg's recovery of the 'Belgian States' was soon ended by the Napoleonic invasion and the inclusion of them into France. The same actually happened with the northern Low Countries that were included in the French empire as the 'Batavian Republic'. At the Congress of Vienna in 1815 – ending the era of Napoleon – the great powers Austria, Russia, Prussia and the United Kingdom decided to create a 'United Kingdom of the Netherlands' under the leadership of the House of Orange (King William). The Congress of Vienna thus more or less reunited the old Seventeen Provinces, this time including the Princebishopric of Liège. The Kingdom covered the territory – except for a few minor alterations – that is today the Benelux: Belgium, the Netherlands and

Luxembourg. The United Kingdom of the Netherlands was very
short-lived though. In 1830 the southern provinces broke away
from it and created a new independent state called Belgium. This
new state had thus never existed before. It was a new entity,
composed however of territories that had before been sometimes
more or less united under the same ruler (Luyckx, 1985; Beaufays, 1998; Wils, 1998; Witte et al., 2005).

The common history of the northern and southern Netherlands
and their early separation in 1648 is very relevant for the further
political development of Belgium. It defines what Belgium is and
what it is not for two important and related elements. Religion is
the first. The Treaty of Münster put the Netherlands on the map
as a Protestant (Calvinist) state, even if there was an important
Catholic minority. The areas that remained under the Habsburg
rule were Catholic and did not tolerate Protestantism. When
Belgium became independent in 1830 it was thus clearly a Catholic country. The Catholic Church indeed played an important role
in the rapid alienation between the northern part of the Low
Countries – a state already dominated by Calvinism for more than
two centuries – and the Catholic south.

The second element that marks the meaning and identity of
Belgium is language. The language of the Netherlands was and is
Dutch. The Dutch language had been standardized by the process
of state formation after 1648 and by Protestantism. Indeed, the
translation of the Bible into the language of the people facilitated
the use of one common variant of Dutch. The language situation
in the southern areas of the Low Countries was much more
complex. First there is the line marking the influence of Latin in
the languages spoken in the south of Europe. This line starts in
the north of France and runs from west to east through today's
Belgium, following then the borderline between Belgium and
Luxembourg, running down into the French region of Alsace and
further into Switzerland and into the north of Italy. In Belgium the
people living south of that line spoke French in 1830 (or French
dialects). The people living north of it spoke Dutch. That is, they
spoke a variety of dialects, but not the standardized Dutch of the
Netherlands. One could assume that elites did master that
language, but elites in the north of Belgium – especially in the
larger cities like Brussels, Antwerp and Ghent – also spoke French.
French was a standardized and written language, a language of

literature and modern philosophy. French was also at that time widely used as the lingua Franca in diplomacy.

In the Kingdom of the Low Countries brought into life by the Congress of Vienna, the most important and dominant language was obviously Dutch. Dutch was also to be the official language in the northern part of the Belgian territories, which alienated the northern Belgian elites, while elites from the south spoke a minority language in the Dutch-dominated Kingdom (McRae, 1986; Witte, 1993; Witte & Van Velthoven, 2000; Witte et al., 2005).

It took thus no longer than 15 years of 'reunification' to see the north and the south of the Low Countries fall apart again. Partly inspired by the events in France where the Bourbon dynasty had to leave the throne to Louis-Philippe d'Orléans, riots broke out in Brussels after a performance of the opera *La muette de Portici* (an aria calling for national pride to the tune of the Marseillaise is said to have triggered the event). A mixture of popular revolt and elite revolt against the Dutch King made King William decide to send his sons with troops to Brussels. They settled in the Brussels Parc, where they were an easy target for the many volunteers who were able to oust them on 27 September 1830. That marked the break-up between the Netherlands and the new country called Belgium. A temporary government was immediately installed and a National Congress was elected in November. Its vast majority wanted an independent Belgian state, although one minority group (the 'orangists') preferred the union with the Netherlands to survive and another wanted Belgium to become part of France. One of the first tasks of the new government and Congress was finding an agreement with the Netherlands on the terms of the separation. In particular, the question of the boundaries of the new state proved quite difficult. After the formal recognition of Belgium by the major powers of the Congress of Vienna, Belgium (reluctantly) agreed to leave the northern part of Limburg – with cities like Venlo and Maastricht – to the Netherlands and the left bank of the Scheldt river. It did receive half of Luxembourg though, basically the part where French was the local language. The remaining part of Luxembourg stayed under the Dutch crown and eventually became independent in 1867. The Netherlands accepted the terms of the agreement only in 1839, after which the new country could finally take off.

Figure 2.1 *The Kingdom of the Low Countries, 1815–1830*

The weight of history

The way in which a state comes into being is of crucial importance for its further political development. Its place on the map, the timing of its creation and the specific characteristics of the elites who take the lead and define the nature of a new state remain visible for centuries (Flora et al., 1999). One of these crucial elements for Belgium is indeed the Catholic religion. The strong position of the Catholic Church in the new country is at the origin of the first political divide and party formation: the conflict between the Church and the liberal free-thinking elites. But there is more.

The new Belgian state is also a monarchy. The Netherlands had been a republic since the very beginning and became a monarchy only after the Congress of Vienna made William of Orange King of the Low Countries and Grand Duke of Luxembourg. After the secession Belgium could have opted for a republican status. It did however prefer a monarchy for very pragmatic reasons. Its very creation was already a serious blow to the subtle equilibrium that had been achieved at the Congress of Vienna in 1815. The foreign powers that had to recognize the new Belgium suggested the Dutch crown prince as Belgian head of state. The Temporary Government did not accept this and actually decided to deny the House of Orange for ever the right to the Belgian throne. Belgium finally decided that – in order not to upset the foreign powers with another revolutionary move – a monarchy would be suitable for the new state. When a search committee finally found Leopold of Saxen-Coburg-Gotha willing to accept the Belgian throne, this choice appeared to be very wise. Leopold was the widower of the British crown princess Charlotte, daughter of George IV. Leopold immediately proved to be a good diplomat and was able to negotiate the final agreements between Belgium and the major foreign powers of the time. In 1832 he married Louise-Marie d'Orléans, the daughter of the French monarch.

Leopold had however only reluctantly accepted the throne. After he had seen the text of the Belgian constitution, Leopold declared: 'Gentlemen, you have badly treated the monarchy that was not there to defend itself. Your text is quite democratic. Yet with some goodwill on either side I do believe that we can make it work' (Luyckx, 1985: 59). He was indeed not too pleased with the general thrust of the Belgian constitution that had been drafted by the National Congress. The constitution was quite progressive and liberal, and introduced, inter alia, the accountability of ministers of the government to the elected parliament and not to the monarch. This choice for a parliamentary monarchy was a direct result of the way in which King William had tried to rule the Low Countries as an almost absolute monarch. Progressive forces seized the opportunity to introduce these liberal ideas in the new constitution. That constitution was indeed a good compromise between the more conservative forces, who mainly tried to secure the power and influence of the Church in the new country, and the progressive forces who were inspired by the ideas of the French Revolution. King Leopold arrived in Brussels and took his constitutional oath on July 21, 1831. July 21 is now Belgium's national holiday.

The King had arrived in Brussels, indeed, because Brussels had been chosen as the capital city of Belgium. This is again something that history almost logically dictates, although the consequences for Belgian politics are quite dramatic. Brussels had been a very important city during the previous centuries. It had been the home of the Habsburg court in the 16th century, making it actually the capital city of the Netherlands, and after the loss of the northern Low Countries the city remained the capital of the Catholic Low Countries. Under the Austrian Habsburgs, Brussels kept that status and that is indeed why it played an important role in the Brabant Revolution of 1790. The riots that presaged the separation of Belgium started in Brussels and King William sent his troops to the city to control the situation. When they were defeated in Brussels, the new Belgium was born. Brussels was therefore the most obvious capital city for the kingdom of Belgium.

The reason why the choice of Brussels as the capital had dramatic consequences is its geographic location. Brussels is indeed situated north of the linguistic division line (see Figure 2.2). Its population therefore spoke the Brabant Dutch dialect. Its elites spoke French though, and French very rapidly became the dominant language

Figure 2.2 *The current territorial organization of Belgium*

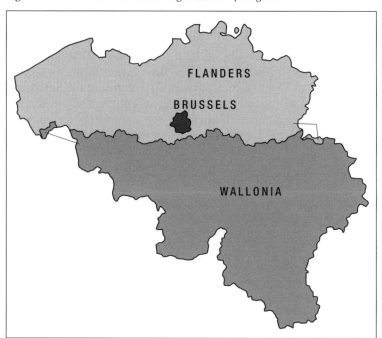

of the city. Before it was the capital of Belgium, Brussels had a population that did not exceed 70,000. As the capital city, it grew fast. It became the administrative centre of a country of which the language of politics and administration was French. French was thus the language of public life and of social promotion. French was the language of formal education. And while the city grew it expanded beyond its old city walls, and thus further into territory where the original vernacular was replaced by French. The use of language in Brussels and the boundaries of Brussels later became one of the major issues in Belgian politics. Even today it is and remains a very divisive issue, but its very location is at the same time one of the reasons why the end and the splitting up of Belgium is not an easy and obvious way out of the conflict.

The conditions of the state's formation turned Belgium into a monarchy, with a liberal constitution that gave guarantees to the Catholic Church. The conditions of the state's formation also turned Belgium into a state where French is the official language and where the capital city is therefore rapidly 'frenchified' (Witte & Van Velthoven, 2000). That is the 'burden' of history that defines and also explains much of the subsequent development of Belgian politics.

The weight of history is clear. What follows is often quite path dependent on these early events and early choices. The creation of the independent Belgian state is a first critical juncture of the country's history. A number of features and institutions are locked into it and will define and limit further choices. The subsequent history of Belgium can also be written by referring to this notion of critical junctures. In particular, the territorial organization crosses a few 'points of no return' that thoroughly shape the future development towards a federal state structure.

1830–1848: Consolidation and 'unionism'

During the first decades of the political history of Belgium, the two major leading forces kept their differences on the back burner. This first period is therefore labelled 'unionism'. The common goal of the creation of a new state and the need to remain united as long as the Netherlands did not accept Belgian independence led to a constitution in which both Catholics and liberals had been able to secure a number of their demands. The strong role of the parliament, the freedom of religion and the freedom of education were principles espoused by the liberals. The Catholics secured the freedom of the Church to nominate the members of the clergy and the guarantee that they would be paid by the state.

A first parliament – a bicameral structure with a House and a Senate – was elected in 1831. It was directly elected, but the number of citizens having the right to vote was extremely limited. In order to obtain voting rights one had to pay a minimal amount of taxes, which gave only 55,000 of the then 3,800,000 inhabitants the possibility of electing members of the parliament. King Leopold was quite free to choose his ministers and he also gave himself the necessary freedom to be active on the international front.

One of the first tasks of the new parliament and government was the normalization of relations with the Netherlands – finalized in 1839 – and the building of the necessary infrastructure for transport and trade. In 1835 the first train connection on the continent was opened between Brussels and Mechelen. The organization of schools and universities also belonged to the early topics dealt with by the new administration. Very interesting and also revealing is the fact that regulations on the organization of primary and secondary schooling proved to be quite difficult. The limits of the role of the Church and the possibilities for the state to organize education divided the liberals and the Catholics. The Church had its Catholic University in Leuven. The freemasonry reacted to that with the creation in 1834 of a free and non-religious university in Brussels: the Université Libre de Bruxelles. It goes almost without saying that both institutions – as well as the state universities of Ghent and Liège – used French as the teaching language.

The young state also had to organize the functioning of its lower tiers of government. Regulations on the powers and institutions of the local municipalities and of the provinces were introduced in 1836. Supporters of a strong central state and supporters of local autonomy reached a compromise, in which the local level would indeed have the powers to deal with all matters related to the local level, but the executive of the municipalities – mayor and aldermen – would be appointed by the government. Symbolically much more important is the statute given to the provinces. The autonomy of the old entities like the Duchy of Brabant, the County of Flanders or the Princebishopric of Liège had been abolished under French rule, and the nine provinces of Belgium no longer coincided fully with the territories' historical powers (with for instance only half of Luxembourg belonging to Belgium). Although Article 1 of the Belgian constitution described the territory as composed of nine provinces, their autonomy was not reinstated. The law of 1836 made a clear choice for a unitary country. Its evolution towards federalism in the late 20th century would thus not be based on these historical entities, but on groups and territories that developed as a result of the choice for French as the principal language of politics, administration and education (see Chapter 3).

Unlike in the Netherlands, the provinces do not have a role in central decision-making either. The Dutch First House of the Parliament indeed refers to the historical 'Staten Generaal' with representatives of the provinces. The Belgian Senate (see also Chapter 7) is set up as a conservative assembly for a unitary Belgium, not as a house where the constituent territorial units are represented. The current Senate – after the reform of 1993 – does reflect the territorial organization, but to represent the language communities and not the provinces.

As soon as these basic institutional choices were made and independence was fully secured, the cracks in the union started to show. Until 1840 governments were composed of ministers of both groups, but after that time executives were formed from only one of the groups and with the other one then clearly in opposition. The awareness of an ideological divide in the parliament and in public opinion – at least among the voters – eventually led to the formal creation of a Liberal party in 1846. It was the very first party to be formed in Belgium. It espoused a better separation between Church and state, a more democratic voting system and better conditions for the working class.

The Liberal party was obviously very much on the side of the liberals and democrats that were causing conservative regimes elsewhere in Europe to accept institutional changes, although not all its members backed the sometimes radical reforms claimed by the gradually growing labour movement. The arrival of the Second Republic in France – bringing down the father-in-law of King Leopold – and the spreading of revolutionary socialism caused some unrest among the Belgian elites. One of their ways to react to it and to avoid the revolutionary spirit moving to Belgium was the extradition of a number of foreigners believed to be dangerous. One of them was Karl Marx, who had been living in Brussels where he wrote his Communist Manifesto. One very visible effect of the democratic revolutions was a change in the Belgian electoral law. Until 1848 the amount of paid taxes required to achieve voting rights could vary between cities. From 1848 on it was made uniform at the lowest level possible. A minimal level was indeed fixed in the constitution, which meant that one could not go further without amending the constitution. The number of citizens now entitled to vote rose to 79,000, or some 2 per cent of the population (Mabille, 1986; Luyckx, 1985; Witte et al., 2000).

1848–1893: The social question and the Flemish question

The unionist period was based on the equilibrium between two groups opposing each other mainly on topics related to the role of the Church and of religion. Matters become more complex though when new tensions come to the fore. These came from outside, from groups so far excluded from participation in the politics of Belgium, primarily the labour movement. Industrial activity was already present under the Dutch rule. One of the famous entrepreneurs of that time was the British-born John Cockerill. He built – with the help of King William – a real steel empire. Its activities were – like many other industrial plants – mainly located in the south of Belgium, between the cities of Liège and Charleroi. In the north the cities of Ghent (textile) and Antwerp (harbour, shipbuilding) were important centres, while the rest of the territory remained essentially rural. The growth of Belgian industry led obviously to a growing labour class and to its gradual organization into a network of cooperatives and trade unions. These networks became the origin of a new political party. After a few failed attempts, due, among other reasons, to the more radical and revolutionary orientation of the workers from the south and the more pragmatic position of those from the north, the Belgian Workers' party was born in 1885. It did however not yet participate in elections, since its potential voters had no voting rights. One of its major demands was of course the introduction of universal suffrage, which was eventually introduced in 1893.

Although the system was called universal suffrage, it was not built on full equality of the voters. Just as before, suffrage was limited to male citizens older than 25. All men now did receive a vote, but some of them received a second or a third, based on property, income or diplomas. The number of voters rose to 1,300,000, of which some 800,000 had only one vote.

Changing the voting rules required a change to the constitution. Its text had remained unchanged since 1831, and the reform of 1893 was mainly meant to allow the introduction of this more or less universal male suffrage. It is interesting to note that the new text also introduced the possibility for Belgium to acquire colonies.

In the parliament elected in 1894 under the new system, three parties gained representation: the Liberal party, the Workers' party and the Catholic party. Indeed, in 1884 the counterpart of the Liberal party during the first 45 years of Belgium's existence had finally decided to formally create a political party. Its full name was the 'Federation of Catholic Circles and Conservative Associations'. These widespread Catholic associations were one of the results of the first major school conflict – sometimes referred to as school war – between liberals and Catholics. After a few Catholic governments, the Liberal party seized power in 1878. It tried immediately to implement its promises on the organization of primary education. These tensions between liberals and Catholics were not new. Both had given a different interpretation of the freedom of education and of the right of the state to have its own schools. For the liberals, it did not mean that the state should just supplement, where needed, the Catholic schools but that it should actively set up a network of schools where religion would not be an automatic part of the curriculum. A new law on primary schools was issued in 1879. It obliged every local municipality to have a public school and forbade the municipalities from subsidizing free (Catholic) schools. In public schools religion was removed from the curriculum. The reaction of the Church was immediate and fierce. Public opinion was mobilized by all means available, and most effectively: Holy Communion was refused to all teachers of state schools, and a Catholic school was set up in each and every parish. As a result of this, public schools in the north of Belgium were almost completely deserted. In the south however the public schools did survive. The Liberal government then suspended diplomatic relations with the Vatican and tried to scrutinize all the accounts of Catholic schools.

At the elections of 1884 the liberals lost heavily, and a new Catholic government came to power. Its first job was to go back more or less to the old system and to restore diplomatic relations with the Vatican. After the 1886 elections, in which the newly created Catholic party participated for the first time, the liberals faced another defeat. The results of these elections are more than remarkable: the Liberal party had not one single member of parliament elected in the northern provinces. All the seats there went to the Catholic party.

The result was remarkable, but not exceptional. The results of the first elections organized under the new rules in 1894, and in which the Workers' party also fielded candidates, reflect this same political division between north and south. The Workers' party was able to elect 28 members to the House of Representatives (out of a total of 152). They were all elected in the south, and this meant at once an absolute majority of all seats in the south. All the seats in the north and thus a full monopoly went to the Catholic party.

This sheds a very clear light on the meaning of territory in Belgian politics, even before the language issue became really salient. After the politicization of the tensions between Church and state and between labour and capital, the so-called Flemish question now also made its way on to the political agenda. It had actually been there from the very beginning, since it was basically built into the Belgian independent state. The choice of French as the sole official language of Belgium was an obvious choice for the political elites, but it was a choice for a language that was not spoken by a small majority of the population. Indeed, the census of 1846 counted 4.3 million Belgians, of which 42 per cent spoke French, 57 per cent spoke Dutch and 1 per cent spoke German (McRae, 1986). The use of language was not distributed at random over the territory, but reflected the century-old division line between the Germanic languages of the north of Europe and the Latin languages of the south. The choice of French for official matters was not meant to ban the use of Dutch. Indeed, Belgian governments subsidized efforts to support the literary and cultural life of the Dutch and they played an active role in the decision to use standard Dutch spelling for the language that was then often called Lower German (Nederduits) or Flemish. Actually some users (especially priests) of the Flemish variant of Dutch – in the territory of the former County of Flanders – did try to have their language chosen as the official *Nederduits*. One should not forget that Dutch was the language of the Netherlands and that it was therefore also the language of Protestantism. Yet the acceptance of the existence of the standard Dutch language was not enough to contain the slowly growing demands for its use in more than only cultural matters. A Flemish Movement (again taking its name from the old County) started claiming the recognition of Dutch as a second official language for administrative matters. These demands were rejected by the francophone Belgian elites. They feared that the official recognition of a second language would be detrimental for the young Belgian nation, in which the generalized use of French could be a marker of a common identity. This refusal to take the demands of the Dutch-speakers into account would however radicalize the movement. It also increased its presence in the political class, among others, as a result of the slow expansion of voting rights. A number of painful events also accelerated the willingness to accept the Flemish demands. The most important is probably the trial, conviction and execution of two men in 1860. They were later proven to be innocent, but had not been able to defend themselves properly in court because they did not speak French while the judges did not speak Dutch. This all finally led to laws in 1872 and 1878 regulating the use of languages in criminal courts and in public administration. Their basic logic also formally allowed the use of Dutch in the northern provinces of Belgium. A new law on higher education obliged the teachers of certain topics in public secondary schools to be able to speak Dutch and allowed the use of Dutch for some courses at the state university of Ghent (Witte & Van Velthoven, 2000; Vos, 1998a; 1998b; Zolberg, 1974).

And while the Flemish question made its way on to the political agenda, the social question became burning hot. Massive strikes in the Walloon industries in 1886 were violently repressed, but led eventually to the adoption of the first social laws. They regulated among other things the use of young children as cheap labour.

By then the political debates and political decisions were becoming a matter for the elites of the political parties, which substantially reduced the role of the King. Leopold had died in 1865 and was succeeded by his son Leopold II. This second King of Belgium was a man of grand and wild ideas. One of his major moves was the acquisition of a colony. Leopold I had already been quite active with attempts to broaden the influence of the Coburg dynasty in the world. He therefore actively backed the attempt of the Habsburg prince Maximilian to become the emperor of

Mexico. Maximilian was married to Leopold's daughter Josephine Charlotte. Leopold had hoped to play a role in the economic development of Mexico and even chose the side of the Confederates during the American secession war in the hope of controlling the cotton trade. When Maximilian was executed in 1867 that was the end of the story. While he was still the prince heir, the future Leopold II was literally looking around the whole world for territories to be controlled by Belgium. He strongly believed that Belgium needed markets for its products and that it could use the cheap labour of oversees territories to further build its own prosperity. Although the Belgian political and economic elites did not follow his reasoning, he did pursue his goal. And by 1885 he had set up the 'Independent State of Congo' in central Africa. The Belgian parliament accepted the move and made sure that there would be a watertight separation between the Belgian accounts and the accounts of the state over which Leopold II could now rule as an absolute monarch. The ruthless way in which he organized the production and trade (especially of rubber) in Congo, however, led to international protest. Congo would not remain the personal property of Leopold II for long (Hochschild, 1998; Vanthemsche, 2007).

1893–1918: The right to vote

In 1908 Congo became a colony of the Belgian state. There was heavy criticism, especially from the UK, about the way in which the Belgian King was exploiting the population of Congo. Leopold was also facing criticism in Belgium. He was often abroad – in the south of France – where he spent time with the young baroness of Vaughan with whom he had two children. He was gradually convinced that the best solution would be the transfer of Congo to the Belgian state. He did try hard though to keep part of it as a purely royal domain. But in 1908 the Belgian parliament finally decided that Congo would become a Belgian colony. Suddenly Belgium possessed a colonial territory that was 80 times its own size.

This short period between the introduction of a first and limited universal suffrage and the end of the First World War is indeed a period of many and deep changes that mark the way in which Belgium would function during the 20th century. Becoming a colonial power is one of these changes. The second is the change of the party system. The new electoral rules already allowed for the election of representatives of the Workers' party and that party fundamentally changed the basic mechanics of the party system. The victim of the change was the Liberal party. Its voters were spread and under the majoritarian system it had become quite difficult to have its candidates elected. The introduction of proportional representation in 1900 – Belgium was the first country to introduce this system – allowed the Liberal party to survive, but from now on there were two large players, both based on a solid and well-organized social movement. The role of the Liberal party remained important until the Second World War, but the beginning of its fading away was around the turn of the century. Also the fact that the two large parties each dominated in one of the two future regions of Belgium further reduced its potential impact.

The further rise and success of the Workers' party was also the result of the industrialization of the country. This period was one of rapid growth and expansion, especially in the coal and steel industry. Belgium became an important exporter of machines, and was for instance well known for the tramways that were built by ACEC (Ateliers de Contructions Electriques de Charleroi) in France, Egypt, Russia and China. While the labour movement in the south was mainly organized by the socialists, the labour movement in Flanders also developed in the Catholic world, which led to some tensions and conflicts in the Catholic party. One well-known story is that of priest Adolf Daens of the city of Aalst who was able to get elected in parliament with a 'Christian democratic' programme. It defended the workers and their language rights, and that marks the beginning of a new position of the Catholic party in Flanders. Although not actually renaming itself as a Christian democratic party until 1945, it now became much more sensitive to the demands of the Flemish population.

And that is another aspect for which this period can be seen as a turning point. Increasing pressure from an increasing number of Flemish organizations – the Flemish Movement – led to a number of crucial decisions. In 1886 a Flemish side would appear on the Belgian coins. In 1888 a speech was held for the very first time in Dutch in the House of Representatives (meaning however that the person speaking was hardly understood). In 1894 a number of elected MPs of the Catholic party took their oath in Dutch. And finally in 1898 came the long-awaited 'Equality Law', stating that

Belgium has two official languages and that thus all laws would have to be published in both languages and that both versions were to be put on an equal footing.

One important demand was not met though: the use of Dutch in universities. The francophone rejection of that idea was fierce, fearing that by using Dutch the Flemish would miss opportunities to keep contact with progress and civilization. Archbishop Cardinal Mercier, especially, voiced this opinion several times in quite crude terms (Boudens, 1975). The question of the use of language in universities stretched into the First World War. The German occupying forces lent their ear to the demands of the Flemish 'activists' who tried to obtain from them what they could not obtain from the Belgian authorities. In 1916 the Flemish University of Ghent was solemnly opened, as the result of an obvious act of high treason. But that action also made many aware of the fact that these demands were not that radical after all. Much more radical demands were voiced during the war years by the 'Council of Flanders', a grouping of prominent members of the Flemish Movement. It wanted the administrative reorganization of Belgium into two regions, a Flemish one including Brussels and a Walloon one. Later the Council even declared Flemish independence, but its members left the country as soon as the German defeat became clear.

The military operations of the war were quite important for Belgium. The First World War on the European continent was very much a war along an almost immobile front running from the west of Belgium into the north of France. The war years were very difficult for Belgium, since it was almost completely occupied by Germany. Conditions of life were quite bad and help was offered by – among others – an American 'Commission for Relief in Belgium' chaired by Herbert Hoover.

Life at the war front was obviously also extremely harsh. On top of the difficult physical conditions came the language situation in the army. Many soldiers stuck at the Western front were Flemish. Attempts to keep cultural activities alive gradually developed into a 'Front movement' that among other things wanted on the graves of the Flemish soldiers the inscription AVV-VVK (Alles voor Vlaanderen/Vlaanderen voor Kristus – All for Flanders/Flanders for Christ). This Front movement also laid the foundations for the Front party, the first party political emanation of the Flemish Movement after the war (Luyckx, 1985; De Schaepdrijver, 1997; Witte et al., 2005).

1918–1945: More consociationalism and territorial division

After the war Belgian politics was thoroughly changed. Belgium had even become a bit larger. Members of the government had made claims to get back the territories that were left to the Netherlands in the agreement of 1839, such as the south bank of the Scheldt and the Duchy of Luxembourg. Yet at the negotiating tables in Versailles Belgium only received a small piece of German land in the east (Eupen, Malmédy, Sankt Vith). These 'East cantons' are today the German-speaking Community of Belgium which has received autonomy as a community in the Belgian federation. Belgium also received the German African colonies Rwanda and Burundi to the east of Congo.

The interwar years were not a period of deep change but of consolidation of the transformations that had occurred earlier. First the principle of prudent leadership typical of consociational democracies found its way into the system. Of the 18 governments between the two wars there were 9 governments of national unity, bringing together the three traditional parties. The willingness to govern together is especially visible during periods of crisis, and the 1920s and 1930s were indeed economically difficult times. The threat of fascism was also countered by closing ranks. There is an interesting anecdote about a by-election in Brussels in 1937. In 1936 the three traditional parties had registered a historically low score, with 25 per cent of the votes going to the Communist party, the Flemish regionalist VNV and Rex, a movement led by the populist and authoritarian Léon Degrelle. His admiration for Mussolini and Hitler was clear and he also espoused a new order for Belgium. His electoral success (11.5 per cent in 1936) was also based on his bringing about several collusions between (Catholic) politicians and financial organizations. In 1937 Degrelle asked the Rex member of parliament for Brussels to resign, together with all the possible successors on the list. A by-election was needed and Degrelle himself was the candidate for Rex. The three traditional parties then decided to ask Prime Minister Van Zeeland – then not a member of parliament – to stand against Degrelle. Degrelle received only 19 per cent of the votes, and that was the beginning of the end of the rexist movement (Luyckx, 1985; Dumoulin et al., 2006).

The three traditional parties gradually become strong mass organizations during this period. Although they all faced some internal divisions (especially the Catholics), they started acting as unified actors, with a party president and with a group leader in the parliament. The parties thus firmly controlled the members of parliament and firmly controlled the members of government. The personnel selection for the government was indeed increasingly made by the party presidents and not by the King. The King himself was the spokesperson of the conservatives who believed that this party democracy was undermining the constitutional order. The King in the 1930s was Leopold III. He had succeeded Albert who had killed himself rock climbing in the Ardennes in 1934. He was quite critical of the way in which parliamentary democracy functioned and often warned of its weaknesses, which was an idea that could be heard in many other places in Europe at that time.

The debates about the use of language and the organization of the Belgian territory also continued and produced outcomes that were fully in line with the earlier developments. In 1930 there was finally a Dutch-speaking university in Ghent. Two years later a set of laws regulating the use of language by public authorities further reinforced the principle that language would be related to territory. In 1921 linguistic areas had been defined, of which the boundaries could be adapted every decade after a census. In 1932 the application of the law was expanded to education. That meant that education in Flanders now had to be organized in Dutch, in both public and private (Catholic) schools. Only in Brussels would parents have the choice for one of the two languages. But the question about the limits of the bilingual area of Brussels and the possible exceptions for francophones living in the Brussels periphery remained unsolved. And this is still the case today.

The Second World War was again a very difficult time for the Belgians. The country was fully occupied and ruled by a German military administration (Gerard-Libois & Gotovitch, 1971). German troops entered the territory on May 10, 1940 and 18 days later the military operations were over. That is exactly the moment of the dramatic schism between King Leopold III and the government. Leopold wanted to capitulate and to see what could be done for the population under German rule. The government – after some hesitation – decided to go to Paris and then to London to continue the war. While technically imprisoned (in his Brussels castle) by the

Germans, Leopold tried to form a new government. He went to Berchtesgaden to discuss the conditions of the occupation with Hitler. He also got married again, after having lost his first wife Astrid of Sweden in a car accident in 1935. The story of the second marriage is politically not that important, but it was used later in the debates about his future role to show that the conditions under which he was 'in prison' were not too bad after all.

When the Belgian territory was liberated in 1944, the King and his children had been taken out of the country by the Germans. The Belgian parliament reconvened and installed Prince Charles, bother of Leopold, as the temporary regent of Belgium. The government expressed its hopes that Leopold could come back soon, but he himself had already made clear that he wanted the government to admit that they had been wrong in 1940. Leopold was a stubborn man, and that would prove fatal for him. He would be cast aside by the prudent leadership of the three traditional political parties.

1945–1995: Towards a federal state

The first half-century after the Second World War was a period full of tensions (Huyse, 1986; Dumoulin et al., 2007). Prudent leadership and consociational practices were often put to the test but were in the end always able to pacify conflicts when they became really explosive. In the social and economic sphere the occupation years had already brought together the leaders of the major interest groups and they had laid the foundations of a solid welfare state, with a generous social security system and a strongly developed social partnership. The old pillar organizations did not disappear, but became active partners in and of the welfare state. That did not at all remove all tensions from labour relations, but it did allow the trade unions and employers to keep in touch and to remain on speaking terms. The permanent presence in power of the Christian democratic party and the almost permanent presence of the Socialist party in power also helped to secure the social peace. Major general strikes such as those in 1960, in 1977 and in 1983 were an exception to the rule.

But first there was the problem of King Leopold III. The political world was deeply divided about what to do with him. Only the Christian democrats fully supported his return to the throne, while socialists, liberals and communists wanted him to resign. Leopold himself wanted to return and convinced the Christian democrats to organize a referendum in 1950. To the question whether Leopold could come back, 57 per cent of Belgians answered positively. Yet in Wallonia the yes vote only got 46 per cent and in Brussels 48 per cent. Leopold came back to the country, but quite rapidly violent riots broke out. All political parties and also the leaders of the major trade unions agreed that Leopold could not come back to the throne and had to convince him to accept that he would be succeeded by his son Beaudoin. That is what he reluctantly did, but he kept on denouncing this injustice until his death in 1983 (Stengers, 1980; Luyckx, 1985; Dumoulin et al., 2006).

The way in which the King's question was solved in 1950 and the way in which the last school war between Catholics and supporters of the public schools was settled in 1958 further illustrates how the Belgian political elite oscillates between a role of preacher and mobilizer in its own world and a role of compromise builder when needed. This capacity was put increasingly to the test when the different views of French-speakers and Dutch-speakers on the organization of the state resurfaced strongly in the 1960s. Concentration on the economic and financial issues, on the King's question and on the school question had kept the language issue at a slightly lower level during the 1950s. The active collaboration of the Flemish regionalist VNV with the Nazi occupation had also very much discredited the Flemish Movement.

In the 1960s the linguistic divide again made its way to the top of the agenda – and remains there today. The 1960s marked the first steps towards the deep transformation of the Belgian state structure. And that has not been easy at all. In 1963 a number of important decisions were taken by a Christian democratic and socialist government – for example the freezing of the language border and the granting of language facilities to local minorities – but that put the survival of the coalition severely at risk. That 1961–65 government was the last one until 1991–95 that went to the end of its term. The late 1960s, the 1970s and the 1980s were a period of extreme government instability. During that period schism affected all the political parties and regionalist parties scored extremely well in Flanders, Brussels and Wallonia. But in the end the state was indeed reformed in five major steps.

During these 40 years one extra development changed the relations between north and south – and not in a way that could make them easier – the decline of Walloon industry. The economic centre of the country shifted from the south to the north. It was one of the elements that triggered a renewal and political strengthening of a Walloon Movement in the 1960s (Destatte, 1997; Dupuis & Humblet, 1998; Kesteloot, 1998; Van Dam, 1998; Hasquin, 1999). Demands for autonomy were based on the fear that the central Belgian state would favour economic development in the north to the detriment of Wallonia (Quévit, 1982; 1988). This economic decline of Wallonia and the strong development of the Flemish economy turned Flanders into a very strong actor. Flanders has for evident historical reasons – the fight for the recognition of its language – a much stronger identity than Wallonia or than the Belgian francophones (Van Dam, 1997; Maddens et al., 1998). Flanders is a demographic majority that has displayed its power from the 1960s on. Devices to block the Flemish majority were urgently asked for by the francophone parties and written into the constitution in 1970. And now Flanders is also the economic leader. That leads on both sides to a questioning of the viability of the Belgian state. Flanders can believe that it can be stronger if it can go alone. And the francophones fear that a state in which they are the weaker part might in the long run not be the best solution.

In 1960 the former Belgian Congo became independent. That was another difficult time for the Belgian government. It was far from prepared to grant independence. Demands voiced by the local elites came as a surprise, since Belgium had only been thinking of possible independence in the very long run, and had not invested at all in the creation of a local elite. Economic development and economic profit were the first goals of colonial politics. The granting of independence had to be organized almost overnight. The relations between the leaders of the former colony and of the former motherland rapidly turned very sour. After half a century of Congolese independence, relations with Belgium are still often very troubled (Vanthemsche, 2006; 2007).

From the 1960s on the closer international environment of Belgium also changed. In 1954 it joined the European Coal and Steel Community and joined the EEC in 1958. Belgium is today and has basically always been a strong supporter of the European Union. Its integrated market is very important for the small Belgian economy. And gradually Belgian elites also espoused the further development of a strong political union. In 1976 Prime

Minister Tindemans wrote a report in which he supported a European Union. All later prime ministers have upheld a similar view. For Belgium, the European Union goes without saying.

After 1995: The federation at work

In 1995 the three regional parliaments were elected directly for the very first time (for Brussels it was a first re-election). This marked an important turning point in the political history of Belgium. Choices made almost two centuries ago about territorial organization and about the identity of the new state have been gradually but thoroughly changed. A new Belgium has been created in an attempt to build political institutions able to govern a society that is culturally divided along territorial lines.

Conclusions

Like all histories, the history of Belgium could have been different. The modern Belgium would then have a different look and feel, a different set of institutions, a different party system, a different territorial organization. Yet its current situation is the clear result of events and choices of the past. Telling its history therefore helps us to understand why things are what they are.

For Belgium there are four major 'turning points' that define the future by building the past deeply into the institutions and procedures. The first is the state formation. The timing and reason for the creation of the new Belgian state built in an almost inevitable language conflict and a deep cleavage between the Catholic and the liberal state builders. The second critical juncture is a series of reforms of the electoral system. The expansion of voting rights in 1893, the introduction of proportional representation in 1900 and the granting of universal male suffrage in 1919 marked the development of a party system in which two parties – the Catholic and the Socialist – were set to dominate the political scene later on. The Liberal party was almost pushed out of the system, but survived because of the proportional electoral system. The two large parties each dominate in their part of the country.

The third critical juncture is the institutionalization of this territorial divide by the geographical organization of the use of language from the 1920s on. A territorial reorganization was set in motion that would become the fundaments on which the federal state would be built. And finally, the shift of economic power from south to north after the Second World War added one more element to the territorial divide. While until that time the distrust of the Belgian central state had been located in Flanders and based on a linguistic identity, now the south has also developed a distrust for the central state where Flanders is seen to dominate on all fronts. A state was born in 1830. A state became deeply divided in the course of the next two centuries.

Table 2.1 *Important dates in the history of Belgium*

1830	Belgium claims its independence from the Kingdom of the Netherlands.
1839	An agreement is reached with the Netherlands and the territory of Belgium is fully defined.
1878	First school war between the Catholic and the Liberal parties
1893	Introduction of a plural universal male suffrage.
1898	The 'Equality Law' puts French and Dutch on an equal footing as the official languages.
1914	German troops enter Belgium on their way to France. The war front is frozen for four years in the 'West Corner' (Westhoek).
1918	The Pact of Loppem brings together the leaders of the three traditional parties. They decide to ease the tensions on the social and linguistic front. Universal male suffrage is introduced.
1932	Laws regulating the use of language in administrative matters and for education confirm the territorial solution initiated in 1921.
1936	First real critical election. The traditional parties only poll 75 per cent of the votes. Challengers are communists, Flemish regionalists and fascists.
1940	German troops invade Belgium. After 18 days the Belgian army surrenders. King Leopold III and the government deeply disagree on strategy.
1944	Liberation of Belgium. Prince Charles becomes regent in the absence of the King.
1949	Introduction of universal suffrage, that is, granting of voting rights to women.

cont'd

1950	Referendum on the possible return of the King. Political three-party agreement to force Leopold to abdicate in favour of his son Beaudoin.
1954	Formation of the first coalition of liberals and socialists. First government without the Catholic or Christian democratic parties since 1894.
1958	The School Pact puts an end to the last major school war.
1963	Agreement of Val Duchesse/Hertoginnedal that freezes the language border and enshrines exceptions to the territorial organization of the use of language.
1968	The Christian democratic party splits along the language division. The Liberal party follows in 1971 and the Socialist party in 1978.
1970	First state reform. Regions and communities are created. Decision-making at the national level now requires formal consensus between the two language groups.
1980	Second state reform. Regions and communities receive more competences, an assembly composed of national MPs and an executive composed of national ministers.
1988	Third state reform. More competences are devolved to regions and communities. Brussels becomes a region and elects its regional parliament in 1989.
1993	Fourth state reform (Saint Michael Agreement). Belgium becomes a federal state. All regional parliaments are elected directly as from 1995.
1999	Formation of a coalition of liberals, socialists and greens. First government without Christian democrats since 1954. First liberal prime minister since 1878.
2001	Fifth state reform. Further devolution of powers and increased fiscal powers for regions and communities.
2007	Longest coalition formation process ever. The government is formed 194 days after the federal elections of June 10.

Chapter 3

Territorial Organization and Reorganization

The first article of the Belgian constitution leaves no doubt about the current nature of the regime: Belgium is a federal state. The new Article 1 was introduced in 1993 to replace the first article stating that Belgium was composed of nine provinces. The new Article 1 goes on to say that the federation is composed of communities and regions. And the next three articles explain what that means. There are three communities: the Flemish, the French and the German Community. And there are three regions: the Flemish, the Walloon and the Brussels Region. And finally there are four linguistic territories: the Dutch, the French, the bilingual territory of Brussels and the German territory (Vande Lanotte et al., 2003; Uyttendaele & Martens, 2005).

And that says it all. Belgium is since 1993 a federal state, but its building blocks are – unlike most other federal states – a quite complex mix of regions and language communities. The federal structure is based on territorially defined substates, but there are important exceptions to that basic logic. The reason for this rather hybrid state structure is simply the fact that there has so far not been a real agreement on the way in which Belgium should be organized. The state structures as described in the constitution of 1993 – and amended again in 2001 – are the temporary result of a compromise between two conflicting views of Belgium. The constitution describes a subtle equilibrium that exists as long as it is not fundamentally challenged by one of the two large language communities. That has been the situation in Belgium ever since the first revision of the constitution in 1970. That was the first temporary compromise, and it has been challenged ever since, leading to a series of consecutive new reforms and debates that continue until today and that will probably continue as long as Belgium remains on the map.

In this chapter we will first look back at the way in which the federal state came into being. The concrete steps towards the current Belgium help us to understand the way in which it has been structured. Next we look at the federated entities – the regions and communities – and at their formal structures: their government, their parliament, their political powers and financial means. We conclude by summarizing and summing up no less than nine reasons why the Belgian federation is a rather special and unusual federation.

The steps towards a federal solution

It is obvious that the Belgian federation is not a 'coming together' federation. It is not a union of formerly existing territories or states like the US American, the Swiss, the Canadian or the Australian federations. Federalism in Belgium is the result of devolution, of a redefinition of the national territory. This process of devolution is not unique to Belgium (Stepan, 1999). Several other European states went through a similar process. Spain formally recognized the existence of autonomous communities in its transition from the Franco dictatorship to parliamentary democracy. In the UK a status of autonomy was given to Scotland, Wales and Northern Ireland. What makes the devolution in Belgium unique though is the fact that the units that after the reform became the building blocks of the federation *have no history before the existence of Belgium.* Unlike Scotland or Catalonia or the Basque country or the regions of northern Italy, and unlike the units of all the 'coming together' federations, the Belgian regions and communities did not exist before Belgium was created.

The names used for the Belgian substates do however have some historic meaning. Flanders has a long history, but it is the history of the County of Flanders, and its territory was limited to the current provinces of East and West Flanders. Parts of the historic County of Flanders belong today to the Netherlands and parts belong to France. There are however three more provinces in today's Flanders. The provinces of Flemish Brabant and Antwerp both belonged to the old Duchy of Brabant, which was cut in two after the creation of the Netherlands in 1648, divided again into Brabant and Antwerp under Napoleon and then in 1993 split into Flemish Brabant and Walloon Brabant. And the fifth Flemish province – Limburg – is also only a fraction of its historic territory, since the northern part belongs to the Netherlands. Parts of it actually belonged to the Princebishopric of Liège, and Liège is today a province of the Walloon Region. The terms Flanders and Flemish are now used to designate these five provinces, but they do not have a common pre-Belgian history.

The meaning of the term Wallonia for the south of the country is less clear. There was never a well-defined entity with that name. One of the (conflicting) explanations is that is refers in the old Germanic language to the people speaking another, that is, Celtic or Roman language. The inhabitants of Wales in the UK were in the same way labelled as 'strangers' (Henry, 1990). In the newly created Belgium, the terms Wallonia and Walloon were rapidly used to refer simply to the French-speaking part of the country, while in the north the terms Flanders and Flemish became the standard way to refer to the Dutch-speaking population.

The Belgian federation is thus not built on historic communities. The building blocks of the Belgian federation are new entities, and these entities came into being as a result of the creation of Belgium in 1830. It is important to note though that the words used to define these entities clearly refer – after the creation of Belgium – to the use of *language*. It is the organization of the use of language that in the 19th century set in motion a process of territorial reorganization (Murphy, 1988; McRae, 1986). When after the Second World War the notion of federalism was put onto the agenda by the regionalist parties in Flanders and then also in Wallonia and in Brussels (see Chapter 4), it referred to a decentralization of the unitary Belgian state into entities defined by the use of language.

The major problem though and the very source of the complex and unfinished nature of the Belgian federation is the fundamental *lack of agreement about boundaries*. When in the 1960s the regionalist movements and parties were putting enough electoral pressure on the traditional parties to take the issue fully into account, they were defending very different and even incompatible views of the future of Belgium.

On the Dutch-speaking side the definition of Belgium stresses the existence of two major language communities. Of these language communities the Dutch-speaking or Flemish community was treated badly by the Belgian state. It slowly claimed full recognition of Dutch as one of the two official languages of the country and gradually pushed back the influence of French in the Flemish part of the country. For this recognition and protection of the Dutch language to be fully secured, the Flemish community wants to receive autonomy (in matters of culture in the first place) within well-defined boundaries. Flanders in the Belgian federation should in this view be composed of the Dutch-speaking territory and of the capital city of Brussels.

This view is however not compatible with the way in which the francophones see the future of Belgium. There are indeed two related conflicts about the borders of Flanders. First there is the idea of fixed and well-defined borders. From the 1920s on, the borderlines between the linguistic regions have been defined on the basis of a census, conducted every decade. Whenever 30 per cent of the population of a local municipality declared that their language was not the language of that region, the municipality moved into the bilingual territory. Given the higher status of French – both in cultural and in economic terms – the language border always moved in the same direction. This process of 'frenchification' led to a gradual geographical reduction of the Flemish region. That was especially the case in and around Brussels. The bilingual Brussels region was in the 1960s much larger than just the capital city. Some 20 former Flemish villages had become part of the expanding urban area and had also been transformed from a Dutch-speaking into an official bilingual status and in practice into French-speaking places. The Flemish Movement refers to this process as the 'Brussels oil stain'. Stopping it would require the abolishment of the census as a basis on which the boundaries were defined. Fixed boundaries would be the only way to define once and for ever where the territory of Flanders begins.

This is exactly the point where francophones have a different view. It is the view of the speakers of a strong language that does not need to be protected, and that therefore defends more easily an individual right to speak the language of one's choice. Freedom of language is indeed entrenched in the Belgian constitution, and therefore a territorially defined limit on that freedom is not acceptable in this francophone view. If reality shows that a clear majority of the population speaks French, the institutional organization of the state should reflect that reality. Fixing the linguistic borderline is therefore not a good idea, and including Brussels into Flanders is out of the question. Brussels is historically a Dutch-speaking city, but that is no longer the case. The city and the wide area around it have a population of which a very large majority of more than 80 per cent speaks French (Janssens, 2001). And Brussels should therefore have boundaries that reflect the reality of the use of language. Areas still outside Brussels should – whenever their population prefers it – be added to the Brussels territory. The two language groups thus start from a very different perspective and reach very different and conflicting conclusions.

The consequence of these different views on the way in which the use of language should be regulated leads to two different proposals for the future of Belgium. On the one hand there is the Flemish proposal of a reform that is based on the language communities. That means that Belgium should give autonomy to two entities. On the other hand there is the francophone proposal to create three regions. One region would be Wallonia, the region south of the language border. The second would be Brussels, since it cannot be part of the Flemish territory. And the third would then be Flanders without Brussels. In this scenario the Brussels territory includes all the significant francophone populations living in its periphery. Brussels should not be squeezed into an unnatural 'carcan', or straitjacket, based only on historical and thus obsolete boundaries. The area around Brussels is generally labelled 'Brussels periphery' by francophones and 'Flemish edge' (Vlaamse Rand) by the Flemish.

These are the ingredients of the institutional debate that started in the early 1960s, leading to a series of quite inventive compromises, but never to a solution than can be seen as fully satisfactory by both language communities. Every institutional compromise is an agreement for the time being. The Belgian federation is therefore not based on a blueprint. It is not based on existing models. It was not even meant to become federal in the first place. The reforms of the state that have been negotiated since the 1960s were basically an attempt to *avoid federalism*. Federalism was a term only used by the regionalist parties. Granting autonomy to both the regions (Flanders, Wallonia and Brussels) and the communities (French, Dutch) was a way to avoid gridlock and further and more radical demands (Covell, 1993).

In the following paragraphs we will describe each of these steps until the latest reform of the constitution in 2001. Each of these reforms and temporary agreements however only came into being after long periods of bitter – always only verbal – conflict and gridlock. In the institutions put into place as a result of these compromises, there is also a place for the German-speaking community of Belgium. This community of some 60,000 people was never really involved in this debate between north and south. But since a new state structure built on the use of language was set in place, the German language community received a far-reaching degree of autonomy, similar to the Flemish and French language communities.

Although Belgian state reform is not the realization of a blueprint, there is some clear logic. Each reform builds on the previous one, by expanding and refining it. None of the consecutive reforms, however, introduced a fundamental change. Some crucial choices made in the earliest phases of the territorial reorganization of the Belgian state – starting in the 1920s – can be considered as critical junctures, as points of no return. The effects of these early choices remain visible today.

Step 1: Freezing the language border

Although there was no reform of the constitution involved, a number of decisions taken in 1963 are extremely important. Many historical agreements or pacts have received a name. For the 1963 reform this is the agreement of 'Val Duchesse' or 'Hertoginnedal' (Witte, 1988). It refers to the castle-like residence in a Brussels park that has often been used for top negotiators to retreat from public and press attention in order to try to find a way out of pressing problems.

The 1963 agreement clearly marked the new strength and confidence of Flanders, and, indeed, the agreement fulfilled a number of important Flemish requests. The most important was the fixing of the language borderline and thus the abolishment of the language census. Actually the last census before Val Duchesse/Hertoginnedal had faced massive protest from the Flemish side, with many mayors simply refusing to organize it. The results of the last census had indicated that again six municipalities adjacent to Brussels would have to move from Flanders into the Brussels bilingual area. After painful discussions, during which the survival of the Christian democrat and socialist government was at risk, a compromise was found.

It stated in the first place that the language border would not change any more. The census would in the future not ask questions about the use of language. This is the point scored by the Flemish. To compensate for this, linguistic 'facilities' were granted to the inhabitants of a number of local municipalities – especially those six municipalities around Brussels. These facilities mean that the inhabitants can communicate in French with the public authorities and that primary school education can be organized in French if a minimum number of parents request it. It does however also mean that these municipalities remain fully in the Flemish territory where the language used by the public authorities and in education is and remains Dutch.

In that same agreement two municipalities were transferred to another province, which meant that they were transferred – albeit with language facilities – to another language regime. One went from Dutch to French (Comines/Komen) and one from French to Dutch (Voeren/Fourrons). In Voeren/Fourrons this gave birth to a political movement 'Retour à Liège' (Back to Liège) that would win all local elections until 2000. Disagreement on the statute of Voeren/Fourrons – a village of merely 4,000 inhabitants – has been the cause of the fall of several governments. The Flemish also asked in Val Duchesse/Hertoginnedal for a reorganization of the electoral districts in and around Brussels. The central district of Brussels – full name being Brussels-Halle-Vilvoorde (or BHV) – indeed also includes parts of Flanders. The Flemish would have liked to see it split into a Brussels district and one for the Flemish part of it (including the six municipalities with facilities). This problem was however not solved, and remained one of the sources of frustration for the Flemish. The non-expansion of Brussels on the other hand is one of the sources of frustration for the francophones.

This agreement was accepted in parliament, but with substantial resistance on the francophone side. On the Flemish side the idea of the language facilities did not go down easily, but the geographical limitation of Brussels and the freezing of the language boundary were a clear victory. The francophones now became very much aware of the fact that being a demographic and thus parliamentary minority was a serious problem. Coupled with the economic power of the north strengthening and the Walloon economy in decline, this situation activated and mobilized both a Walloon and a Brussels regionalist party. The Brussels FDF mobilized basically on the right to freely speak the language of one's choice, on the right of Brussels to become a fully fledged region and on the right of municipalities outside of Brussels to join Brussels (see also Chapter 4). The incompatible demands for the future of Belgium were now clearly on the table.

Step 2: A constitutional reform in 1970

The Belgian constitution had for a very long time remained basically unchanged. In the 19th century it was changed once to expand voting rights and again in 1919 to further expand voting rights (see Chapters 2 and 5). The reform of 1970 was therefore the very first major reorganization of the Belgian state. The 1970 reform is important and even crucial for two reasons. In the first place it lays the foundations of the future federal Belgium. It is a point of no return. The freezing of the language border in 1963, the split along language lines of the public broadcasting company in 1960 and the split along language lines of the Department of Education are other markers of an evolution that was picking up momentum and that would soon lead to the end of all the Belgian political parties. The second reason why the reform of 1970 is crucial is in the way in which it defines the procedures for future reforms.

The 1970 reform enshrined the existence of regions and communities. There was hardly any agreement on what exactly they might do, but the acceptance of the principle was quite important. Actually, there was more agreement on the communities than on the regions, because the latter supposed an agreement on Brussels. Could it really be a region like the two others? What would its boundaries be? Could it be a francophone region or should the Dutch-speaking minority receive guarantees? All this was postponed to a later phase.

But the acceptance of a double structure for the new Belgium is quite important. It is an incredible compromise between the two incompatible definitions of Belgium. The regions follow a strictly territorial logic: Wallonia, Brussels and Flanders are defined in geographical terms. In this regional organization Brussels is a region and is not part of the Flemish Region. At this point there was no real agreement on the boundaries of Brussels, but those accepted after the freezing of the linguistic borderline in 1963 were the basis to work on.

As can be seen in Figure 3.1 the communities follow to a large extent the territorial logic, but overlap in the Brussels region. The Flemish Community is composed of the inhabitants of the Flemish region and of the Dutch-speakers in the Brussels region. The French Community is composed of the inhabitants of the Walloon region and of the French-speakers in Brussels. In the territory of

Figure 3.1 *The territories of regions and communities*

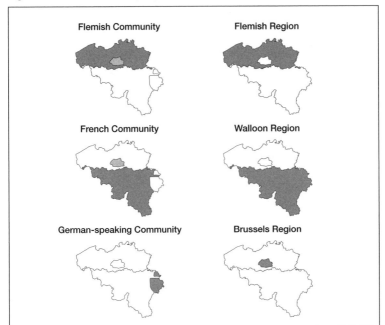

the Walloon Region there is however also the area in which German is the official language: although part of the Walloon Region, it is a separate German Community. This compromise between regional and communitarian logic does not produce easy and straightforward new institutions, but it allows the Belgian state to move on, to hold off, for the time being, the demands for further autonomy. And the compromise can survive as long as both large communities *agree to disagree* about the exact place and meaning of Brussels.

After the acceptance of these constitutional reforms, Prime Minister Gaston Eyskens declared solemnly that a major step had been taken. He told parliament that 'the Belgium of our fathers' did not exist any more and that a new Belgium had been put into place, a Belgium in which the existence of regions and communities was officially and formally recognized. And the hope was that this would be enough for a real new start. It was however only the beginning.

The reform of 1970 also introduced a number of measures to protect the francophone minority. From 1970 on, both houses of the parliament are neatly divided into two language groups. All MPs elected in a unilingual district automatically belong to that language group. Those elected in the mixed district of Brussel-Halle-Vilvoorde can make a choice by taking their oath in the preferred language. The division in language groups is needed for three protective measures, the first of which refers to the composition of the government. From 1970 on the Belgian government needs to respect the rule of 'parity' which means that there have to be an equal number of Flemish and francophone ministers. The prime minister is not counted in this parity. Since 1970 all prime ministers – except for two very short-lived governments (see Chapter 6) – have been Dutch-speakers.

The second measure is the 'alarm bell procedure'. It states that when three-quarters of the members of one language group declare that a proposal is being discussed that will harm their interests, the parliamentary procedure must be interrupted. The issue goes to the government in its fifty-fifty composition and the government has 30 days to come up with a solution. If there is no solution, there is no government any more. And to form a new government, an agreement between the two language groups is required.

The third measure is a new legislative technique. The constitution created new types of laws called 'special majority laws'. These are actually constitutional laws, but do not have to go through the long procedure needed for a change of the constitution (see Chapter 7). They can be used to further fill in the general principles laid down in the constitution, for example the structure and competences of the regions and communities. For a special majority law to be accepted or amended, special majorities are needed. A special majority law requires a two-thirds majority of all members of parliament and a majority of the members of each language group.

This 1970 reform of the constitution, meant in the first place to cool down the tensions between the two language groups and to reduce the pressure from the regionalist parties demanding a deep reform of the state, is a historical landmark. It marks the institutionalization of a *power-sharing logic* for the managing of the linguistic tensions.

Building into the institutions the obligation to govern together has a double effect. First, it puts into place, step by step, a federal system that has to function according to the rules of consociational logic. And second, it defines the rules of the game for any further reform of the system. After 1970 – and this is very important for the francophone minority – all institutional reforms need this double majority. All reforms have to take into account the fact that the two language communities are mutual veto players. Using the demographic majority of the Flemish has now become impossible. And that is another source of frustration for the Flemish Movement. The 1970 constitution is usually referred to as the 'bolt constitution', for the way in which it puts a lock on the potential demographic power of Flanders.

Step 3: The reform of 1980

After a decade of failed attempts to give some concrete meaning and substance to the regions and communities that had been defined in the constitution of 1970, a large coalition of Christian democrats, socialists, Volksunie and FDF was formed in 1977. It controlled the required large and double majorities in the parliament and it took on board the two most radical forces on each side, both prepared to settle for a compromise. This 'Egmont Pact' would not be immediately implemented though. After only 18 months the government collapsed. It took a few more attempts to implement the reforms and finally a large three-family coalition of Christian democrats, socialists and liberals was able to amend the constitution in 1980.

This time formal institutions were set up for the French, Flemish and German language communities and for the regions of Flanders and Wallonia. For Brussels there was no solution. There was no agreement on the boundaries, on the exact status and on the way in which the Flemish minority could be protected in a Brussels region. The new institutions were however still fairly thin. The regions and communities – except for Brussels – now had a parliamentary assembly. These were not directly elected, but based on the existing language groups in the national parliament. The Flemish and the French Communities had a parliament that was thus composed of the Flemish and francophone members of both the House of Representatives and the Senate. The Walloon regional assembly was composed of the national members of House and Senate elected in Walloon districts.

At this point, the institutions of region and community are merged on the Flemish side, introducing an important asymmetry into the system. Indeed, there would be only one Flemish assembly, responsible for both the Region and the Community. Actually this allows Flanders to stress the community as the first and most important component of the Belgian state. The Flemish assembly is the assembly of the Flemish Community, and without the few members living in Brussels it is the assembly of the Region. This is symbolically important for Flanders but also practically feasible. The difference between the Flemish Community and the Flemish Region is Brussels, but in Brussels the number of Dutch-speakers is quite small. Of all the members of the Flemish Community no more than 3 per cent live in Brussels. This ratio is quite different on the francophone side. Of all the members of the French Community, almost 20 per cent live in Brussels. Furthermore there is a historical and thus symbolically important link between Flanders and Brussels that does not exist between Wallonia and Brussels. Brussels is geographically not located in Wallonia.

After the 1980 reform, the assemblies of the regions and communities also have a government that is called 'executive'. It is however not elected by these assemblies. Actually a number of ministers in the Belgian government receive a portfolio with competences relative to one of the regions or communities. Thus post 1980, the Belgian government has a Minister President, a Minister of Finance and a Minister of Education for each community. This is a rather hybrid and clearly unfinished situation, but – like in 1970 – it is enough to agree that for the time being this should be able to function. The most difficult question – What about Brussels? – is postponed. The Brussels issue is put 'in the fridge'.

Step 4: A solution for Brussels

During the 1980s the political agenda shifted more to economic and financial matters. Tensions related to the reorganization of the state did not disappear though. The Brussels issue remained unresolved and the little village of Voeren/Fourrons, especially, continued to bother the Belgian government. At the local elections of 1982, the list 'Back to Liège' once more won the elections. The leader of that list, José Happart, should therefore have been appointed mayor of the village. At that time the appointment had to be decided by the national government, in which the Flemish parties did not want to see Happart – who declared proudly that he would not speak or learn Dutch – become the mayor of a municipality in which the official language of the public authorities is Dutch (with language facilities for the inhabitants). The Parti Socialiste put José Happart on its list for the European elections of 1984 where he received a very solid 235,000 preference votes. The Happart issue eventually brought down the Belgian government in 1987.

Forming a new government after the early elections thus required a new agreement on a number of burning issues and growing frustrations on both sides of the language border. Together with an extremely complex compromise about the required language knowledge of public authorities at the local level, the Belgian state moved further in the direction of a federal system. And its institutions became ever more complex.

First there was a solution for Brussels. The boundaries remained unchanged, but the region received – with some minor exceptions (see below) – the status of a real region. Although the Flemish did not like the idea, they could accept it because of the interesting compensations. These include the acceptance of a close link between the Dutch-speaking inhabitants of Flanders and Brussels. Furthermore the Brussels regional institutions are set up as a kind of mirror of the Belgian institutions. The Brussels regional parliament is divided into two language groups. The Brussels regional government must be composed of an equal number of Dutch-speaking and French-speaking ministers, with exception made for the regional prime minister. And for crucial votes – like the election of the prime minister – a majority in each language group is required. Brussels is a region that can only be governed as long as both language communities find a common ground to govern together. If there is no agreement, there is no government. In 1989 the first Brussels regional parliament was directly elected by the Brussels population.

After the 1988 reforms it was clear that one crucial element was missing in the Belgian state structure. While the Brussels regional parliament was directly elected in 1989, the other assemblies of regions and communities were still composed of national MPs having 'two hats' and sitting in both parliaments at the same time. And again after difficult and painstaking discussions and negotiations and one more government that collapsed without being able to solve the puzzle, another constitutional reform was agreed upon in 1993. This one was called the 'Saint Michael Agreement' because it was on Saint Michael's day (29 September) that the final compromise was struck.

This agreement actually put the roof on the house and trans-formed Belgium into a state that can be called federal. While federalism was, in the 1960s, considered a heresy and rather something to be avoided, it is now the official label of Belgium. There are three achievements that need to be mentioned here. The first and most important is the direct election of all the regional parliaments. After Brussels in 1989, Flanders and Wallonia elected their first regional parliament in 1995. The second change is the reform of the Senate. The second house of the Belgian parliament, which had become in its composition almost a copy of the House of Representatives, was transformed into a Senate of the Communities. And finally the territorial organization of Belgium was adapted to the new federal logic by splitting the central province of Brabant into Flemish Brabant and Walloon Brabant, meaning that both Flanders and Wallonia are now divided into five provinces. The Brussels Region is not divided into provinces and no longer belongs to a province. As in previous constitutional reforms, in 1993, the regions and communities received additional competences and financial means, further reducing the powers of the central state. Of importance here is the fact that competences with respect to international relations were also devolved to the regions and communities.

Another and less important constitutional reform was agreed on in 2002. This involves the expansion of financial and fiscal auton-omy for the regions and communities and the strengthening of the guarantees for the Dutch-speakers in the Brussels Region. The number of seats for each language group in the Brussels regional parliament is now fixed. And again powers are devolved to the regions and communities, including the transfer of the competence to fully organize and supervise the local municipalities.

The distribution of powers

The double federation of regions and communities and the need to find an acceptable solution for a Brussels Region that is, for community matters, linked to both (and especially the Flemish) communities, has put into place a quite complex set of interlock-ing institutions. These come on top of the fact that there are two different types of substates. They each have their own compe-tences, and it is quite important to note the difference between the two – albeit a difference based on a rather straightforward principle. The communities have powers related to *people*. They offer services. The regions have powers related to *territory*. In practice the distinction between them is not always tenable, since people live in territories while politics related to territories affect the people living there.

The powers of the regions and communities are listed in a number of special majority laws, that is, laws that have been accepted by a two-thirds majority and by a majority in each language group in the federal parliament. They need the same double majorities to be changed.

The main competences of the regions (Flanders, Wallonia and Brussels) are:

- Area development planning (for example town planning, monuments and sites, land policy and so on)
- Agriculture
- Environment (protection, waste policy)
- Rural development and nature conservation (parks, forests, hunting, fishing and so on)
- Housing
- Water policy (production and supply, purification, sewerage)
- Economic affairs (economic policy, export policy – not included are monetary policy, price and income policy, labour law, social security)
- Energy policy (except for national infrastructure and nuclear energy)
- Local and provincial authorities (institutional organization, administrative control, finance of public works)
- Employment policy (partially)
- Public works and transport (roads, ports, public transport but railways not included)
- International cooperation within the limits of these competences.

The main competences of the communities (Flemish, French and German-speaking) are:

- Cultural matters (defence and promotion of language, arts, libraries, radio and television broadcasting, youth policy, leisure and tourism and so on)
- Education

- So-called 'personalized' matters (health policy, assistance to individuals and so on)
- Use of language (except for the localities with a special status, that is, with language 'facilities')
- International cooperation within the limits of these competences.

The powers of the federal state are not explicitly listed in the constitution or in special majority laws. This means that in practice the *residual powers* belong to the federal level. All powers not devolved remain federal. The major powers of the federal state are:

- Justice (the organization and functioning of the judicial branch)
- Social security (finance and organization) and labour law
- Monetary policy (although mostly transferred to the European Central Bank) and public debt
- Security and defence
- Civil law (marriages, contracts, nationality and so on)
- Foreign affairs (except for those matters devolved to regions or communities).

These lists show clearly to what extent the different steps in the reform of the state have devolved quite substantial powers to the regions and communities. For the communities, the competence to organize education is the most important in terms of money and in terms of visibility. Regions also have a number of competences that make them conspicuous in people's daily lives; one of the most important being public transport. All three regions have their own regional transport company (bus, tram and metro) that clearly belongs to the region. Environmental policy, nature conservation, area development planning and housing are other very visible policies on which the regions can build a distinctive profile.

Regions and communities have also received a high degree of autonomy in international relations. The basic principle in this respect is very simple: *in foro interno, in foro externo*. When a competence belongs to a region or community it also confers the power to organize the international contacts and to make treaties. International trade is also a competence that belongs to the regions. All three regions thus have a minister with international affairs and international trade in his or her portfolio. This devolution of international powers to regions and communities has multiplied the antennas of Belgium in other countries. In addition to the national embassy and consulates, the regions and communities have their own representations. These do not function at the diplomatic level, but are meant to promote the culture and economy of all the composite parts of the federal Belgium (see also Chapter 9).

Overall the competences are neatly distributed in fairly homogeneous packages, which is the result of the very logic of the reform. It is meant to grant autonomy and not to foster cooperation. There are however a number of competences for which some matters are shared between the federal level and the regional or community level. This is especially the case for economic and labour policy. Prices, salaries and unemployment (part of the social security system) are federal, while the regions have some competences in labour policy and the communities are responsible for education and formation. Flanders, in particular, would like economic and social policy to be put together into more homogeneous packages, and that these should be given to the substates.

The institutions of the federal state

The long march from the freezing of the language border to the new Article 1 of the constitution was a very erratic process. It did however end in a set of institutions that have already achieved a short tradition. Competences and financial means will still move between levels, but the basic organization of the federal state is here to stay for a while. We will first describe each of the federated entities, and then discuss their political powers (Deschouwer, 2005a).

At the substate level Belgium has five federated entities: Flanders, the Walloon Region, the Brussels Region, the French Community and the German Community (see Figure 3.2). The structure of the Walloon Region is the simplest. It is one of the three regions, with regional institutions and with control over the powers granted to the regions. Wallonia has chosen Namur as its capital city, and that is indeed where the Walloon parliament and Walloon government are based.

The Walloon parliament has 75 seats and is elected directly by all the voters living in Wallonia. Like the other regions, its term is

Figure 3.2 *The structure of the Belgian federation*

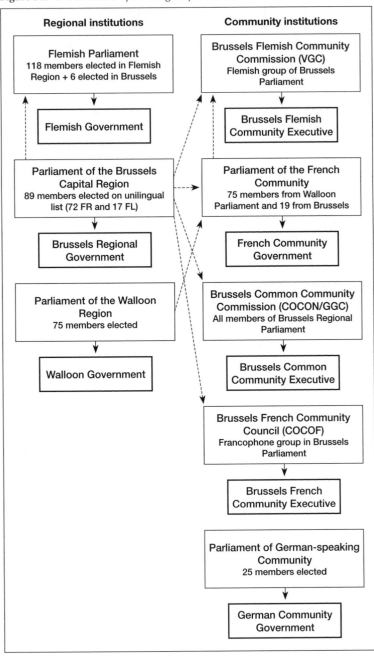

five years. The regional elections are always organized in June, on the same day as the elections to the European Parliament. The Walloon government is elected by the Walloon parliament, and has a maximum number of nine ministers. This number has been fixed by the Walloon Region itself (actually increasing the number from the original seven to nine in 1999). The Walloon government and parliament issue *decrees* to deal with the matters devolved to the regions. The Walloon Region also has its own administration. Actually, civil servants formally belonging to the central Belgian administration have been gradually transferred together with the competences moving from the centre to the devolved entities.

Flanders is both a region and a community. Technically speaking both a Flemish Region and Flemish Community exist, but the Flemish government and parliament have the powers of both entities. There is thus one single Flemish parliament, which is located in Brussels, because Brussels has been chosen by the Flemish parliament as the capital city of Flanders. It might seem awkward to opt for Brussels – being another region – as the capital city, but since Flanders wants to be a community in the first place, it can choose Brussels because Brussels belongs to the territory on which the powers of the Flemish Community can be exercised.

There are 124 members in the Flemish parliament. Of these a total of 118 are elected directly by the voters living in the Flemish Region. Six of them are elected in Brussels, and together they form the parliament of the Flemish Community. The voters who in Brussels cast a vote for the parties competing for the seats of the Flemish language group can, subsequently, cast a vote to elect the Brussels members of the Flemish parliament. When the Flemish parliament deals with matters strictly related to the region, the members elected in Brussels do not have the right to vote. The Dutch-speakers of Brussels are in fact, with 5 per cent of the seats, slightly overrepresented in the Flemish parliament. Reducing the number of seats would however raise the threshold for one seat to at least 20 per cent, and that would severely limit the possibility for smaller parties to have a representation from Brussels in the Flemish parliament.

The Flemish government has a maximum number of 11 ministers. Of these one has to be an inhabitant of Brussels. His or her competences should be strictly community competences such as culture or sports or tourism. The Brussels minister in the Flemish parliament normally also has the competence of Brussels affairs and is the liaison with the institutions of the Flemish Community in Brussels (see below). The Flemish government is elected by the parliament.

Like the other regions and communities, Flanders has its own administration dealing again with both regional and community matters. It implements the decrees issued by the Flemish parliament and government. This Flemish administration is also located in Brussels. In doing so, Flanders clearly demonstrates its attachment to Brussels. Flanders is visibly present in Brussels with a series of official buildings like the parliament, the official and working residences of the ministers and the buildings of the administration, all displaying the Flemish lion flag.

The German Community is also a fairly easy and simple structure. It has a parliament of 25 members, who have been directly elected since 1990. Only the inhabitants of the German-speaking territory – in Wallonia – have the right to vote. The parliament elects a government that is composed of up to five ministers (usually three), one of whom is the prime minister. The government and parliament issue decrees dealing with the community matters for the inhabitants of the German territory. For regional matters, the German-speaking Belgians belong to the Walloon Region.

The French Community has a parliament of 94 members. It is not directly elected. The members of the French Community parliament are first elected in the Walloon or the Brussels parliament. Of the 72 francophone members of the Brussels parliament, the first 19 elected also have a seat in the French Community parliament. Together with all 75 members elected in the Walloon parliament they represent the French Community of Belgium. The French Community parliament elects a government of a maximum eight members (raised from the original four in 1999 to be able to distribute more easily the ministerial posts in a three-party coalition).

The French Community parliament and government issue decrees on community matters, valid for the population of Wallonia (except for the German language territory) and for the inhabitants of Brussels. The French Community can however decide to transfer some of its competences to the Walloon Region or to the institutions of the French Community in Brussels (see below). The most important of these transfers to have been realized is education, where the Brussels francophone institutions have received full powers to organize francophone education in Brussels.

Some competences of the French Community have also been transferred to the Walloon Region. Actually this reflects the difficulties of having two separate entities – a region and a community – serving to a large extent the same population. In Flanders this was easily solved by simply merging the region and the community. The importance of Brussels in the French Community makes this simple merger much more difficult on the francophone side, and it would also go against the idea that it is the regions and not the communities that are the most important building blocks of the Belgian federation. Confronted though with the rather smooth functioning of the merged Flemish institutions, several attempts to better link the Walloon Region and the French Community have been tried out. This is done mainly by the choice of ministers for both governments. A member of the Walloon government can at the same time be a member of the French Community government. A francophone member of the Brussels government can also be a member of the French Community government. So far the composition of all these coalitions has been the same, which allows the francophone political parties to move their ministers between these governments and to share them between the governments. In 2008 a quite radical choice was made by the Parti Socialiste: it put the same person in the position of prime minister of the Walloon government and of the French Community government.

And finally there is the Brussels Region. Formally it is called 'Brussels Capital Region', to symbolically mark (on the request of Flanders) the difference between the Flemish and Walloon Regions on the one hand and the Brussels Region on the other. The Brussels Region needs to be a mixed and bilingual one and form a bridge between the two language communities. The Brussels Region has received the same powers as Flanders and Wallonia, but there are a few minor but significant exceptions. The rules produced by the Brussels regional parliament are called 'ordinances' while the other regions (and communities) issue 'decrees'. The federal government can in principle nullify an ordinance, although this is politically unthinkable because of the linguistic balance to be respected in the federal government. Courts can also check the constitutionality of ordinances, but not of federal laws or decrees. Contrary to the two other regions, Brussels has no 'constitutive autonomy', which means that it cannot decide on the way in which its institutions function. The reason for that is the protection of the Dutch-speaking language group in Brussels. The way in which this minority is represented and protected is entrenched in the federal constitution.

In the Brussels regional parliament, 17 out of the 89 seats are reserved for Dutch-speakers, as are also two ministerial positions out of five. The competence to change this logic belongs to the federal government only. Flanders and Wallonia, in contrast, can decide themselves on the number of seats in their regional parliament, the number of ministers, the electoral system.

The Brussels regional parliament has 89 seats, which is quite a large number, given the size of the region. Wallonia has a parliament of 75 members for some 3.5 million inhabitants. Brussels has one million inhabitants. The larger size of the Brussels regional parliament is simply meant to give the Flemish minority a reasonable representation. The original size of the parliament was 75, and the number of seats going to each of the language groups was computed on the basis of the number of votes cast for each of them. That meant for the Flemish Community either ten or eleven seats. Six of them also had to sit in the Flemish parliament. From 2004 on, the number of Flemish seats is fixed at 17, and the number of francophone seats is fixed at 72. The Brussels parliament is thus directly elected by two separate sets of voters, each electing their part of the parliament. That is exactly the way in which the federal parliament is elected, since there are no statewide parties. In Brussels though the neat separation between the two groups is an institutional obligation. When a list is presented to the election of the Brussels parliament, a choice has to be made on which of the two language groups it will run. Whoever is a candidate on a list of one language group can never in the future be a candidate on a list of the other language groups. And in order to be able to stand for election on one of the lists a candidate needs to have an identity card in that language.

Inhabitants of Brussels can choose whether the first language on their identity card is French or Dutch (the third and fourth are always German and English). For inhabitants not running for elections this has no further consequence. The choice of a language for the identity card does not lead to a formal registration as belonging to one of the language groups. Inhabitants of Brussels remain free at all times to make use of whatever is being offered by each of the two communities. At each election, the voters are free to choose. The candidates can make a language choice only once.

This is indeed the basic logic of the Brussels institutions. At the level of the institutions, everything is strictly divided into language groups. At the level of the citizens, there is no formal division. There is no subnationality. All inhabitants of Brussels can go and watch theatre shows sponsored by either the French or the Flemish community. Each inhabitant of Brussels can choose whether he or she wants to send the children to a school of the Flemish or the French Community. And that choice can change over time and can be different for the first and the second child.

The Brussels regional parliament elects a government of five ministers: two from each language group and one prime minister. The prime minister of Brussels is – given the overwhelming majority of French – always a French-speaker. The Brussels parliament and government issue ordinances on regional matters only. For community matters on Brussels territory, the Brussels parliament splits up into no fewer than three different institutions.

First there is the COCOF: the 'Commission de la Communauté Française' (Commission of the French Community). It functions as a parliamentary assembly that can issue 'rules' (not decrees or ordinances) to organize the policies of the French Community in Brussels. These policies of the French Community originate from the French Community Parliament of Belgium. The COCOF has a government composed of the francophone members of the regional government, each having some community matters in their portfolio (arts, culture, education and so on). For matters that have been formally transferred from the French Community to the COCOF, it can issue decrees. This is the case for the organization of francophone schools in the Brussels region.

There is of course a Flemish counterpart to the COCOF, but its relation to the larger Flemish Community of Belgium is different. Fully into the Flemish logic that there is only one Flemish Community and that it includes the Dutch-speaking inhabitants of Brussels, the Flemish Community Commission or VGC (Vlaamse Gemeenschapscommissie) has no real law-making power. It implements and executes Flemish decrees on community matters in Brussels. The organization of Flemish schools in Brussels is thus basically decided in the Flemish parliament and government and executed in Brussels by the VGC. Like the COCOF, the VGC has a government composed of the Flemish members of the Brussels regional government.

And finally there is also a Common Community Commission (COCON in French and GGC in Dutch). It is composed of all the members of the regional parliament. It has no competences in the realm of culture, arts or education, but deals with welfare organizations that do not have a clear unilingual status. The most important of these are the local social welfare organizations OCMW/CPAS (see below), the management of some public hospitals and homes for the elderly. These can opt for a bilingual status. The executive of the COCON/GGC is composed of all the members of the Brussels regional parliament.

It is clear that very few people really grasp all the subtle differences between these institutions, all making policy for the inhabitants of Brussels. These have thus seven public authorities taking care of them: the federal state, the Brussels Region, the French Community and the COCOF, the Flemish Community and the VGC, and finally the local municipality.

Financing the regions and communities

The way in which fiscal and financial powers are exercised in the Belgian federation clearly reflects its nature: a double federation of regions and communities and an open-ended and constantly adjusted process of piecemeal changes. The devolution of the financial powers did not follow the pace of the devolution of policymaking powers, which meant that until 2002 the basic logic was one of redistribution to the regions and communities of centrally collected taxes. Before 2002 the autonomy of regions and communities in matters of taxation and fiscal policy was extremely limited. A reform of the special majority law regulating the financial processes in 2002 introduced a somewhat higher level of fiscal and financial autonomy. The Flemish side wanted even more. This demand was very much inspired by the better economic situation and stronger fiscal capacity in Flanders. Francophones are very reluctant to see an increase in subnational fiscal and financial autonomy because they fear the fiscal competition that could result from it and that would put Flanders – the only region really able to reduce taxes – in an even stronger position. The degree of fiscal and financial autonomy of regions and communities thus remains fairly limited (Deschouwer & Verdonck, 2003).

The double federation has a number of direct consequences for Belgium's fiscal and financial organization. The two communities are both present in the Brussels Region, but the inhabitants of Brussels are not required to choose a community identity. The communities therefore do not know who their own citizens are. The total figures of taxes paid in the Brussels region are known, but not the amount coming from members of each of the communities. Thus, for Brussels, one needs to agree that tax money is considered to come from both communities according to a virtual 80–20 balance, reflecting more or less the weight of each community in Brussels: 20 per cent Dutch-speakers and 80 per cent French-speakers. Basically, taxing powers are transferred to the regions rather than to the communities, precisely to avoid this Brussels problem. If a community were to decide to raise a tax, it could only do so in cooperation with the other community, which means that it is not really an autonomous taxing power.

The communities are thus predominantly financed by federal funds. These funds are composed of three elements: financial transfers, a compensation for former shared taxes (radio and television tax), and a fund related to the number of foreign students in each community's education system. This mixed and very ad hoc logic illustrates perfectly how the financial organization is the result of subsequent piecemeal political compromises and not of some well-defined principles.

The financial transfers are composed of VAT transfers and a personal income-tax transfer. Each year an amount is determined for the communities, based on the level of the transfer in 1989 and adapted to the consumer price index. In 2002, it was agreed that from 2012 on the amount would also be adapted to the growth in gross national income. Until 2012, the difference between the old and the (more generous) new technique will be compensated for by an annually increasing fixed amount. The total amount given to each community is also adapted to changes in the total student population (the major expenses of the communities being indeed the organization of their school system). There is no solidarity mechanism for the distribution of these funds because they were based on the needs (number of students) of each community. The 2002 reform did not introduce such a mechanism either, but simply increased the amount given to each community and linked it not only to the communities' needs but also to the communities' taxing capacity. The first clearly responds to a demand from the French Community, the latter to a demand from the Flemish Community.

The transfer of personal income-tax revenue is an amount fixed by special majority law and adapted annually to the growth in national revenue. The proportion given to each community is determined on the basis of each community's contribution to the personal income tax, with a fixed 20–80 distribution key for taxes collected in the Brussels region. The VAT transfers and personal income-tax transfers constitute the bulk (some 90 per cent) of the communities' financial means.

The regions also receive transfers from the federal state, but have had since 2002 a greater fiscal and financial autonomy. The transfer of the federal income tax is similar to the one given to the communities. There is a total amount set in 1989 and adapted annually to the evolution of the consumer price index and to the growth in gross national income. The distribution between the regions is based on each region's fiscal capacity. An equalization transfer is given to the regions with a personal income-tax revenue level that is below the national per capita average. The amount is a fixed sum set in 1989 (indexed), multiplied by the number of inhabitants of that region and by the difference in percentage between the per capita income-tax revenue of the region and the per capita amount in the country as a whole.

The regional autonomy introduced in 2002 takes the form of lump-sum reductions or increases of the personal income taxes. Regions also have the right to reduce taxes in matters related to the regional competences. This means, for instance, that they can use their own fiscal incentives for environmental policy. The fiscal autonomy of the regions has, however, been bound by measures that seek to prevent too much fiscal competition between the regions. The margins of the autonomy are set at 6.75 per cent of the personal income tax localized in each region. The special majority law of 2002 also states that regions must refrain from unfair tax competition, but fails to define exactly what that means.

Regions also control a number of taxes of their own: taxes on gambling and betting, the opening of drinking establishments, automatic betting devices, gifts, registration of property, automobile registration, and possession of radio and television sets. All these taxes used to be federal taxes, and the federal state deducts the amount that it loses by giving it to the regions from the general transfer of the personal income tax to the regions. The regions can also autonomously set the base for real estate taxes (also taxed by the federal state and by municipalities). All these measures allow the regions to conduct a fiscal policy of their own, although within strict limits.

All these regulations of the fiscal and financial organization of the Belgian federation are written down in special majority laws and not in the constitution. The constitution does not even give a general principle or guideline. Indeed, the special majority laws do not implement such a principle, but reflect the temporary agreement between regions and communities that are economically different and that voice different demands in this respect. The north pushes for more autonomy, the south for more solidarity. The only possible outcome is a detailed agreement right in the middle.

Dealing with conflicts

The autonomy of regions and communities is thus far-reaching and they do not have to account for their actions at the federal level. Since in a federal state a minimal level of mutual goodwill is needed to make its complex institutions function more or less smoothly, the Belgian constitution requires all authorities to act in a spirit of federal loyalty. Actually, the notion only enters Belgian debates when one of the constituent entities feels that the other is going beyond the limits (that is, when a conflict of interest seems to be building up). This would typically be the case when Flanders pushes for further autonomy and tries out the limits of its designated powers, or when the francophones try to get around the obligation to keep the actions of the French community limited to Wallonia and Brussels or when they try to get around requirements for bilingualism.

The creation of regions and communities has led to new instruments of policymaking. While the federal level issues 'laws', the regions and communities issue 'decrees' or 'ordinances'. These different instruments are however treated on an equal footing. There is no such thing as a hierarchy of norms, giving precedence to the rules of the higher level. For policies that require cooperation between the levels or between regions and communities, the normal instrument is that of intergovernmental cooperation agreements stating clearly who will do what.

The regions, the communities, and the federal state can draft such agreements of cooperation in view of the creation and common management of common services and institutions, the joint exercise of competences or the development of joint ventures. Agreements can be horizontal (between the region and communities) or vertical (between the federal state and regions or communities), and they can be optional or compulsory. The latter might seem strange, but the technique has often been used to make sure that the transfer of powers to a lower level does not lead to major discontinuities. A transfer is then agreed on, but becomes effective only when the regions and/or communities have concluded an agreement of cooperation to deal with the details of the transfer and the details of the way in which the task will be performed in the future. This was done, for instance, when public transport was transferred.

The Belgian federation is the result of numerous attempts to avoid ongoing conflict. Yet, even though the federal structure has reduced the tensions between the language groups, the level of potential conflict remains high. On top of that and mixed with it are the typical conflicts occurring in federal states: conflicts of competence and conflicts of interest.

Conflicts over the distribution of powers are settled in a judicial way. This can take two forms. First, conflicts can be prevented by the legislation section of the Council of State (Raad van State/Conseil d'État), which renders a prior opinion on all proposed legislation whether it emanates from the federal or the federated entities. The Council checks whether the laws, decrees, and ordinances comply with higher legal rules, including of course the constitution. The advice of the Council of State is not binding, but it is an important warning, and does have a political impact. Second, if a conflict over distribution of powers is signalled after a law, decree, or ordinance has been issued, it is settled by the Constitutional Court (Grondwettelijk Hof/Cour Constitutionnelle). This court is composed of twelve judges, six Dutch-speaking and six French-speaking, all appointed by the federal government, on proposal of the Senate. Half the judges are former politicians, and half belong to the judicial profession.

Conflicts of interest (that is, conflicts involving lack of agreement on the substance of laws, decrees, or ordinances) are more problematic because they need a political solution in an institutional setting that is complex, full of subtle equilibriums, and full of diverging interpretations. The conflicts here are likely to occur between the two major communities and will then in practice have to be solved by an agreement between them. Typically, this will be a projected law or regulation by one entity or by the federal government, which another entity fears will affect it negatively. In order to formally deal with conflicts of interest, the 'Concertation Committee' was created. It is composed of the federal prime minister, five ministers of the federal government, and six members of the governments of regions and communities. It also needs to be perfectly linguistically balanced. Either the federal government or the government of one of the federated entities can signal a potential conflict to the committee. This move suspends the debated decision for 60 days. During that time, the committee can try to find a solution by consensus. If this is not found after 60 days, the suspension is lifted and the conflict remains unsolved. If the conflict is serious, that is the most likely outcome.

The fact that federal Belgium is basically built on two language groups means that the difference between conflicts of interest and conflicts over the distribution of powers are often blurred. If the two language communities disagree on the way in which the constitution, a law, or a decree has to be interpreted, a ruling by a court does not solve the problem. The problem is at the same time then a political problem, a divergence of views, and hence a conflict of interest. If the interpretation of a rule remains unclear, it needs to be reformulated and thus renegotiated. It needs a political solution (Jans & Tombeur, 2000; Poirier, 2002).

A peculiar federation

The Belgian constitution declares formally that Belgium is a federal state, but the least one can say is that it is a rather special federation. Its political institutions do not really resemble those of the classical 'come together' federations. Other federal or federal-type countries that are the result of processes of devolution – like Spain – also display a number of very peculiar features. Typical for these more recent federal or regionalized states are institutions *à la carte*, adapted to sometimes widely varying demands from different parts of the national territory. Summing up, we can say that there are at least nine aspects making the Belgian federation a peculiar one.

In the first place it is a federation *by default*. Belgium was never designed to become a federal state. The federal structure is the outcome of a long series of difficult compromises between conflicting views on the organization of the state and its territories. These compromises were meant to cool down the conflict, not to deliberately build a federal state. And because it is a federation by default, it is also an *unfinished* federation. Put differently: nobody knows exactly where these reforms are finally heading. Is there an end point? And what could or should it be? Fixing an end point does however require some fundamental agreement on the very nature of the Belgian federation, on its essence, on its fundamental composition. And there is no such agreement. On crucial issues like the boundaries of the substate entities and on the role to be played by the federal state there are only different and sometimes strongly diverging views. This is nicely illustrated by the very confusing way in which the powers of the federal state and the residual powers are defined. Article 35 of the constitution says that the federal state only has the competences given to it by the constitution itself, which means that residual powers belong to the regions and communities. But there has been so far no introduction of such an article in the constitution because there is no agreement on a list of minimal federal powers. The same Article 35 says that regions and communities have the residual powers, under the conditions written down in a special majority law. But there is no special majority law so far, and the constitution says that this special majority law needs to be adopted after the introduction of the list of federal powers in the constitution. In practice then, the regions and communities have only the powers given to them explicitly by the constitution and by the special majority laws, and the residual powers remain with the federal state, although the constitution says that they do not lie there. This is confusing and unfinished, but it is a way to keep on going without having to agree on matters on which no agreement seems possible.

Third the Belgian federation is clearly *bipolar*. Its real political building blocks are the Flemish and the francophones. Different views between them, including on their territory and on the status of Brussels, lie at the origin of the introduction of language territories in the 1920s on which the regions and communities were built. The division in two is visible and institutionalized in many places: political parties belong to only one language group, members of parliament and members of the federal government are divided into language groups, the Belgian members of the Senate and of the European Parliament are elected per language group, the alarm-bell procedure protects the minority language group, and so on and so on. Decision-making on a daily basis and especially decision-making on the future structure of the Belgian state thus always involves two actors who are each other's veto players. The federal decision-making in Belgium thus resembles much more a confederal than a federal logic. The only way to govern and to agree on the working principles of the state is common agreement.

And that is a typical characteristic of *consociational democracy*. The Belgian federation is a copybook example of a consociational system. It involves power sharing at the central level and veto power for all major actors. And it uses the principle of autonomy to avoid ongoing conflict at the centre level. If no agreement on a common policy can be found at the federal level, the obvious solution is to split it up, to give each region or community the possibility of conducting its own policy, without having to agree with the others.

This also means that the Belgian federation is *centrifugal*. All reforms so far have gone in the same direction: contracting the central state and devolving ever more powers – but not many taxing powers – to the regions and communities. The centrifugal tendency also follows directly from the absence of federal political parties. And it is illustrated by the fact that each language community considers itself as being a periphery, as being a minority that needs to protect itself against the federal state where the other community is seen as the dominant one. The centre is left without defence (Hooghe, 2004).

The Belgian state structure is federal by default. It is unfinished but without a clear end point, it is bipolar, consociational and centripetal. And furthermore it is a unique *double* federation of both regions and communities and it is an *asymmetric* federation. Regions and communities are not fully the same and are linked to each other in varying ways. This asymmetry also means – and this is peculiar characteristic number eight – that it is a highly *complex* federation.

The Belgian state is also a typical *dual* federation (Watts, 1999). That means that the powers between the central and the substate level are clearly divided. There is not much room for shared competences. This type of federation is referred to as a 'layer cake' federation. Wherever one cuts into the cake, the two layers are clearly visible. If competences are less clearly separated, federations are not like a layer cake but like a marble cake (Grodzins, 1966).

The Belgian federal system has been put into place because a unitary system did not function any more and it has been refined any time when the existing federal system faced gridlock. And therefore the existing system also simply works and it works quite well. The policy outputs of the federal state and of regions and communities keep Belgium in the high categories of all indexes measuring the quality of life. And probably even more important: the tensions between the two language groups have been and remain strictly verbal tensions, with no significant acts of physical violence. Highly complex state structures are then a fairly reasonable price to pay.

Chapter 4

Political Parties

Political parties play a major and central role in modern representative democracies. Parties are present at the input side of a political system, where they mobilize the voters and define the meaning and structure of the electoral competition. They form the government and decide on ministerial portfolios. Belgian political parties fulfil all these functions. But they do more. Belgium is a typical 'partitocracy' (De Winter, 1998a), where the parties are by far the most important political actors. Parties are present in society, not only as membership organizations but also through a variety of social, economic and cultural organizations that are directly and visibly linked to the parties. The parties also fully control the government, where ministers need the approval of the party leadership for most of their actions. The Belgian parties have a strong grip on public administration, where – especially for top functions – appointments and promotions are distributed between them.

In this chapter we present the Belgian parties. We first describe the origin and further development of each of the parties and party families. Next we look at party organization, at the very important position of party president and at the (declining) party membership. We conclude with a discussion of the way in which parties have secured a large amount of financial support from the state.

The political parties

In Belgium one makes a clear distinction between two types of political parties. First there are the 'traditional' parties. These are the Christian democratic, the liberal and the socialist parties. They are indeed the oldest parties, all going back to the 19th century. Actually these three parties have now become the three traditional party *families*, since each of them split into two different unilingual parties. There are thus six traditional parties. These traditional

Figure 4.1 *The evolution of the total score for the three traditional party families (Christian democrats, socialists and liberals), 1919–2007*

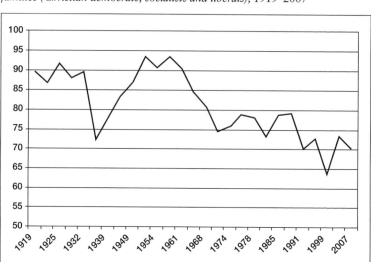

parties are the backbone of the party system (Van den Brande, 1963; Delwit & De Waele, 1997b). The largest party is always one of them, and a coalition is always formed by at least two of these traditional parties or party families. Together they have always polled at least 63 per cent of the votes, with a high point of 93 per cent in 1950 and 1958. As Figure 4.1 clearly shows, there have been ups and downs in the electoral domination of the traditional parties.

The periods of lower scores for the traditional parties obviously mean that other parties managed to be successful. These were Flemish regionalist parties and then fascist parties in the 1930s, the Communist party in the late 1940s, regionalist parties again and stronger in the 1960s and the 1970s, green parties from the 1980s on and right-wing populist parties since the 1990s. It is interesting to note though that none of these new parties has ever been able to take the place of the traditional parties. Even if some of them – especially the regionalists in the 1970s – were able to grow larger than one of the traditional parties, they were never able to keep up that level. New parties tend to come and go, while the older parties survive. That is indeed why they are still labelled traditional parties.

The Christian democrats

The Christian democratic party family is the heir of the old Catholic party that was formed at the end of the first major school conflict in 1884. Its position at that time was mainly conservative. Gradually a Christian labour movement challenged the party from the inside, asking it to pay more attention to social issues. In the small Flemish industrial city Aalst, especially, the conflict between the so-called Christian democrats and the party leadership was fierce, with local priest Adolf Daens choosing the side of the workers and being able to get elected to parliament in 1894. He not only questioned the free-market orientation of the Catholic party, but also its lack of affinity with the demands of the Dutch-speakers.

After the introduction of universal male suffrage, a new party was created in 1921 under the name 'Catholic Union'. It was actually a fusion of four building blocks: the old Catholic party, the Union of Christian Workers, the Farmers' Union and the Smallholders' Union. Even today, these four building blocks – called *'standen'* – remain to a certain extent the basic components of the party. Its further history is quite complex though (Gerard, 1985). In 1936 the party changed its name again to become the 'Catholic Block'. Interestingly, the Catholic Block was composed of two sections: The Dutch-speaking 'Catholic Flemish People's party' and the French-speaking 'Catholic Social party'. The linguistic divide disappeared again after the Second World War when in 1945 the CVP-PSC was created (Christelijke Volkspartij – Parti Social Chrétien) (Van den Wijngaert, 1976; Gerard, 1985; 1995; Beke, 2005). It declared itself a 'unitary' party, which meant that the old *standen* would no longer be its components. That was however only a matter of formal organization, since the Christian labour movement, the farmers and the smallholders – each also having their own Christian organizations – remained very powerful. All members, and especially the elected office-holders of the CVP-PSC, had a clear label, and whenever positions had to be distributed – for instance portfolios in government – a neat equilibrium between them was respected. In 1945 the CVP-PSC also clearly adopted Christian democratic principles, based on 'personalism' and on moderation – a centre position between liberals and socialists – in matters of social and economic policy

The division between two unilingual sections was abolished in 1945, but soon the two language groups within the party developed their own organization. Gradually the CVP-PSC split into two new political parties. The issue finally breaking it up was the discussion about the use of language at the Catholic University of Leuven. Leuven is situated in Flanders, and the once francophone and then bilingual university was split into a Dutch-speaking one in Leuven and a francophone one – still called Université de Louvain – for which a new campus was built in a new Walloon town called Louvain-la-Neuve.

The two new Christian democratic parties obviously still belong to the same family and today sit together in the European People's party. Yet there are a number of clear differences (De Winter, 1997; Georges, 1997), the first and most important being size. Christian democracy has always been much stronger in Flanders. With the Flemish electorate also being larger than the francophone, the CVP was more than two times the size of the PSC. While in 1974 the CVP polled 23 per cent of the Belgian votes (40 per cent of votes in Flanders), the PSC polled only 9 per cent of the Belgian votes (23 per cent of the votes in Wallonia).

Both parties had already been facing electoral decline for some time. In 1950 the CVP-PSC polled close to 50 per cent of the Belgian vote. In 1961 this was down to 41 per cent. The combined score of the two Christian democratic parties dropped below 30 per cent in 1991 and below 20 per cent in 1999. The 1999 elections were dramatic for Christian democracy. CVP lost its number one position in Belgium and in Flanders and lost power for the first time since 1954. Both CVP and PSC then went through a moment of deep crisis and tried to reposition themselves. In 2002, the francophone PSC renamed itself as CDh or 'Centre Démocrate Humaniste' (Democratic Humanist Centre). It thus dropped the 'Christian' from its name, but remained loyal to the centrist position it had upheld before. While in the past a strong conservative tendency had always been present and visible in the PSC, the new CDh positions itself more to the left, both on ethical and on social and economic issues. The electoral results of the CDh have, however, not really improved since then.

The disarray after having lost power was much stronger in the Flemish CVP. Indeed, it had been the leading party of the country for more than 40 years, occupying during most of these years the position of prime minister (see Chapter 5). Like the PSC the CVP decided to change its name, to get rid of the association of CVP with governing and the necessary compromises with other parties that had made the CVP lose its credibility. After some discussions about the Christian label in the name, the CVP renamed itself as CD&V (Christendemocratisch en Vlaams – Christian democrat and Flemish). The adding of *Vlaams* to the party name is quite revealing for the new orientation of the party. Having been pushed into opposition, the Flemish Christian democrats found themselves suddenly in a position where they could leave behind the more prudent attitude that was imposed on them as long as they were in power and leading the Belgian government. While the old CVP – especially since 1968 and under pressure from the Flemish regionalist party – had moved towards a federalist position, the party documents after the change to CD&V in 2001 began using the term 'confederation' for the desired future structure of Belgium. It actually means an increased power for the regions and language communities and thus a further reduction of competences at the central level. For the elections to the Flemish regional parliament in 2004 and again for the federal elections in 2007, CD&V decided to form a pre-electoral coalition and present common lists with N-VA, a Flemish regionalist party claiming full independence for Flanders. It brought the party back to power at both levels, with a much more radical regionalist profile. The electoral alliance fell apart in 2008 because N-VA felt that CD&V was after all too soft (in government) on the regionalist Flemish demands.

The socialists

In terms of political influence the socialist party – now two parties – comes second. And while for the Christian democrats the most important player was the Flemish party, in the socialist family the Walloon wing is much more important. This asymmetry was present from the very beginning in 1885, when the newly created Belgian Workers' party (BWP-POB) was based mainly on the strong labour movement in the south of the country, with only a few urban centres of industry in the north. The first elections with a more or less universal male suffrage law returned 28 MPs for the BWP-POB, all elected in Walloon districts. When the labour movement became more important in Flanders, it was heavily dominated by the Christian organizations, which eventually found their secured place as one of the *standen* of the Catholic party.

The BWP-POB remained an outsider for quite a while. It entered parliament in 1894, but was only accepted as a governing party during the First World War, because Catholics and liberals then felt that a government of national unity was needed. Between the wars the socialists were an occasional governing partner, but the major players were still the Catholics and the liberals. After the Second World War, though, the then renamed Belgian Socialist party (BSP-PSB) was in power quite often. From the 1960s on an alliance between Christian democrats and socialists became the almost 'natural' governing coalition. With these two – and later four – parties the two largest forces of the country were allied and thus each language group was represented by the largest party. Until 1965 the two even secured a solid two-thirds majority in the parliament.

Like most labour parties, the original structure of the Belgian Workers' party was indirect, that is, its original members were not individuals but organizations. That remained so until the reorganization of the party in 1944. Close links with the labour organizations did not, however, disappear: the socialist trade union, especially, kept a secure place in the major party organs (Deschouwer, 1994a; 1999; Delwit, 1997; Govaert, 1997b).

The BSP-PSB tried hard not to be torn apart by the linguistic divide, but was of course not able to ward off the pressure. Regionalism in Wallonia was very much based on the labour movement – see below – and the regionalists were excluded from the party. In Brussels the Dutch-speaking socialists presented their own lists as 'Red Lions' (the lion referring to the Flemish lion flag). Gradually the socialist party started to recognize in its internal organization the presence of two language groups (and of three regions – see Chapter 3), and in the 1970s it had a double presidency, with one party leader from each language group. In 1978 two new parties were created: PS and SP. Of these two the PS was by far the largest and the strongest. In 1978 the PS secured 37 per cent of the votes in Wallonia, while the SP polled only 21 per cent in Flanders. The two parties of the socialist family not only are of different size, they also have a slightly different orientation. In Wallonia the PS was and remains very strongly based on the traditional labour movement and on the socialist trade union. On the Flemish side the distance from the trade union is larger, and the general ideological orientation of the party is more pragmatic. When in the 1990s Tony Blair launched his New Labour and a 'third way', the socialists in Flanders were very enthusiastic. That was not the case in Wallonia, where militants and leaders considered this to be a dangerous move towards neoliberalism.

The further electoral fate of the two socialist parties has also been quite different. In Wallonia the PS has remained quite strong. Only in 1999 and in 2007 did it drop just below 30 per cent of the Walloon votes, with peaks up to 44 per cent in 1987. In 2007 though, the relative low score meant that for the very first time since universal suffrage the PS was no longer the largest Walloon party. It was beaten by the liberals.

Being the largest party in Flanders has never even been close for the SP. It usually polls just above 20 per cent, except for dramatic results in 1999 with only 15 per cent and 2007 with just over 16 per cent of the votes in Flanders. The Flemish socialist party is actually one of the smallest socialist parties in Europe, with only the Irish socialists as serious competitors for this role.

The francophone PS is one of the very few parties (with the francophone greens) not to have changed its name. It only dropped the B when it separated from the BSP-PSB. The Flemish party did however go through a process of internal evaluation and rethinking after the electoral defeat of 1999. Its campaign leader Patrick Janssen – a professional marketeer – was elected as party president and he rebranded the SP as SP.a. This stands for 'Socialistische Partij anders' or Socialist party *different*, but can also be read as Socialist Progressive Alternative. The idea was that the Flemish green party and possibly even the Christian labour movement and the progressive wing of the Flemish regionalists (Volksunie) could be brought together in one large left-wing alliance. Yet only the progressive wing of the regionalists, and then only after the Volksunie had fallen apart (see below), eventually formed an electoral alliance with the SP.a. At the federal elections of 2003 and 2007 and at the regional elections of 2004 common lists were presented under the label SP.a-Spirit. In 2009 this was again changed into 'Socialisten en Progressieven Anders' (socialists *and* progressives different) to allow members of the Vl.Pro (see below) to join the party without having to label themselves 'socialist'.

Within the socialist family the Communist party also needs to be mentioned. It has however not played an important role in Belgian politics. The labour movement has been electorally represented by the socialist parties and by the Christian democrats. The

Communist party thus never became a mass movement. It was created in 1921 as Parti Communiste de Belgique/Belgische Kommunistische Partij (PCB/KPB), and its strength was limited to the urban and industrial areas, where it sometimes polled up to 10 per cent. That also meant that its presence and strength were much stronger in Wallonia than in Flanders. At the national level its score never went beyond 6 per cent (in 1936). At the first elections after the Second World War however, the Communist party polled almost 13 per cent. The role played by the Communist resistance during the German occupation had earned it political respect. This was also shown by its presence in a few post-war governments (see also Table 6.1). Yet in 1949 its score went down and at the beginning of the Cold War it dropped below 5 per cent. Gradually the Belgian Communist party disappeared, although it remained present and strong until the 1980s in the old Walloon industrial areas.

The liberals

The Liberal party is Belgium's oldest party. It has a history of more than 160 years. It played an important role in the 19th century, as long as the only competitor was the Catholic party. The Liberal party was able to win absolute majorities on several occasions, but the electoral breakthrough of the Workers' party after the electoral reform of 1893 marked the beginning of its way down. The Liberal party was stronger in the urban areas, and that meant more success in Brussels and in Wallonia than in Flanders (where basically all seats went to the Catholics). When the Workers' party entered the scene, it pushed the Liberals out of their strongholds, except for Brussels where liberalism remained clearly the strongest movement.

The introduction of proportional representation in 1899 saved the Liberal party. It could survive next to the larger parties – the Catholics and the socialists – each based on a broad social movement. Until 1945 the Liberal party was still the preferred coalition partner of the Catholic party. After the war its relevance faded away. This led the party to a thorough rethinking of its position in the Belgian system. Its origins lay in the opposition to attempts by the Church to be a force in the Belgian state, and in education in particular. During the last school conflict between 1954 and 1958 this was still part of the core identity of the party, especially since it then governed with the socialists against the CVP-PSC. The pacification of the school conflict was however a turning point. The party leader, Omer Vanaudenhove, renamed the party the PVV-PLP (Partij voor Vrijheid en Vooruitgang – Parti pour la Liberté et le Progrès – party for freedom and progress) and – more importantly – left the anti-clerical identity behind. Economic liberalism became its central identity and the PVV-PLP explicitly tried to convince Catholic voters who believed in the free-market economy to vote for it. Indeed, a poster for the 1965 elections shows a church with the parishioners at the end of Mass and the text saying: 'You can also vote liberal. The Liberal party respects religion'.

And it worked. The move to the new PVV-PLP was relatively successful, be it more in Wallonia than in Flanders. It marked the beginning of a slow but steady growth of the party. While the two other traditional parties – and especially the Christian democrats – faced a gradual decline, the PVV-PLP moved upwards. At the end of the 1990s it finally reached a position in which it could play a leading role again.

On the road towards that renewed strength in Belgian politics the PVV-PLP also had to face the increasing conflict between its francophone and Flemish wings. While the Christian democrats had felt the pressure in Flanders to move into the regionalist position and the socialists had responded to that pressure in Wallonia, the liberal party on either side had never been very sensitive to regionalist demands. In the Flemish Movement the acronym PVV was jokingly referred to as 'Pest Voor Vlaanderen' (Pestilence for Flanders). Actually the pressure on the PVV-PLP came mainly from Brussels. The Brussels regionalist party FDF (see below) endorsed basically a liberal ideology and defended fiercely the linguistic rights and freedom of the francophone inhabitants of Brussels. The Brussels section of the PVV-PLP first saw the defection of its Dutch-speaking members and office-holders who called themselves 'Blue Lions'. The francophone PLP, not knowing how to counter the rising FDF, split into several smaller groups, some of which sought to ally themselves with the FDF. While on the Flemish side an autonomous PVV was created, it was 1979 before the francophone liberals in Brussels and in Wallonia could reunite into one single party, which took the name PRL (Parti Réformateur Libéral – Liberal Reform party) (D'Hoore, 1997).

While the liberal family, and both liberal parties, generally fared well at elections, its political relevance remained limited. The basic handicap of the liberal family was the fact that both in Flanders and in Wallonia it was not the largest political force. Electoral victories – meaning electoral growth – were often not translated into participation in power. This greatly frustrated the Flemish party leader Guy Verhofstadt. He had taken over the PVV in the early 1980s and made it move towards a fairly radical neoliberalism. The removal of the PVV from government in 1987 to make place once again for a coalition between Christian democrats and socialists further fuelled his frustration about the dominance of these two parties and of their allied organizations (primarily the trade unions). In 1992 he revamped the PVV into a new party called VLD (Vlaamse Liberalen en Democraten – Flemish Liberals and Democraten) (Deschouwer, 1997).

The 'Flemish' in the name is again revealing of what happened. The VLD endorsed the neoliberal ideas of its leaders and introduced a number of quite revolutionary rules for the election of party president and party executive (see below). At the same time it moved into a more Flemish regionalist direction, among other reasons because a number of figureheads of the Flemish regionalist Volksunie (including its former party leader) were willing to join the new party. It would however take eight more years and two more elections before the VLD could – at last – remove the Flemish Christian democrats from their leading position in Flanders and in Belgium.

In 1999 Guy Verhofstadt became prime minister of a coalition with the socialist and green parties. That meant that the hard neoliberal line had to be softened a lot. Eagerness to remove the Christian democrats from power for the first time since 1958 was an important motivation for accepting the compromise with the left. As the leading party of the country the VLD would, however, quite rapidly pay the price for its concessional attitude. After having accepted the granting of local voting rights to non-European citizens it faced a major defeat at the regional elections of 2004 and again at the federal elections of 2007. One of the previous candidates to the party presidency – the former national judo coach Jean-Marie Dedecker – had been kicked out of the party and presented a list under his own name in 2007. His 'Lijst Dedecker' claimed to be really liberal and really Flemish, which indeed hurt the VLD at the polls. The 2004 defeat led the VLD to – once again – change its name. Since 2007 it has called itself 'Open VLD'.

While on the Flemish side the liberals moved closer to a regionalist position by welcoming former leaders of the Volksunie, the francophone liberals also moved towards a more francophone position. The Brussels FDF, which had caused so much damage to the francophone liberals in the 1960s and 1970s, had remained a meaningful force in Brussels, but not at the federal level. PRL and FDF then decided from 1995 on to present common lists to the voters. That guaranteed the FDF a few seats in the federal parliament and it also strengthened the position of the PRL in Brussels (especially in the Brussels regional parliament). From 2003 on this alliance of PRL and FDF – also formally allied to a Christian democratic movement led by a former party president of the PSC – has participated in elections under the label MR (Mouvement Réformateur – Reformist Movement). Changing party names and labels has become a very common feature in Belgian politics. Losing one election can be enough to leave the old name behind.

Regionalist parties

After the short-lived fascist parties that shook the system in 1936 and the also short-lived early post-war successes of the Communist party, from the 1960s on, the regionalist movement challenged the monopoly of the traditional parties. The impact of the regionalist parties has been quite important. They have put regionalist demands really high on the agenda. As a result, the traditional parties have not been able to contain the differences between the Flemish and francophone views on the future of Belgium. And with all parties basically agreeing that the Belgian state had to be reformed, the longer-term impact of the regionalist parties is also visible in the way in which the Belgian state is now organized (Deschouwer, 2009c).

The story of the regionalist parties is one of rapid electoral success with peaks in the early 1970s. After that, while the Belgian state was changing its nature and while all parties became regional and regionalist parties, the story is one of electoral decline towards almost irrelevance. Electoral alliances with the traditional parties have however secured their presence in parliament. It is also interesting to note that in all parties in Flanders former members of the Volksunie are present in quite important positions. While the party itself gradually disappeared, its leaders gradually left and joined other parties.

Flanders

The Flemish regionalist party Volksunie was created in 1954 (Govaert, 1997a; De Winter, 1998b). It was however not the first party-political presence of the Flemish Movement. Immediately after the First World War the 'Front party' (Frontpartij) was able to secure a few seats in the Belgian parliament. It asked for a full recognition of Dutch as the language of education and of the public authorities in the northern part of the country. At that time the Flemish Movement also started to have its effects on the three traditional parties. In each of them the number of Dutch-speaking officeholders increased as a direct effect of the introduction of full male universal suffrage in 1919. The Catholic party even formally acknowledged in its structure that language and territory were intimately linked. In 1937, the Front party joined the VNV (Vlaams Nationaal Verbond – Flemish National Union), a much more radical and also outspoken pro-Nazi party. It was able to gather no less than 12 per cent of the votes in Flanders in 1936. During the occupation of the country by Nazi Germany between 1940 and 1944 the VNV actively collaborated with the German administration, also hoping that a German administration would be more willing to listen to Flemish demands than the old Belgian administration. This choice of the party-political wing of the Flemish Movement during the Second World War remains a liability for the Flemish Movement today. It does, however, itself keep that link alive by its claims ever since the end of the war that the Flemish collaborators were acting out of sheer idealism. Many of the active militants of the VNV were of course punished by the Belgian state after the war, and the Flemish Movement has continued to ask for a full amnesty for them. The link between the Flemish Movement and Nazi Germany has always been a clear-cut argument used by Belgian francophones to discredit the Flemish Movement as being basically a fascist movement, even if many and prominent members of the Flemish Movement did not follow the VNV and opted for resistance against the German forces.

Recreating a Flemish regionalist party after the Second World War was thus not very easy and not very successful. In 1954 the VU (Volksunie – People's Union) was created and this party would indeed become a very important actor in Belgian politics. After a slow start it broke through in 1965, with 12 per cent of the Flemish votes. Further successes in 1971 and 1974 made it important enough to be invited to participate in negotiations about the reform of the Belgian state and eventually to participate in government. This confronted the VU with a major dilemma, that would divide the party until its very last days into a group of moderates who were willing to participate in the Belgian government and to strike compromises on partial and piecemeal changes, and a group of more radical supporters who fundamentally distrusted the Belgian establishment and who defended a clear and full realization of Flemish demands, including far-reaching autonomy for Flanders and the recognition of Brussels as a Flemish city. The very different view of the francophones on the status of Brussels (see below and also Chapter 3) required major compromises on this issue. After having participated in the Belgian government coalition in 1977–78, the VU lost severely at the polls and was challenged by a new and radical regionalist party called Vlaams Blok (Flemish Block).

From the 1980s on, the VU struggled with its identity and strategy. Its impact has been important, since it pushed the other parties to take regionalist claims into account. It put enough pressure on them to reform the unitary Belgian state into a federation granting autonomy to the Dutch-speaking community. It pushed the traditional parties so far that they themselves split into two unilingual parties. But these new unilingual parties have now also taken away the very *raison d'être* of the VU, since they all support the Flemish cause. The consequence was a gradual but clear electoral decline, a constant internal debate between the moderates and the radicals, with the latter seeking to differentiate the VU from the other parties by no longer upholding federalism but instead more far-reaching forms of autonomy (Govaert, 2002; De Winter, 1998b; 2006a). Internal debates between left and right further eroded the party from within. In 2001 an internal referendum was held about the future of the party. Three groups offered the party members a choice: a radical regionalist wing, a more moderate and more leftist wing and a group asking that the party would not be split. The radical group won the internal referendum and thus became the official heir of the VU. It calls itself N-VA (Nieuw-Vlaamse Alliantie – New Flemish Alliance). In 2003 it presented lists for the elections of the federal parliament, but polled only 4.8 per cent of the Flemish votes, which meant exactly one singe elected MP. From then and until 2009, the N-VA did not present lists of its own. It was able to strike a pre-electoral alliance with the Flemish Christian democrats of CD&V, and received a number of more or less secure places on the common lists of this so-called 'Flemish cartel' (Noppe & Wauters, 2002; Wauters, 2005; Van Haute & Pilet, 2006). In 2009 it again presented its own list at the Flemish regional elections.

The second group that remained after the end of the VU – the more moderate and leftist wing – called itself SPIRIT (Social, Progressive, International, Regionalist, Integral-Democratic and Future-oriented). It never participated in elections, but soon decided to present common lists with the Flemish Socialist party SP.a. Spirit changed its name to Vl.Pro (Vlaams Progressiven – Flemish Progressists) in 2008. The combination of moderate regionalists and socialists did well in 2003 and 2004, but after the federal elections of 2007 Vl.Pro was not able to have one single elected member of the House of Representatives. The alliance was ended in 2008, after which the party took yet another name: Social Liberal party or SLP. The one minister in the Flemish regional government (Bert Anciaux) and many members did not stay in SLP but joined the SP.a, which slightly changed its acronym to welcome them (see above).

Wallonia

The life of the other regionalist parties is less complex. In 1965 the RW (Rassemblement Wallon – Walloon Rally) was formed. It defended autonomy for Wallonia, mainly because the economic strength and wealth of the country had been moving north, leaving the once prosperous Walloon economy in dangerous decline. Unlike the Flemish Movement with its long history and dense network of organizations, the Walloon Movement was never a mass movement (Dupuis & Humblet, 1998; Kesteloot, 1998). And the RW was – although also based on a social movement called MPW (Mouvement Populaire Wallon – Walloon Popular Movement) – in the first place the instrument of its leader, François Perin. This smart and pragmatic party leader rapidly brought the RW into government. Since that meant also accepting very liberal economic policies, the party immediately faced deep internal conflicts. Perin then created a new Walloon liberal and regionalist party that would subsequently merge into the francophone liberal PRL. The RW did not survive this move (Van Dyck & Buelens, 1998). It rapidly fell into electoral insignificance, which is also due to the fact that its first competitor – the Socialist party in

Wallonia – had in 1978 become a new and unilingual party also upholding the interests of the Walloon Region.

The Walloon regionalist movement was originally a leftist movement, with deep roots in the Walloon labour movement. That is exactly why the leadership of the pragmatic but rather liberal Perin was difficult to accept for the rank and file. Finding the way back to the Socialist party was an almost natural thing to do. Just like the VU, the RW appears to have been the victim of its own success (Van Haute & Pilet, 2006). Its impact on the other parties has simply taken away its electoral niche.

Brussels

The third regionalist party of Belgium is a Brussels-based party. The FDF (Front Démocratique des francophones – Democratic Francophone Front) defends the rights of the French-speakers of Brussels. It is very clearly a reaction against the claims and increasing strength of the Flemish Movement and parties in the 1960s. The Flemish demand to incorporate Brussels into a Flemish substate is countered by the demand to make Brussels a fully fledged third region in a Belgian federation. The main argument for this is the fact that a large majority of the Brussels population is francophone. Very significant minorities of francophones – in some local municipalities even majorities – live in an area just outside Brussels, and therefore the FDF wants Brussels to be enlarged in order to allow them to live in a region in which the official language is not Dutch. The rapid rise and success of the FDF also occured in the 1960s and early 1970s. Like the two other regionalist parties the FDF quite rapidly accepted an offer to join a coalition government. It did so in 1977 – a government that agreed the 'Egmont Pact', a major compromise that laid the basis for further reform towards a federal Belgium. Unlike the two other regionalist parties the FDF was not torn apart by this move from protest to power. The FDF is still an important political force today, but only in its Brussels region. There it has become primarily a local party, present in the government of many of the 19 local municipalities of the Brussels Region. At the national level and in the national parliament, the FDF is a very small party. It has secured its presence in the Belgian parliament and sometimes also in the Belgian government by linking its fate to the francophone Liberal party. Ever since 1993 it has participated in all elections on a common list with the PRL. The alliance of both is called MR (Mouvement Réformateur – Reformist Movement) (Crisp, 1971; Kesteloot, 2004; Kesteloot & Collignon, 1997; Deschouwer, 1984; Van Dyck & Buelens, 1998).

Three regionalist parties have thus emerged in Belgium, one in each of today's regions of the Belgian federation. All three reached their electoral peak in the early 1970s and subsequently participated in government. All three started their electoral decline after that, being confronted with the fact that other parties – now fully split – had taken over their demands for more autonomy. Only on the Flemish side does a meaningful regionalist force remain in place, but the party defending the most radical Flemish position – Vlaams Belang – is also a radical-right populist party.

Populist radical-right parties

Christian democratic, liberal and socialist parties have a very long history in Belgium. The regionalist parties are (and, for some, have been) a more recent phenomenon, rising and shaking the party system in the 1960s and 1970s. In 1978 the last Belgian party fell apart. Since then, new parties develop separately in each of the two party systems. The birth of Vlaams Blok (VB) is a borderline case. Originally the party was created as a breakaway from the Volksunie, after it had accepted participation in the coalition government of the Egmont Pact in 1977. There is no counterpart of this phenomenon on the francophone side.

The first years of VB were actually not successful at all. Throughout the 1980s it polled between 1 per cent and 3 per cent of the Flemish votes. But towards the end of that decade it started to make its way into the party system. This happened after the party added – mainly on the initiative of the young Filip Dewinter – a strong anti-immigration and law-and-order discourse to its separatist programme. This combination of (Flemish) nationalism with the typical mix of immigration and security issues – explicitly copied from the French model of Jean-Marie Le Pen and his Front National – first worked at local elections in the city of Antwerp. The local coalition of socialists and Christian democrats – in power since 1918 – was heavily criticized and held responsible for all the problems with which this major harbour city was confronted. The 18 per cent vote in Antwerp for a party with a very radical and extreme discourse was quite a shock.

The next step was the European elections of 1989, where 6.5 per cent of the Flemish voters opted for VB. And the real break-through came in 1991, when more than 10 per cent of the Flemish votes went to VB. The election day of November 24, 1991 was quickly labelled 'Black Sunday' and the (more or less) sudden success of VB led to heated debates about what was wrong with Belgian and, more specifically, Flemish politics (Bouveroux, 1996; 2003; Swyngedouw, 1992). Journalists, opinion makers, sociologists and political scientists tried to understand why voters could fall for a party that actually campaigned on the idea that immigrants had to be sent back to their homeland. The direct line between the fascist wing of the Flemish Movement and the elite of VB – indeed present in the person of its president Karel Dillen – was heavily publicized. All other parties agreed that they would lay a so-called cordon sanitaire around VB, meaning that cooperation and certainly coalition formation with VB was out of the question.

VB proudly accepted this outlaw status and went on winning votes at every subsequent election. At the local elections in Antwerp in 1994 it became the largest party, with 28 per cent of the votes. It was however kept out of the city government by a broad all-party coalition against VB. And VB again improved its score at the next election.

A high point was reached at the regional elections in Flanders in 2004. Actually, the party had been convicted in court a few months before the elections for its systematic use of racist propaganda. In order not to lose its subsidies from the state (see below) it had to change its name. Vlaams Blok became Vlaams Belang (Flemish Interest) and continued to play the underdog role, while blaming the establishment for using whatever it could find to silence a party wanting to use its right to speak out (Erk, 2005). The federal parliament had also, not long before the regional elections, accepted a law giving non-European citizens voting rights in local elections. The combination of these elements proved an ideal cocktail for an electoral boost. With 24 per cent of the votes in Flanders, the freshly renamed Vlaams Belang became the largest party in the Flemish parliament. With the 'cordon sanitaire' still being respected, an all-party coalition (except the greens) was put together to keep VB out of government.

The 2004 result was so good, that it actually triggered internal debates in the party. Doing even better would become quite difficult. And although VB again did very well in most places at the local elections of 2006, it lost its first place in its hometown Antwerp. After 15 years of winning elections, there was suddenly a perspective of failure and of course still complete exclusion from power. Antwerp could have been the place where VB could force its way into power, but that failed. Several strategies have since been discussed, for example becoming a more moderate party with a more friendly image, or forging a broad alliance of all right-wing forces in Flanders. Such an alliance would include the N-VA and the liberal breakaway party Lijst Dedecker (to which VB has already lost a number of its elected members). Whatever happens in the future, it is clear that VB lost its momentum in 2006. It does remain a powerful political actor though, still exercising fully its blackmail power on the political system (Sartori, 1976). Ever since the breakthrough of 1991 it has been watched closely by the other parties, all desperately trying to find a way to stop its growth.

Right-wing populism is very much a Flemish affair. On the francophone side there is a right-wing party – its name is Front National (FN) – but its success does not compare with that of VB (Coffé, 2005a; 2005b; Rea, 1997). While VB is a well-organized machine that has been able to build on networks of the Flemish Movement, FN barely has an organizational base. While VB was always a united and disciplined party, FN is constantly going through bitter internal debates. There have been numerous splits and recreations and disputes about the right to use the name and to spend the money. While VB has become a strong brand in the political market in Flanders, FN is associated with these internal problems and a very uneven electoral showing. While VB improved its score and position at every election, FN did well in some elections and lost again at the next. While the strength of VB in Flanders has given it – after a first period of attempts to avoid it – a high visibility in the Flemish media, FN is totally silenced by the francophone media. If right-wing extremism is discussed (but never invited) in francophone media, it refers to the VB.

Green parties

Belgium has two green parties. Of course it does. And just like all the other party families, its strength and significance is different in both language groups. The stronger of the two is Ecolo, the francophone green party. Both green parties scored their first electoral success in 1979, at the European elections – and that was especially the case for Ecolo, immediately securing 5 per cent of the francophone votes. Building on the classic green electorate of younger and well-educated voters supporting non-materialist issues, Ecolo was able to grow steadily. In 1991 it was the largest green party in Europe (votes obtained within the francophone community), and it has remained one of the largest of the family. When in Flanders the right-wing extremist party VB appeared to be able to attract voters moving away from the traditional parties, Ecolo did so on the francophone side with a quite spectacular 13 per cent of the francophone votes.

The high point came in 1999. A problem with dioxin in cattle and chicken feed that was discovered a few weeks before the federal elections created a major scandal. Both green parties immediately seized the opportunity to focus on their core environmental business. The green family obtained 14.4 per cent of the votes and Ecolo polled a solid 18 per cent on the francophone side. This electoral high point was also a major turning point, since the green parties were invited to participate in the government coalition with liberals and socialists. Ecolo had clearly announced that it was ready to make that move, but the period in government (1999–2003) was nevertheless a difficult one. The party could barely make a choice between government and opposition. It even invented the word 'participopposition' to define its very ambiguous position (Delwit & Van Haute, 2008; Deschouwer & Buelens, 2002). During that time in government Ecolo twice went through a leadership change. This meant a replacement of the leaders who had accepted participation in government by leaders who were very critical of the actions of the coalition. A few days before the 2003 elections Ecolo even decided to leave the government after a (new) dispute with the other parties about managing the noise around Brussels airport. The results of the 2003 elections were disastrous. During the campaign the greens had been portrayed as quite unreliable partners, and their late exit from government did not help to redress that image. After this not particularly pleasant experience in government, Ecolo decided to stay in opposition. At the local level however, where it actually participated quite early in local governments (among which was the city of Liège in 1982), Ecolo is one of the potential coalition partners and does participate in local governments.

The Flemish green party also seized the opportunity of the European elections of 1979 to present a list to all the voters in Flanders. Its result (2.3 per cent) was beyond expectations, but clearly lower than Ecolo. The party presented lists under the name of 'Agalev', which stands for 'Anders gaan leven – Living differently'. The success at the European elections made the name stick. During the 1980s and early 1990s Agalev gradually secured its position in the Flemish party system, be it as a relatively small party. The high scores of Ecolo in the south were never within reach for Agalev. Its highest score also came in 1999, after the dioxin crisis. For Agalev, this also meant the beginning of a first term in government. Unlike Ecolo, Agalev was able to make a relatively smooth transition from opposition to government. With a strong party leader who had a good relationship with the prime minister, the party was a very loyal partner in the coalition. It did go through a difficult moment though when a decision to export weapons to Nepal was too easily accepted by the federal Agalev minister. She resigned and was replaced.

The real blow fell at the 2003 federal elections. Both Ecolo and Agalev lost heavily, but for Agalev this meant the loss of all federal MPs. This was not only a serious psychological shock but also a financial one, since parties need to have representatives elected in order to receive state subsidies (see below). At the 2007 federal elections Agalev did recover a bit, but remained in opposition. In 2007 it participated in the elections under a new name. Like many other Belgian parties it felt that the old name was too easily associated with the past and thus with losing the election. Today the Flemish green party is simply called Groen! (with the exclamation mark as part of the name) (Delwit & De Waele, 1997b; Rihoux, 1997; Delwit & Van Haute, 2008).

Summary

The Belgian party system is based on a fairly simple basic structure. There are six party families: Christian democrats, socialists, liberals, regionalists, greens and right-wing populists. For each family there are two parties, one in each language group. From there more complexity is built in. First the parties of the same family generally have a different size and strength in each language group, which produces two party systems with quite different dynamics. The recent evolutions of the regionalist parties also add to the complexity. The Walloon RW has disappeared and the VU split into two parties. And these two remaining parties and the Brussels regionalist FDF do not always participate in elections on their own. They form common lists with other parties. And finally, party names tend to change easily. The split of the traditional parties led to some name changes, and most parties changed their name again at least once. Reading and understanding Belgian election results is thus not a very straightforward exercise. Table 4.1 should be a good guide to finding one's way in the party political labyrinth.

Party organization

Structure

Belgian political parties all have a very similar structure. This reflects the territorial organization of the state and of the electoral system and a tradition of fairly high centralization of power in the hands of the party leadership. The smallest units are the local sections. These exist at the level of the local municipalities. Some local sections are based on smaller units, reflecting the older municipalities before their number was drastically reduced by the fusion of 1976 (see Chapter 6). The most important role for the local sections is their participation in local elections and consequent involvement in politics at the municipality level. These local sections of political parties used to be very visible and active organizations, playing an important role in local social and cultural life. This role has however declined during the past few decades (Deschouwer & Rihoux, 2008). Local party sections have become more purely political organizations, being highly active during local campaigns, but focused mainly on local policymaking in between. Local sections are quite independent though. They draft the lists for local elections and decide on the party strategy at the local level. That includes the formation of pre-electoral alliances, the formation of coalitions and the selection of the members of the local executive (Deschouwer & Wille, 2007).

Local sections are grouped at the next territorial level for elections, but there are differences between francophone and Flemish parties. Indeed, in Flanders the provinces are the electoral districts for both the election of the federal House of Representatives and of the Flemish parliament. The provinces are therefore (except for the

Table 4.1 *Belgian political parties*

Acronym	Full name	Family	Language	Origin and short history
CD&V	Christen-democratisch en Vlaams	Christian democratic	Dutch	Created in 1884 as a Catholic and Conservative party. Reformed and renamed as CVP/PSC in 1945. Became independent Flemish party in 1968. Adopted current name in 2001.
CDh	Centre Démocrate Humaniste	Christian democratic	French	Created in 1884 as a Catholic and Conservative party. Reformed and renamed as CVP/PSC in 1945. Became independent francophone party in 1968. Adopted current name in 2002.
Open VLD	Open Vlaamse Liberalen en Democraten	Liberal	Dutch	Created as Liberal party in 1846. Renamed as PVV/PLP in 1961. Became independent Flemish party in 1971. Renamed as VLD in 1992. Renamed as Open VLD in 2007.
PRL	Parti Réformateur Libéral	Liberal	French	Created as Liberal party in 1846. Renamed as PVV/PLP in 1961. Became – after several splits and mergers – the francophone 'Party Libéral Réformateur'. Since 2003, participates in elections (together with FDF) as MR – Mouvement Réformateur.
SP.a	Socialistische Partij Anders	Socialist	Dutch	Created as the Belgian Workers' party in 1885. Renamed as BSP/PSB in 1945. Became independent Flemish party SP in 1978. Renamed as SP.a in 2001.
PS	Parti Socialiste	Socialist	French	Created as the Belgian Workers' party in 1885. Renamed as BSP/PSB in 1945. Became independent francophone party PS in 1978.
Groen!		Green	Dutch	First participation in elections in 1979 as Agalev (Anders Gaan Leven). Renamed as Groen! in 2005.

cont'd

Acronym	Full name	Family	Language	Origin and short history
Ecolo		Green	French	First participation in elections in 1979.
N-VA	Nieuw-Vlaamse Alliantie	Regionalist	Dutch	The official successor of the Volksunie. Participated in regional elections of 2004 and federal elections of 2007 on common lists with CD&V.
FDF	Front Démocratique des Francophones	Regionalist	French	Created in 1963. Participates in elections on common lists with PRL. Since 2003 this alliance is called MR – Mouvement Réformateur.
SLP	Sociaal-Liberale Partij	Regionalist and left-liberal	Dutch	One of the two parts of the former Volksunie. First name in 2001 was Spirit. Renamed as Vlaams Progressieven in 2008 and renamed again as SLP in 2008. Participated, until 2007, in elections on common lists with SP.a.
VB	Vlaams Belang	Radical-right and regionalist	Dutch	Created in 1978 as Vlaams Blok. Is a breakaway from Volksunie. After conviction for racism VB was renamed as Vlaams Belang in 2004.
FN	Front National	Radical-right	French	First participation in elections in 1991.
LDD	Lijst Dedecker	Liberal	Dutch	Former candidate to the presidency of Open VLD breaks away and first participates in federal elections of 2007.

old Brabant province – see Chapter 5) the most important building blocks of the party. The provinces are the level at which recruitment and election of the political personnel needs to be organized.

For the francophone parties, the organization between local municipalities and national level is more complex. For the election of the federal House of Representatives the provinces are the electoral districts, but the election of the Walloon parliament is organized in smaller districts in two of the five Walloon provinces. Francophone parties also have an important structure in Brussels. Since almost one in five francophones in Belgium live in Brussels, the Brussels regional sections of the parties have an important weight. They are furthermore involved in the election of the Brussels regional parliament.

The national party congress is formally the most important structure of the party. It decides party strategy, which includes the possible approval of an agreement to enter a coalition government at the federal or at the substate level. Traditionally the party congress was composed of representatives of the district sections, but most parties now allow all individual members to participate and to vote in the congress.

The party president

One crucial task of the congress has however disappeared: the election of the party president. This competence has now been given to the individual party members. In 1969, when it had become a new unilingual party, the francophone Christian democratic PSC (now CDh) introduced direct election of the party president by the members. The smaller Brussels party FDF also used that procedure. Other parties followed in the 1990s.

The direct election of the party president sometimes leads to real and intensive internal debates between strong candidates. That has been most often the case for Open VLD, which was actually the trendsetter of this procedure for the Flemish parties. In 2004 the incumbent party president Somers was challenged by the former national judo coach Jean-Marie Dedecker, who was able to win 38 per cent of the votes but remained a very critical outsider and was eventually excluded from the party in 2006. He participates with his own list 'Lijst Dedecker' in the elections since 2007.

The more usual system though is one in which the members can approve a choice that has already been made by the party leadership. Party presidents are obvious candidates to become ministers in a government. They not only belong to the party elite but are also in the most powerful position to decide who can become a member of the government. The party statutes do not allow for the function of party president to be combined with a ministerial position (although exceptions are possible – see below), which means that a vacant position in the party needs to be filled rapidly. Formally the vice-president can take over, but if this is not really a leading figure, a replacement will be sought. This can be done in one broad decision on the way in which the available positions will be distributed among the party elite. A person not selected for a position in the government can then be placed at the head of the party. There is a formal call for candidates and a free election in which all members can participate, but the party leadership's candidate is always the winner.

The party president is the real leader of the party (Fiers, 1998). He or she is the spokesperson of the party, the one to be called by journalists whenever the party is involved in political initiatives or debates. The party president is also the person who needs to keep the profile of the party clear and visible, which is especially important when it participates in a coalition government. At the same time the party president is the first contact for the prime minister or for the presidents of the other parties in government when the coalition's policies need to be coordinated. The party president also needs to coordinate the activities of the party at the federal and at the substate level. There is indeed no substate level of the parties. The substate level is the highest level and is the national level. Coordination between what the party does at both levels is therefore crucial. The only easy situation is the one in which the party is in opposition at all levels. If a party governs at both the federal and the regional level, its partners can be different, and this requires careful communication both with the coalition partners at both levels and with the outside world. Governing at one level and being in opposition at another one – possibly with or against the same partners – also requires a careful coordination and communication. This is the role of the party president.

The question whether the most important leader of a party needs to be the party president or a member of the government or governments in which the party participates, is a constant tension. In the 1970s and 1980s – a time when the life of coalitions was often in danger because of tensions between the language groups – the meeting of the party presidents who very often had to sit together to try the save the coalition was referred to as the 'junta' of party presidents. Indeed, it showed very openly to what extent the parties make and break a coalition government (De Winter, 1996). But it also led to a devaluation of the decision-making power of the members of government themselves, since they constantly had to double-check with the party presidents. This gradually changed and today it is habitual to have the most important person enter the government.

When a party leads a government, the role of its president is clearly reduced. The most important person in the party is then the prime minister, even if he is not formally the party president.

The party bureau

The party president is the formal chair of the party bureau – the central executive – that meets every week on Monday. The party bureau is composed of representatives of the lower levels, elected either by these party structures or directly by the members. In the party bureau the party in parliament (group leaders) and the party in government (ministers) are also present. The bureau discusses government politics and decides on the position of the party.

The party bureau is also typically the place where social organizations related to the party have a secure place – this is especially the case for the Christian democratic and for the socialist parties. Members of the liberal pillar organizations also have their place in the francophone liberal party, but Open VLD abolished this practice in 1992. It even allows all party members to elect the party bureau.

In most parties there is also a smaller group of people who actually lead the party on a daily basis. This group obviously includes the party president and the most important ministers in the different governments. They are (internally and sometimes by the press) given names like 'the G4' or 'the teletubbies'. This practice again makes it very clear that the Belgian parties are centralized organizations, in which the role of the party president is absolutely crucial.

Party membership

Political parties in western democracies are losing members. That is a well-known and well-documented phenomenon (Katz, Mair et al., 1992; Mair & van Biezen, 2007). Belgium should fit into

that general picture. It has two typical mass parties – the Christian democrats and the socialists – for which membership numbers
have always been quite high. Being a member of one of these
parties was linked to the membership of the many other organizations and associations that belong to the Catholic and socialist
pillar. The deep penetration of the parties and the pillars in the
Belgian state (see also Chapter 8) made membership an attractive
feature. Being a party member meant that one could count on the
party representatives in the elected assemblies, in the governments
and in the public administration to make sure that state services
would be provided correctly and rapidly.

The clientelist practices are today less important than before.
Many local party sections still organize 'surgeries' or 'clinics'
(*zitdagen/permanences*) where party representatives are at the
disposal of the public for helping them find their way through the
public administration, but the practice is increasingly seen as
belonging to an 'old political culture' and going against deonto-
logical rules for politicians (Maesschalck et al., 2002; Deschouwer
& Rihoux, 2008).

One can thus expect a gradual decline of party membership
numbers in Belgium, especially for the traditional mass parties. The
picture is however a bit more nuanced. The decline is quite evident,
but has been preceded – as can be seen in Figure 4.2 – by a period
of increasing membership numbers until the early 1980s. There are
two explanations for these growing numbers at a time where in
many other countries the decline had already started. Both reasons
refer to the creation of new parties. All the traditional parties in the
1970s went though a phase of recreation and renewal. The split of
the old parties was indeed a moment of crisis, but also involved a
fresh start for each of the new parties. And second, the 1970s are
the time when the regionalist parties reached their highest electoral
peaks, and that was also reflected in their growing membership
numbers. The new parties never mobilized the very high membership numbers of the traditional parties, but their arrival in the political landscape could certainly compensate for the potential overall
decline. When the regionalist parties began their way down, there
was no other new party family that could compensate the decline.
Green parties have very few members. In 2007 both green parties
together had only 8,000 members. Vlaams Belang does have sizable
membership numbers (22,000 in 2005), but these do not replace
the very high numbers of the traditional parties.

Figure 4.2 *Evolution of the total number of members of the Belgian parties, 1960–2005*

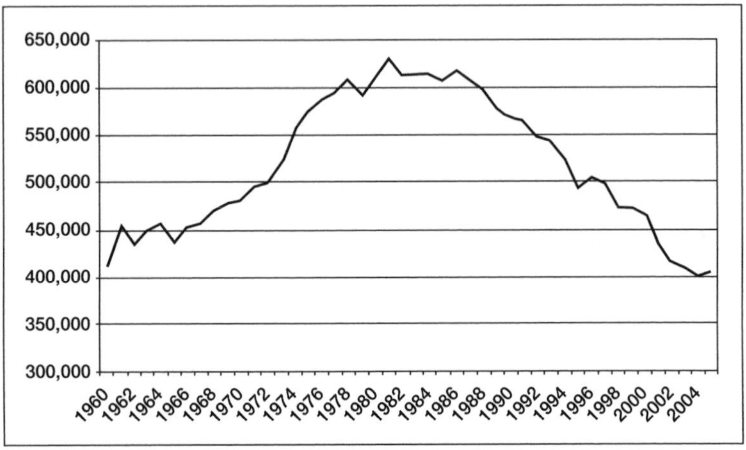

Sources: Maes (1988) and *Res Publica* political yearbooks

The absolute numbers as shown in Figure 4.2 are always a bit misleading. A more accurate assessment of the size of membership numbers is the total number of members as a proportion of the electorate, that is, of all citizens entitled to vote. Figure 4.3 shows that evolution. The highest point is then still 1978, but the subsequent decline is quite spectacular and reaches in 2003 a membership/electorate ratio that is by far the lowest ever.

Breaking down the figures per party family also shows to what extent the loss of members has been a matter primarily for the two traditional mass parties. Figure 4.4 shows the evolution for Christian democrats, socialists and liberals. Until 1980 the socialists were able to increase their membership numbers, but from then on the evolution has been negative. Christian democrats experienced heavy losses in the early 1960s. That was also a time during which they faced serious electoral decline and challenge from the renewed Liberal party, which tried explicitly to attract religious voters. After some two decades of stability, the membership numbers for the Christian democrats started going down from the 1990s onwards. And here again that coincided with further electoral losses.

For the liberal family the picture is different. The liberal parties' numbers began to rise in the early 1960s and reached a high point

Figure 4.3 *Evolution of party membership as a proportion of the total electorate*

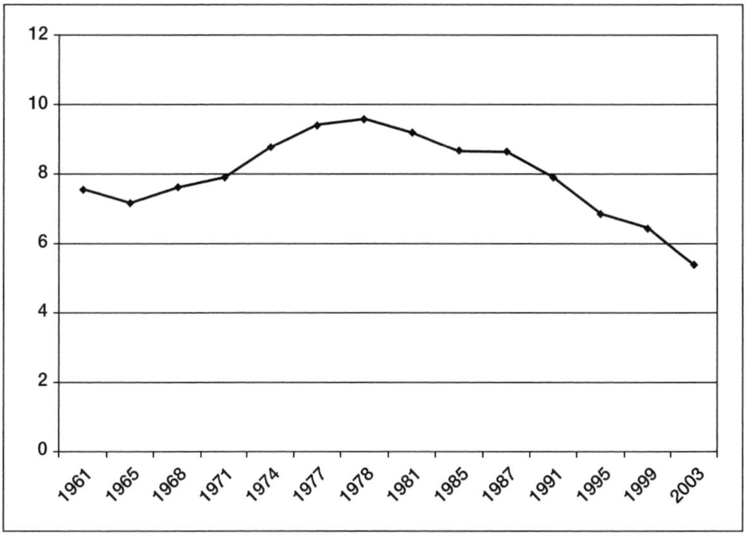

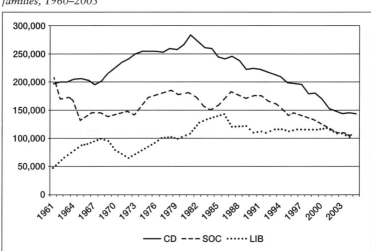

Sources: Maes (1988) and *Res Publica* political yearbooks

Figure 4.4 *Evolution of membership numbers for the three traditional party families, 1960–2005*

Sources: Maes (1988) and *Res Publica* political yearbooks

thirty years later. Since then the membership numbers of the liberal parties have not gone down significantly. It is interesting to note that the numbers for the liberal parties were always far below those of the socialist and Christian democratic parties, but the latest figures show the liberals and the Christian democrats at the same level, and the socialists only slightly above them.

Party finance

Political parties in Belgium are to a very large extent financed by the state. More than 75 per cent of their income is provide by state subsidies (Van Bunder, 1993; Weekers et al., 2005). The notion of 'state' is however very broad in this respect. Parties have indeed secured flows of money coming from several sources. The number of sources has systematically increased since the 1970s and the sums provided by each of them have also been upgraded several times. Meanwhile the possibilities for attracting other – private – sources of income have been drastically reduced.

The first and the oldest source of income is the support given to the party groups by the Senate (from 1970) and by the House of Representatives (from 1971). The logic is that each party group receives an amount per member of parliament. These amounts have been increased over time. In the Senate the party groups now receive 70,000 euro per member and in the House 45,000 euro. Although these subsidies were originally meant to pay for parliamentary assistants, the money can be used freely by the party groups. In practice it means that these subsidies are pooled with other sources of income with which activities and personnel can be paid.

Until 1989 the subsidies for the party groups were the only important state subsidy, together with some support going to study centres or party-related broadcasting companies. After many proposals and many debates a law was adopted – the so-called law Dhoore – that introduced four new principles. The first is the direct subsidies given by the federal state to the party organizations. That money is sent to the central party office and not to the party in parliament. Every political party having at least one MP elected in each of the houses of parliament receives a fixed amount of 130,000 euro and a variable amount of 1.3 euro per voter in the last federal elections. The introduction of these direct subsidies (and a first substantial increase in 1992) more than doubled the amount of state money going to the parties. At the same time – that is the second principle – the parties' ability to receive gifts from private persons or from companies was almost completely abolished. Only individuals can still give a very limited amount of 2,000 euro per year to a political party.

This drastic reduction of the capacity to accept gifts is the direct consequence of a number of party finance scandals that were revealed in the early 1990s. The most important is probably the one in which the Italian helicopter manufacturer Agusta appeared to have paid both socialist parties as a reward for an important order placed by the Belgian army. Several socialist ministers had to resign and were eventually convicted by the Court of Cassation. Willy Claes, who was Minister of Economy at the time of the deal, even had to resign from his post of secretary general of NATO.

The new rules forbid parties to accept gifts and that is compensated by a very comfortable amount of money provided by the state. The parties' need for money, and one of the reasons why they went beyond the legal and ethical limits for getting it, was the ever-increasing cost of election campaigns. And that is where the third principle comes in: expenses for election campaigns are severely limited. A maximum amount is set for each party per election campaign and the use of expensive campaign means, for example hiring large billboards, is forbidden. Individual candidates also have to limit their expenses and both parties and elected candidates have to report to a parliamentary commission on the way in which their campaign has been organized and financed. And that is the fourth principle. Parties have to publish their accounts and show how they have spent the money that they have received from the state.

Meanwhile the new levels of government have also introduced public subsidies for the parties. The parliaments of regions and communities have since 1980 – when these parliaments were not yet directly elected – decided to offer party groups the same kind of subsidy as the one offered in the federal parliament. It means that subsidies are given to the party groups. These subsidies have gradually grown and have been substantially increased after the first direct election of the regional parliaments in 1995. Depending on where they have participated in elections, the parties can thus receive money directly from the federal state and indirectly to the party groups in the two houses of the federal parliament, in the Flemish parliament, the Walloon parliament, the French Community parliament, the German Community parliament and the Brussels regional parliament (and its separate Community Commissions). This amounts to some 40 million euro per year, or approximately 6 euro per member of the voting population (Weekers et al., 2005).

The direct election of the regional parliaments in 1995 marked the start of the federal state and thus also the coming of age of the substate levels of government. First the Walloon Region introduced direct subsidies to parties in 1996. Flemish parties followed suit and the Flemish parliament has paid direct subsidies since 2001. It gives all the Belgian parties another 10 million euro per year.

The federal law Dhoore obliges the parties to write into their statutes their formal acceptance of the Universal Declaration of Human Rights. This was meant as a possible means of avoiding having to give money to the populist radical-right party Vlaams Belang. A perverse effect of the way in which the traditional parties have secured their income and regulated their expenses is indeed the ability of a growing party to receive substantial amounts of money. Vlaams Belang has written into its mission statement the required respect for human rights, making that device completely harmless. Attempts to make the rules harder have not really been successful. Since 2005 the law states more clearly that subsidies can be made dependent on a party's accept-ance in words and in acts of a non-racist attitude. For the franco-phone parties this is seen as an important device that should indeed be used to cut off Vlaams Belang and Front National from the state subsidies. Flemish parties are generally more reluctant to push Vlaams Belang once more into an underdog position that might increase its vote. Furthermore the party is by now well prepared for a possible loss of its state subsidies. It has enough reserve to survive for a while. The existing rules have indeed been and are still quite generous for all parties able to attract a minimal number of voters (Maddens & Weekers, 2006).

Smaller parties especially have to count on the direct subsidies to the party organization paid by the federal state. It is therefore crucial for them to have at least one MP elected in each house of parliament. The introduction of an electoral threshold of 5 per cent per district has had severe effects for the Flemish greens and for N-VA. At the federal elections of 2003 the Flemish greens lost all their federal MPs, while they would have retained two members of the House without the threshold (Hooghe et al., 2006). The loss of the direct subsidies on top of the loss of the subsidies to the federal parliamentary groups obliged the party to drastically reduce its personnel expenses.

N-VA was able to secure one MP in the House but none in the Senate. That one member proposed an amendment to the Dhoore law and was able to have it accepted. From 2004 on a party can therefore receive direct state subsidies if it has at least one elected member of at least one of the two houses.

Conclusions

During the past four decades the party landscape in Belgium has changed radically. The traditional parties fell apart and new parties appeared on the scene. Yet behind this turmoil there are a number of interesting elements of stability. In the first place the parties have remained strong organizations with powerful party leaders. The parties have themselves made sure that they receive enough money from the state at all levels to survive comfortably. In the second place the traditional parties have remained the most important players. Regional parties have come and are almost gone. Green parties have entered the scene, but they remain smaller parties. Only Vlaams Belang has been able to become – to Belgian or Flemish standards – a fairly large party, but it remains to be seen whether it can keep that position.

One element of change has however deeply affected the parties: the gradual disappearance of electorally dominant parties. In both language groups the electoral competition is now very hard, with no party ever being sure of its future position in the party system. That is one of the reasons why parties in Belgium have almost all gone through at least one change of the party name. Changing the name is seen as a way to communicate to the voters that a party is willing to change and renew itself, in the hope of keeping its voters and of winning new voters.

Chapter 5

Voting and Elections

Since Belgium has become a federal system, the number of elections has increased. Not only the federal parliament but also the regional assemblies have to be elected and after 2003 this has been done with a different timetable for each level. Yet since all the Belgian parties are split along language lines, the meaning of both types of elections is scarcely different. It also means that the Belgian parties find themselves almost permanently preparing for the next elections.

This chapter first presents the electoral system that is used for the elections of the different assemblies, giving special attention to the size of the districts and the electoral formula. It also discusses the degree of fragmentation of the party system, the increasing volatility and the very different electoral results produced in the north and in the south of the country.

The electoral system

Proportional representation

All parliaments and assemblies in Belgium are elected in a proportional way. The constitution simply obliges the electoral system to be proportional. The principle of proportional representation was introduced in 1899, which makes Belgium the very first country to use a list PR system. During the 19th century, members of parliament had been elected in a two-round majority system with a run-off election of the two best-placed candidates or list.

Proportional representation was introduced shortly after the expansion of voting rights to all male citizens in 1893. The immediate effect of giving all men the right to vote was the rapid rise of the Workers' party. Until then only two parties – the Catholic and the Liberal – had played a significant role. Very soon the Workers' party took the second place and it could have reduced the Liberal party to a very small size. Proportional representation actually allowed the Liberal party to survive.

Today all parliaments at all levels thus use a proportional logic. Yet not all of them use the same formula to distribute seats and the size of the districts also varies widely.

Provincial districts

For the election of the federal House of Representatives the country is divided into 11 electoral districts (see Figure 5.1). These coincide with the provinces, except for the old province of Brabant where three smaller districts are used. Before 2003 most provinces were also further divided into smaller districts, although the final distribution of seats per party was computed per province. In the old Brabant there was a district comprising Brussels and 35 municipalities of Flemish Brabant. This district – called Brussels-Halle-Vilvoorde or BHV – has for a very long time been at the centre of heated debates (see Figure 5.2). It crosses the language border and therefore Flemish parties have asked for it to be split

Figure 5.1 *The division of the country into electoral constituencies for the House of Representatives*

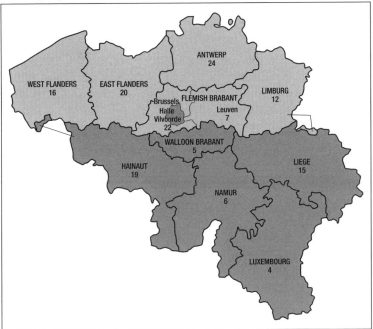

Figure 5.2 *The constituency of Brussels-Halle-Vilvoorde*

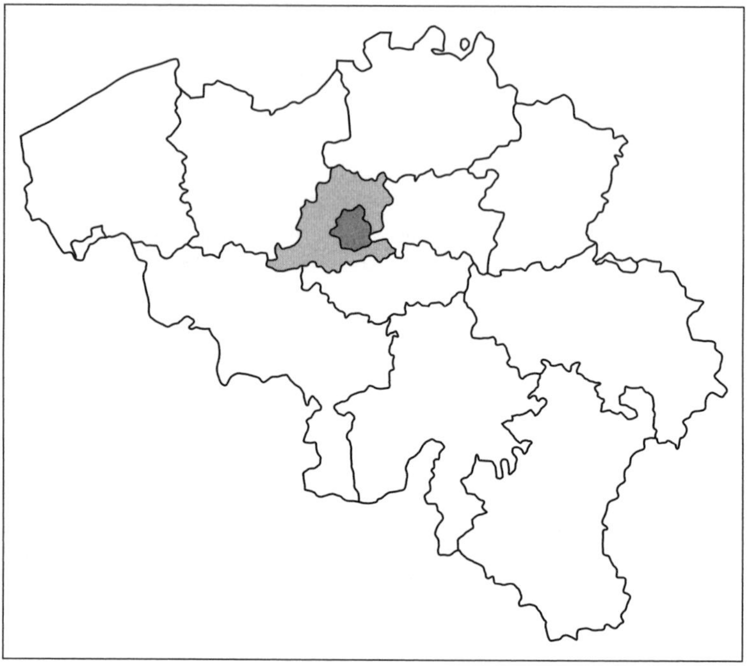

along that border, thus creating a district for the Brussels region only and one for the province of Flemish Brabant. Francophone parties however want to retain the possibility of attracting francophone voters living outside Brussels. When in 2003 all smaller districts were aggregated into provincial districts, no agreement could be found for the old situation in Brabant. A hybrid compromise was nullified by the Constitutional Court, and the old situation was restored. Since 2003 though, the issue of the split of BHV has been very high on the political agenda and it is one of the elements that made the formation of a government after the 2007 federal elections extremely difficult. Postponing the issue has been the only way out of gridlock ever since the freezing of the language border in 1963 (Luyckx, 1985; Pilet, 2005; 2007).

The number of seats available per province reflects the weight of that province in the total number of inhabitants of the country. It is not only the population of voting age and with voting rights that is counted for this purpose, but all inhabitants. That means that in provinces with a higher number of non-voting (foreign) inhabitants the number of votes per seat is lower. It is also interesting to note that the district magnitude – the number of seats per district – is smaller in the Walloon provinces. There is indeed the same number of provinces for a smaller population. In Namur and Luxembourg the number of available seats is quite low, which means that the degree of proportionality is also lower (see below).

Drafting the lists

Parties register their lists per district. The maximum number of candidates per list is the number of seats to be elected in that district. To this list of 'effective' candidates, a party adds a list of 'successor' candidates of up to half the number of seats available, which is put on the ballot paper below the list of effective candidates. Whenever one of the elected candidates has to be replaced, the list of successors is used. A candidate can actually be present on both parts of the list. It is quite usual to give a candidate the first place on the successor list if the place on the effective list does not guarantee election. If one of the elected candidates resigns or simply decides not to accept the new mandate, the first successor can enter the parliament.

That means that for both the effective and the successor list the order of the names is important. It is not an alphabetical or a random order, but a clear rank order decided by the party. Depending on the party and on the type of election, the party members have a say in the selection and ranking of candidates. The old tradition of organizing meetings of the party members at which they could vote for the potential candidates (De Winter, 1988) has been replaced by written procedures (except for the green parties).

The introduction of provincial districts has reduced the number of lists per party. Before 2003 the Flemish parties presented candidates in 11 districts and the francophone in 10 districts. With the smaller number of lists it is much easier for all parties to make sure that the important candidates are elected. Even if the provincial level of the party has a say in the drafting of the lists, it is basically the national party leadership that decides who will be the figurehead on each of the lists. That is not necessarily an incumbent candidate of the parliament to be elected. Candidates able to attract many votes are typically called to 'serve the party' for any election, irrespective of the level at which it is organized. They do not necessarily take up their seats when they are elected, which is where the successor list becomes quite important (see below).

Drafting a list does not only mean following internal party rules and strategies – there are some hard legal obligations too, not least being the *gender quota*. These have been gradually introduced and today oblige all lists to have an equal number of male and female candidates. Furthermore the first two places on the list cannot be taken by candidates of the same gender. The law does not oblige parties to further alternate male and female candidates on the list. Only the green parties systematically present a so-called 'zipper list' (Meier, 2000; 2004; 2005a; 2005b).

The introduction of gender quota from 1999 on had an effect on the number of female candidates elected in the different assemblies (see Chapter 7). The enlargement of the electoral districts has however also softened the effect. The larger parties can now indeed count on more than one or two seats per district. The obligation to alternate candidates is however limited to the first two places. And choosing a female candidate to top the list is not the most common option. In 2007 only one out of four lists (of parties that achieved representation) had a female candidate on top.

The act of voting

All Belgian citizens from the age of 18 have the right to vote. They are automatically registered as a voter in the local municipality where they have their official domicile. A few weeks before the elections a card arrives with the address of the voter's assigned polling station. The network of polling stations is dense, giving all voters the possibility of voting very close to where they live. The invitation also makes clear that voting is not only a right but also an obligation. Voting in Belgium is compulsory. That means: a voter must show up at the polling station. It is however possible to cast a blank or an invalid vote. The latter is not possible where a computer is used for the voting act, which is the case for some 40 per cent of voters living in a municipality that has invested in the acquisition of voting machines. The computer accepts a blank vote, but warns if the vote will be invalid.

This obligation to turn out was written into the constitution in 1893. It was actually a mechanism intended to soften the effect of the expansion of voting rights to all male citizens. The expectation was that all new voters would massively go to the polls, while those who already had the right to vote would not necessarily show up. The article of the constitution that says that voting is compulsory (and secret) has since then never been changed. For the past two decades there have been discussions between parties about the possibility or need to remove that obligation. The liberal parties particularly believe that one should not force the voters to vote but force the parties to make sure that they are able to turn out the vote. The socialist parties are opposed to abolishing the obligation, because they believe that abolishing the compulsory vote would alienate less-informed and less-educated people from politics. With the socialist parties in government since 1987, no initiative has so far been taken. Voting remains compulsory (Hooghe & Pelleriaux, 1998). Turnout thus also remains high, although the risk of being sanctioned for not showing up to vote is very low. Once in a while actions are undertaken in some judicial districts, but generally this is not a first priority for the courts.

Only citizens holding Belgian nationality have voting rights for the election of the federal and of the substate parliament. For local elections (municipal level) non-Belgians also have the right to vote. Citizens of member states of the European Union received local voting rights in the Maastricht Treaty and have participated in local elections since 2000. Since 2006, non-European citizens who have lived for at least five years in Belgium can also register to vote. However, both European and non-European foreigners have to register first, while Belgian citizens are automatically registered as a voter of the municipality in which they live. Unlike the Belgians, foreign voters can thus decide whether they want to be a voter and whether they want to vote.

Casting a valid vote can be done in four different ways. The first and most straightforward way is to tick the box on top of a list. This is called a 'list vote' and means that the voter not only supports this party but also that he or she agrees with the rank order of the candidates, both the effective and the successor candidates. The second way to vote is for individual candidates. Instead of accepting the list order, the voter then indicates who from the list should be elected first. A voter can cast as many preference votes as there are candidates on the list. A third way of voting is to cast preference votes for candidates on the successor list. And the fourth way combines both types of preference voting, that is, voting for candidates on both the effective and the successor list (see Figure 5.3).

Figure 5.3 *An example of a Belgian ballot paper*

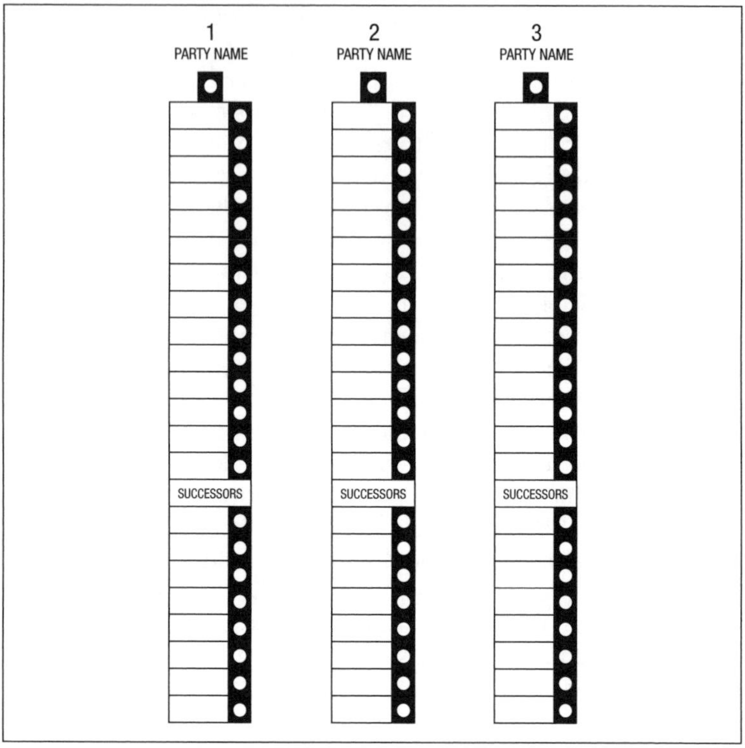

Distributing the seats

All types of votes for a list (see below) are first counted as a vote for the list in order to distribute the seats between the parties, which is done by using the divisor list suggested in 1899 by the Belgian Victor D'Hondt. The results per party are divided by 1, 2, 3, and so on as shown in the example in Table 5.1. It shows the distribution of seats in the province of Liège after the federal elections of 2007. There are 15 seats to be allocated. The first seat goes to the largest number in the list, that is, the PS result divided by 1. The second seat goes to the second number, which is for MR. This logic is followed until all 15 seats have been allocated. The last seat is the sixth seat for the PS.

Before starting the seat allocation, however, one needs to check which parties have reached the electoral threshold, which is set at

Table 5.1 *The distribution of seats using D'Hondt divisors in the province of Liège*

Federal elections of 2007 (rank order of allocated seats in brackets)					
Divisor	PS	MR	CDh	Ecolo	FN
1	200,450 (1)	190,699 (2)	88,874 (5)	84,604 (6)	28,177
2	100,225 (3)	95,350 (4)	44,437 (11)	42,302 (12)	14,089
3	66,817 (7)	63,566 (8)	29,625	28,201	9,392
4	50,113 (9)	47,675 (10)	22,219	21,151	7,044
5	40,090 (13)	38,140 (14)	17,775	16,921	5,635
6	33,408 (15)	31,783	14,812	14,101	4,696
Total seats	6	5	2	2	

5 per cent per district. Unlike Germany where the 5 per cent threshold is a statewide threshold, or Austria where 4 per cent is needed, the threshold in Belgium is checked for each of the districts. The reason for that is the absence of statewide parties. Since parties limit their presence to only one language community, a national threshold of 5 per cent would actually be higher for francophone parties than for Flemish parties.

The 5 per cent threshold was introduced in 2003, together with the enlargement of the districts at the provincial level. The idea of introducing a threshold mainly came from Flanders, where the party system is more fragmented than in Wallonia (see below). Furthermore the size of the provincial districts in Wallonia does not require the introduction of a formal threshold. In the example of Liège there are 15 seats to be distributed, which means that in a perfectly proportional distribution a party needs at least 1/15 of the votes or 6.67 per cent. The largest – most populated – Walloon province is Hainaut with 18 seats. That means that the theoretical threshold is 5.6 per cent. Only in Antwerp (24 seats) and in the central district of Brussels-Halle-Vilvoorde (22 seats) can the new threshold really make a difference.

The 5 per cent threshold did not have important mechanical effects, precisely because the size of most districts imposes a higher threshold than 5 per cent. Its psychological effects have however been important (Hooghe et al., 2006), especially for the two parties which were created after the split of the Volksunie and which have been deeply affected by the threshold. One of the two parties – originally called Spirit, then Vlaams Progressieven and finally SLP – had never participated in elections alone before 2009. In 2003, the party immediately decided to present common lists with the Flemish socialists under the label SP.a-Spirit. By putting enough Spirit candidates into good positions on the common list, it was able to secure a number of representatives in the different assemblies. In 2007 however the poor score of the common lists meant that not one single Spirit candidate was elected.

The second successor party of the Volksunie – N-VA – did participate with its own list in the 2003 elections. It polled 4.8 per cent of the Flemish votes and had only one single member of the House elected (in the home province of the party president). It would have had a second one and a member of the Senate without the threshold. For the regional elections of 2004 and for the federal elections of 2007, N-VA formed an alliance with CD&V and that allowed the party to remain present in the Flemish and in the federal parliament.

These electoral alliances between two parties can work because the parties can negotiate and agree on where to put the candidates on the common list. The list order is one way in which parties can, to a large extent, decide who has the best chances of being elected. The allocation of seats within the parties takes both the number of 'list votes' (top of the list) and the number of preference votes into account. The use and importance of preference votes is another topic related to the electoral system that has been discussed during the past two decades. The liberal parties, who also prefer the abolishment of compulsory voting, keenly defend the idea that preference votes should be the primary means of deciding who is elected. This would give the decision on who is elected wholly to the voters. The major argument against this is that parties need not only very popular candidates but also experts and good MPs who are not necessarily strong and popular personalities often appearing in and liked by the mass media.

The voters themselves have shown an increasing willingness to vote for candidates rather than for the party (Wauters & Weekers, 2008). In the 1950s only 25 per cent of the voters decided to vote for a candidate. Between 1970 and 1990 numbers remained more or less stable at 50 per cent. A sharp increase occurred in 1995, when multiple preference voting was introduced. Since then one can indeed cast a preference vote for more than one candidate. The highest proportion of preference votes was registered in 2003, with almost 70 per cent.

One other reason for this increase is the presence of common lists of more than one party. One can obviously expect supporters of one of these parties to vote for their own candidates. For the smaller partner this is particularly important, since the number of preference votes can assure the election of their candidates. The extremely high proportion of preference votes in 2003 was also the result of the fact that for once the top candidates of the parties could be on the list both for the Senate and for the House. This was again abolished in 2007, and the proportion of preference votes then dropped to 60 per cent.

There are important differences between parties though. Table 5.2 shows the percentage of preference votes per party in 2007. The greens and populist right-wing parties in particular both score below average. These are parties with a strong and clear ideology but with a limited number of figureheads to be put on the lists. Parties who are in government at the federal or at the substate level can always use their most visible ministers to attract votes.

Together with the introduction of provincial districts the importance of the list vote was reduced from 2003. As explained in Table 5.3, the number of votes not showing a preference for individual candidates is divided by two. That gives extra weight to the preference votes and allows candidates to 'jump the queue'. As long as the list vote counted for its full weight and before the most recent rise of the number of preference votes cast, the result was

Table 5.2 *The use of preference votes per party at the federal elections of 2007*

	%		%
CD&V – N-VA	67.2	CDh	72.4
SP.a – Vl.Pro	65.2	PS	73.0
Open VLD	64.9	MR	68.5
Groen!	47.0	Ecolo	48.4
Vlaams Belang	45.0	FN	34.3
LDD	44.9		

Source: Wauters & Weekers (2008)

Table 5.3 *Distributing the seats within political parties*

When counting the votes for the distribution of the seats within the parties, the ballots are divided into four categories:

1. Ballots with only a list vote
2. Ballots with preference votes for effective candidates only
3. Ballots with preference votes for both effective and successor candidates
4. Ballots with preference votes for successor candidates only

For the allocation of list votes to the effective candidates the ballots of categories 1 and 4 are taken into account. These contain votes for the list but no preference votes for effective candidates. For the allocation of list votes to the successor candidates, the ballots of categories 1 and 2 are taken into account.

Imagine a party that has received 72,000 votes and that is entitled to allocate four seats. This is done in four steps.

Effective candidates	Preference votes	Transfer of list votes	Total votes	Ranking
Jean	12,000	+ 2,400	14,400	4
Wendy	17,000	–	17,000	2
Marc	20,000	–	20,000	1
Linda	5,000	+ 4,100	9,100	–
Paul	15,000	–	15,000	3
Pierre	14,000	–	14,000	–
Maria	6,000	–	6,000	–
		6,500		

Successor candidates	Preference votes	Transfer of list votes	Total votes	Ranking
Pierre	13,000	+ 1,400	14,400	2
Wendy	25,000	–	25,000	1
Quentin	8,000	+ 6,400	14,400	3
Johan	1,000	+ 8,200	9,200	4
		16,000		

Step 1: Classifying the ballots into the four categories
The votes per category for this party are as follows:
1. Ballots with only a list vote: 7,000
2. Ballots with preference votes for effective candidates only: 25,000
3. Ballots with preference votes for both effective and successor candidates: 34,000
4. Ballots with preference votes for successor candidates only: 6,000

Step 2: Number of votes needed to obtain a seat
The total number of ballots for this party is 72,000. The number of votes needed to be elected is 72,000 divided by 5 (number of available seats plus 1), which is 14,400.

All candidates with at least 14,400 votes thus automatically obtain a seat. Effective candidates Marc, Wendy and Paul are elected. They do not need the list votes to reach the number of votes needed for election.

cont'd

Step 3: Transferring the list votes
There are 13,000 ballots (categories 1 and 4) confirming the list order. This number is divided by 2, which means that 6,500 list votes are available to be transferred. Candidate Jean needs 2,400 extra votes to reach the threshold for a seat, and these are transferred to the list votes for that candidate. The remaining 4,100 list votes are transferred to Linda, who is the highest not yet elected on the list. That is not enough for Linda to be elected.

Step 4: Ranking the successor candidates
The ranking of the successor candidates defines the order in which they can replace an effective candidate if needed. There are 32,000 ballots (categories 1 and 2) confirming the order of the successor list. That number is divided by 2.

The number of votes needed to be ranked is the same as the number of votes needed to be elected, that is, 14,400. Candidate number 2 reaches that threshold and is ranked first. The 16,000 list votes are then transferred in function of the list order. Candidate Pierre needs 1,400 extra votes, and receives them from the list votes. Quentin needs 6,400 and the remaining 8,200 list votes are transferred to Johan. The total number of votes obtained by each successor candidate defines their ranking.

that the list order was perfectly respected. Between 1919 and 1999 only 30 of the 5,019 elected members of the House (or 0.6 per cent) were able to break the list order. Both in 2003 and in 2007 no fewer than 17 candidates were elected with their personal votes (Wauters & Weekers, 2008).

It is interesting to note though that in 2007 only three of them did not occupy a so-called 'visible' place on the list. It is in fact common to have not only a strong leader of the list but also a strong candidate on the very last place to 'push' the list. As long as the list votes are fully counted, these candidates push the list up without being elected themselves. In 2007 fourteen of these candidates on the last position were elected, but only six of them accepted the mandate. The others were replaced by candidates from the successor list.

This illustrates the great importance of that successor list but also its perverse effect. The well-known candidates are on the effective list and attract an increasing number of preference votes. The increased weight of the preference votes should give voters more freedom to decide who will represent them. Yet the order of the successor list – on which only a few preference votes are cast – also defines who will be in parliament. And that means the parties and not the voters decide.

The phenomenon of 'false' candidates is also the result of the way in which the parties have adapted – or not – to the transformation of Belgium into a federal state. As long as federal and regional elections were organized on the same day (as happened in 1995 and in 1999), the parties had to spread their candidates over the lists for the House, the Senate and the regional parliament. A candidate for the region could however also be a candidate for one of the federal assemblies. When the final results were known, the parties could decide who would take up a seat in which assembly and who could become a member of one of the governments. In 1999 not one single prime minister of regions or communities had been elected in that substate parliament. They had all been elected at the federal level. When elections were disconnected, as was the case in 2003, candidates on the list could already have a seat in another parliament, and wait for the result (and for the availability of successors at both places) before deciding which seat to refuse or to accept or to keep (Versmessen, 1995; Deschouwer, 2000).

The Senate and the European Parliament

For the election of the members of the Senate and for the election of the Belgian representatives in the European Parliament the size of the districts is much larger. Both elections are organized on a language community base. For the Senate, the number of directly elected members is fixed per language group: 25 Dutch-speakers and 15 French-speakers. For the European Parliament – where Belgium has (as from 2009) 22 seats – the distribution is 13 and 8 seats, plus one reserved seat for the German Community. All inhabitants of Wallonia (except in the German area) and of the central district BHV can vote for the lists presented by the francophone parties. The Flemish parties are on the ballot paper in all Flemish provinces and in BHV. That means that only the inhabitants of BHV have the choice between the two language groups. The total number of potential voters for each language group is thus not known beforehand. It depends on the choices of the inhabitants of Brussels and of the Flemish municipalities around Brussels. The inhabitants of the little village of Voeren – which was moved from the Walloon province of Liège to the Flemish province of Limburg in 1963 – can vote for the French Community lists in the nearby village Aubel, situated on the other side of the language border.

The seats within each language group are distributed in the same way as for the districts of the federal House of Representatives. The D'Hondt divisors are used to allocate the seats between parties with, however, a 5 per cent threshold in each language group. Once again, the threshold has no real meaning in the francophone community, where winning one of the fifteen Senate seats or one of the eight European seats requires a higher score than 5 per cent. Just as for the House of Representatives, the lists for the Senate and European Parliament have a set of effective candidates and a set of successor candidates. The gender quota rules also apply.

Since the creation of the new Senate in 1995 (see Chapter 7), the ability to be on an electoral list that covers the full territory of a language group has proved quite attractive for the top party leaders. The election to the Senate is the ideal popularity poll, and the number of preference votes obtained for the Senate (or for the European Parliament) is a clear indicator of the political strength of a candidate. At the first European elections former Prime Minister Leo Tindemans obtained close to one million preference votes. The second highest was for Yves Leterme who obtained 800,000 votes for the Senate elections in 2007.

The way in which the Senate is elected also has perverse effects. Indeed, the top leaders of the parties that subsequently enter the coalition are most likely to become ministers and have to be replaced by successors. Those who end up in the opposition find themselves elected to the wrong assembly, since it is not the Senate but the House of Representatives that controls the federal government.

The regional parliaments

The parliaments of the three regions are also elected in a proportional way by using the D'Hondt system. The elections of the Flemish and Walloon parliaments are quite similar. The major difference between the two is the size of the districts. For the Flemish parliament the provinces are the electoral districts. Contrary to the federal elections, there can be one single district for Flemish Brabant, since the voters of Brussels elect a Brussels regional parliament. The francophone inhabitants of Flanders must obviously participate in the elections to the Flemish parliament. They can however cast a vote for a party espousing the francophone cause, 'Union Francophone', which is actually an alliance of the francophone liberal, Christian democratic and socialist parties. The Union Francophone has been able to elect one representative (of the 124) at each election since 1995.

Like the federal elections, parties need to pass a threshold of 5 per cent per province to be able to participate in the distribution of the seats. This is not the case for the election to the Walloon parliament. It has retained the electoral system that was used for the federal level until 2003: smaller districts and a second-tier distribution of the seats at the provincial level in Hainaut and Liège. The other three provinces form one single district. The quota rules – which have been defined in a federal law – also apply for the elections of the regional parliaments.

The Brussels Region has the most complex system. The number of seats per language group is fixed: 72 French-speakers and 17 Dutch-speakers. Being a candidate on one of these lists is only possible if one's identity card has been issued in that language. A candidate who once stood on a Flemish list can never in future be on a francophone list and vice versa.

The voters first make a choice between one of the two language groups, and then cast their vote for one of the parties and or candidates of that language group. The number of potential voters for each group is thus not fixed. It depends on the choice of the voters, and it gives an indication of the strength of the Dutch-speaking minority in particular. This is quite small, since the percentage of the votes for the Flemish lists was 14.9 per cent in 1989, 13.8 per cent in 1995, 14.2 per cent in 1999 and 13.5 per cent in 2004. Irrespective of these numbers, 17 seats are allocated among the Flemish parties. Three members of the Flemish group and five members of the francophone group can become a member of the regional government, and are then replaced by a successor (that is, if the ministers are chosen among the candidates elected in that parliament).

Election results

Proportionality

The results of elections in Belgium display a few basic features. The first is the very strong proportionality of the distribution of seats. For all elections at the federal or regional level the D'Hondt system is used, which gives only a small advantage to the larger parties. Like all formulae for the proportional distribution of seats, the degree of proportionality decreases when districts are smaller. That is the case in the Walloon provinces, with only four seats in the federal House in Luxembourg, five in Walloon Brabant and six in Namur. For the Walloon regional parliament the size of the districts or district magnitude is also smaller than in Flanders, which is reflected in variations in the degree of proportionality for the election of each of the parliaments.

Table 5.4 computes the degree of proportionality by using the Gallagher index, based on the difference between the proportion of votes obtained by a party and the proportion of seats (Gallagher, 1975). The highest degree of proportionality is found in the Brussels Region, where the district magnitude is very high (for the francophone parties who can fill up 72 seats). The federal and the Flemish parliament have a similar degree of proportionality. The districts used for the election are the same, with only a few more seats for each of them for the election of the Flemish parliament. Elections in Wallonia are (a bit) less proportional. A total of 75 seats are distributed in nine districts.

This high proportionality is a permanent feature of Belgian elections. Changes in the electoral system have never affected the basic logic of proportionality. To the contrary, whenever changes were made, the possible negative effects were deliberately neutralized. In 1995 the size of the federal House of Representatives was reduced from 212 to 150 seats. That could have had an effect on the degree of proportionality, but it was compensated by enlarging the smaller districts and by lowering the threshold needed for participation in the second-tier provincial distribution of the seats. Only the introduction of a 5 per cent threshold per district in 2003 was a deliberate attempt to slightly reduce the proportionality, but since only three districts have more than 20 seats to distribute, its effect has been quite limited.

Fragmentation

A second interesting characteristic of election results in Belgium is the gradual increase of the fragmentation of the party system. In the 19th century there were only two parties: Catholics and liberals. At the end of the century the expansion of voting rights allowed the Workers' party to gain representation and to grow rapidly. The introduction of universal suffrage at the beginning of the 20th century transformed Belgium into a 'two and a half' party system (Blondel, 1968), with two strong mass parties and a

Table 5.4 *The degree of proportionality of elections to the federal and regional parliaments*

Federal House of Representatives (results of 2007)		
	% votes	% seats
CD&V	18.5	20.0
CDh	6.1	6.7
Open VLD	11.8	12.0
MR	12.5	15.3
SP.a – Vl.Pro	10.3	9.3
PS	10.9	13.3
Groen!	4.0	2.7
Ecolo	5.1	5.3
Vlaams Belang	12.0	11.3
FN	2.0	0.7
Lijst Dedecker	4.0	3.3
Others	2.8	0
Gallagher Index of proportionality	3.84	

Flemish parliament (results of 2004)		
	% votes	% seats
CD&V – NVA	26.1	28.2
Vlaams Belang	24.2	25.8
Open VLD	19.8	20.2
SP.a – Vl.Pro	19.7	20.2
Groen!	7.6	4.8
Union Francophone	1.1	0.8
Others	1.6	0
Gallagher Index of proportionality	3.01	

Walloon parliament (results of 2004)		
	% votes	% seats
PS	36.9	45.3
MR	24.3	26.7
CDh	17.6	18.7
Ecolo	8.5	4.0
FN	8.1	5.3
Others	4.5	0
Gallagher Index of proportionality	7.95	

cont'd

Brussels parliament (results of 2004)		
	% votes	% seats
PS	28.8	29.2
MR	28.0	28.1
CDh	12.1	11.2
Ecolo	8.4	7.9
FN	4.7	6.7
CD&V – NVA	2.3	3.4
Vlaams Belang	4.7	6.7
Open VLD	2.7	4.5
SP.a – Vl.pro	2.4	3.4
Groen!	1.4	1.1
Gallagher Index of proportionality	2.73	

now much smaller Liberal party. The rise and success of right-wing parties in the 1930s disturbed the basic pattern which, however, fell back into place soon after the Second World War.

A major change occurred in the 1960s. The rise and success of the regionalist parties caused a sharp increase in the degree of fractionalization of the party system (Rae, 1968). Figure 5.4 shows

Figure 5.4 *The degree of fractionalization in the Belgian party system (dotted line uses party families as units of analysis)*

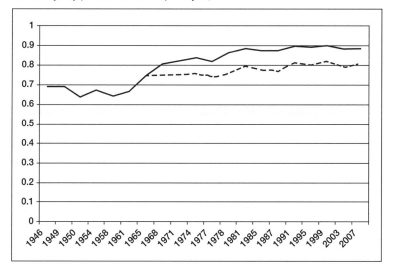

how the fragmentation of the party system has further increased ever since, to stabilize at a very high level in the 1990s. One of the events adding to the fragmentation of the party system is of course the splitting apart of the three traditional parties and the subsequent development of new parties in each of the language groups. The dotted line in Figure 5.4 shows the degree of fractionalization using the party families as units of analysis. It obviously shows a lower level, but the difference between the two lines is not large. Even if the parties of both language groups are counted as one single party, the Belgian electorate has increasingly cast its vote on a wider variety of parties. It basically means that the traditional parties have lost their monopoly. This can also be seen in Table 5.5, showing the results for all (significant) parties since 1946.

In 1950 the Christian democrats polled almost 48 per cent of the votes, the socialists 35 per cent and the Liberal party 11 per cent. Together these three traditional parties controlled no less than 93 per cent of the votes. Figure 5.5 shows, however, how this almost full control of the electoral market by the three traditional political forces has declined since that time. First their monopoly was challenged by the regionalist parties. They reached their peak

Figure 5.5 *The evolution of the electoral results for the three traditional political families*

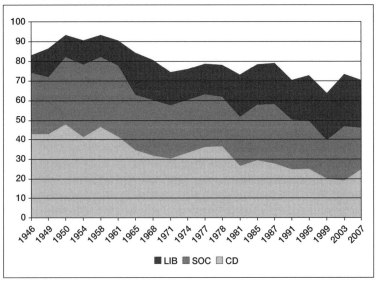

Table 5.5 Election results for the federal House of Representatives since 1946

	1946	1949	1950	1954	1958	1961	1965	1968	1971	1974	1977	1978	1981	1985	1987	1991	1995	1999	2003	2007
CVP-PSC	42.5	43.5	47.7	41.1	46.5	42.3	34.8													
CD&V								22.3	21.9	23.3	26.2	26.1	19.7	21.3	19.5	16.8	17.2	14.1	13.3	18.5
CDh								9.4	9.0	9.1	9.8	10.1	6.7	8.0	8.0	7.7	7.7	5.9	5.5	6.1
BSP-PSB	31.6	29.7	34.5	37.3	35.8	36.7	28.2	28.0	27.2	26.7	27.1									
SP.a												12.4	12.6	14.5	14.9	12.0	12.6	9.6	14.9	10.3
PS												13.0	12.6	13.8	15.7	13.5	11.9	10.2	13.0	10.9
PVV-PLP	8.9	15.2	11.3	12.1	11.1	12.3	21.6	20.9	16.5											
Open VLD										9.6	8.5	10.3	13.1	10.7	11.5	12.0	13.2	14.3	15.4	11.8
PRL / MR										5.6	7.0	6.0	8.2	10.2	9.4	8.1	10.3	10.1	11.4	12.5
KPB-PCB	12.7	7.5	4.7	3.6	1.9	3.1	4.6	3.3	3.1	3.2	2.1	3.3	2.3	1.2	0.8	0.1	0.1			
VU				2.2	2.0	3.5	6.4	9.8	11.1	10.2	10.0	7.0	9.9	8.0	8.0	5.9	4.7	5.6	3.1	
FDF							1.3	2.5	4.5	5.1	4.3	4.2	2.5	1.2	1.2	1.5	-			
RW							1.1	3.5	6.7	5.9	3.0	2.9	1.7	0.2	0.2	0.1	-			
Groen!													2.3	3.7	4.5	4.9	4.4	7.0	2.5	4.0
Ecolo													2.2	2.5	2.6	5.1	4.0	7.4	3.1	5.1
Vlaams Belang												1.4	1.1	1.4	1.9	6.6	7.8	9.9	11.6	12.0
FN																0.5	2.3	1.5	2.0	2.0
RAD-UDRT												0.9	2.7	1.1						
ROSSEM																3.2				
Lijst Dedecker																				4.0
OTHERS	4.3	4.0	1.8	1.8	2.8	2.1	2.1	0.3	0.0	1.3	2.0	2.4	2.4	2.2	1.7	2.0	3.8	4.1	4.2	2.8

in the early 1970s, when together they were able to attract more than 20 per cent. The regionalist parties did not survive, however. By 2007 there was no longer any trace of electoral results for them. They have either disappeared or decided to join forces with the old traditional parties. However, the traditional parties did not reclaim the 20 per cent that they had lost. Their total remains between 70 per cent and 80 per cent. This is because new challengers have appeared in the market: in the early 1980s the green parties entered parliament and in the early 1990s populist radical-right parties started their electoral success.

The loss of the monopoly of the traditional parties is clearly an indicator of the decline in importance of the societal segments or pillars. These networks of organizations and associations linked to the three traditional parties provided a more or less stable and well-defined reservoir of voters. Membership of one of the societal segments was almost automatically linked to voting behaviour. The closed pillar worlds provided all kinds of services, including a party to vote for.

This stable and predictable voting behaviour is now gone. Voters are becoming increasingly volatile (see below). Voting behaviour is of course not completely randomized. Churchgoers vote significantly more for the Christian democrats than for the others. Self-employed and employers vote more for the liberal parties and manual workers vote more for the socialists. But the numbers of churchgoers and manual workers are smaller than ever before. And voting for the familiar party is not necessarily automatic. There are alternatives. These include one of the other traditional parties or one of the newer parties in the party system. Voters won at one election are easily gone a few years later. It is however interesting to note that Vlaams Belang has been able to build a very loyal electorate. The 'cordon sanitaire' excluding the party from the political mainstream has probably helped in this. Deciding to vote for VB is crossing a symbolic line, and coming back into the mainstream is less easy than moving between parties of the mainstream (Frognier et al., 1994; 1999; Swyngedouw et al., 1993; 1998; Swyngedouw & Billiet, 2002).

Whether greens and radical-right parties are here to stay is impossible to say. Greens have proved to be a fairly stable force in many European countries and that is indeed what they are in Belgium also. The Flemish greens lost all their federal seats in

1999 but were able to come back. The electoral strength of the greens is however not very considerable. As in other European countries, they generally poll between 5 per cent and 10 per cent. That means that they are constantly in danger: they do not have a large reservoir of loyal voters.

Volatility

The decline of the traditional parties and the increasing fragmentation of the party system is therefore a very straightforward story. We should however also not exaggerate the amount of change. Even after the electoral challenges of regionalist, greens and radical-right parties, the three parties that were created in the 19th century, and that had by 1919 captured the votes of all (male) citizens, are still there and are still the backbone of the system. Belgium is a very good example of what Lipset and Rokkan (1967) have labelled the 'freezing' of a party system. It means that despite deep and sometimes radical changes in society, the major party actors are still the same.

Behind or under the relative long-term stability of the party system, there is however a quite volatile electorate. Again since the 1960s there have been a number of elections at which large numbers of voters moved from one party to another. The net volatility (Pedersen, 1979) reached double-digit values in 1965, and then again in 1981, 1991, 1999, 2003 and 2007 (see Table 5.5). Of the last five elections only 1995 showed a lower volatility. Voter surveys have however revealed that in 1995, 30 per cent of voters made a different choice from 1991. More important than the long-term stability of the system is the immense short-term uncertainty that all the parties are facing. Votes are easy to win, and therefore they are also very easy to lose again.

North and south

For the discussion of electoral behaviour so far we have looked at national results. That is, we have looked at the scores of the parties or party families at the statewide level. For all parties this national or federal result is obtained by competing in one of the language groups only. That severely limits their potential electoral score, and is one of the ingredients in the increasing fragmentation of the electoral results.

Looking at election results from a national or statewide perspective is however not the usual way for Belgium. Political parties themselves and the media always present and discuss results within each language group only. Doing so reveals a very fundamental feature of electoral behaviour in Belgium. North and south do indeed vote very differently. This is not a recent phenomenon or a new feature in Belgian politics. It has always been there. When in 1894 the first MPs of the Workers' party were elected, this happened only in Walloon districts. All the Flemish seats went to the Catholic party. The introduction of proportional representation produced a 'two and a half party system'. Its composition had however a very strong territorial variation. The two large parties – Christian democrats and socialists – were each even stronger in their 'own' region. This was still the case in 1950, as can be seen in Table 5.6. In Flanders the Christian democrats polled a solid 60 per cent of the votes, while in Wallonia they polled only 34 per cent. In Wallonia the dominant party was the socialist party. Its 45 per cent of the Walloon votes contrasts with the mere 26 per cent of the votes in Flanders. Only for the smaller 'half' party was the score in the two parts of the country more or less the same: 11 per cent in Wallonia and 9 per cent in Flanders.

Table 5.6 shows how the parties and later the components of the party families scored in the two large regions. It also shows the difference between the two per party family. These figures reveal a number of interesting elements. The first is illustrated in Figure 5.6. It shows the evolution of the overall difference between Flanders and Wallonia. In order to do this, we have computed a dissimilarity index. This is similar to the volatility index that is used for comparing two consecutive elections in the same party system: the absolute values of the differences between the two elections are summed and then divided by two (Deschouwer, 2009b).

The evolution over time is one of fluctuation, with some ups and downs. There are three high points: 2007 with a dissimilarity index of 32.1 per cent, 1946 with 29.3 per cent and 1965 with 29.2 per cent. Both the oldest and the youngest results belong to this highest trio. We can therefore repeat that electoral results in Flanders and Wallonia are very different, and that they have always been different. It is not the reform of the institutions granting autonomy to the regions and language communities (see Chapter 3) that has created the differences. The institutional reform has rather acknowledged these differences.

Table 5.6 Results of federal elections in Flanders and Wallonia per party family and difference between the two regions, 1946–2007

	Christian democrats			Socialists			Liberals			Regionalists			Greens			Radical-right			Communists		
	Fl	Wall	Diff	Fl	Wall	Diff	Fl	Wall	Diff	Fl	Wall	Diff	Fl	Wall	Diff	Fl	Wall	Diff	Fl	Wall	Diff
1946	56.2	27.0	29.1	27.4	36.3	8.9	7.7	9.3	1.6										5.5	21.5	16
1949	51.9	31.9	20.0	23.7	37.8	14.1	13.1	14.7	1.6	3.4	0.2	3.2							3.6	12.6	9
1950	60.3	33.8	26.6	26.0	44.6	18.6	9.4	11.4	2.0										2.5	7.8	5.3
1954	52.0	30.5	21.5	28.8	47.7	19.0	10.7	11.7	0.9	3.9		3.9							1.5	6.7	5.2
1958	56.5	35.1	21.5	27.8	46.2	18.4	9.8	10.4	0.6	3.4		3.4							0.1	4.5	4.4
1961	50.3	30.9	19.4	29.6	46.4	16.8	12.1	11.8	0.4	6.2	0.2	6.0							1.1	6.4	5.3
1965	43.8	24.6	19.3	24.6	35.2	10.6	16.6	25.4	8.8	11.9	1.9	10.0							1.7	10.3	8.6
1968	39.1	21.0	18.1	26.0	34.5	8.5	16.2	26.7	10.5	17.1	10.5	6.7							1.4	2.9	1.5
1971	37.8	21.0	16.8	24.6	34.4	9.8	16.5	17.7	1.2	19.2	20.9	1.6							1.5	0.4	1.1
1974	40.5	23.4	17	22.6	38.3	15.7	17.5	15.6	1.9	17.4	19.3	1.9							1.7	2.1	0.4
1977	43.9	25.7	18.2	22.4	39.1	16.7	14.5	19.1	4.6	16.7	9.1	7.6	0.1	0.7	0.6				1.3	5.4	4.1
1978	43.7	26.9	16.7	21.1	36.7	15.7	17.3	16.8	0.5	11.9	9.2	2.7	0.2	1.2	1.1	2.1		1.8	1.9	5.8	3.9
1981	32.1	19.6	12.5	20.7	36.2	15.5	21.3	21.8	0.5	16.2	5.5	10.7	3.9	5.9	2	1.8		2.2	1.3	4.2	2.9
1985	34.7	22.6	12.1	23.9	39.5	15.6	17.7	24.2	6.5	12.8	0.2	12.6	6.2	6.2		2.2		3	0.5	2.5	2
1987	31.4	23.2	8.3	24.4	43.9	19.6	18.7	22.2	3.5	13.0	0.8	12.2	7.4	6.5	0.9	3		8.1	0.4	1.6	1.2
1991	26.9	22.5	4.4	19.6	39.2	19.6	19.2	19.8	0.6	9.5	1.2	8.3	7.9	13.5	5.6	10.4	2.3	6			
1995	27.4	22.5	4.9	20.2	33.7	13.5	21.6	23.9	2.3	7.4		7.4	7.2	10.3	3.2	12.3	6.3	10.5			
1999	22.4	16.8	5.6	15.2	29.2	14	23.3	24.7	1.4	8.8	0.6	8.2	12	18.3	6.8	15.4	4.9	12.4			
2003	21.2	15.4	5.8	23.9	36.4	12.5	25.1	28.4	3.2	4.8		4.8	4.0	7.4	3.4	17.9	5.6	13.4			
2007	29.6	15.7	13.9	16.3	29.5	13.2	18.7	31.1	12.4				6.2	12.7	6.5	18.9	5.5				

Figure 5.6 *The dissimilarity between election results per party family in Flanders and Wallonia, 1956–2007*

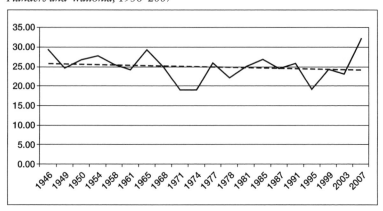

The second conclusion is – rather surprisingly – that the differences are not increasing, at least not if we look at the full period. The four most recent elections do show an increase. In 1995 the regional parliaments were elected directly for the very first time, and since then one can indeed say that the national election results have moved further apart. But 1995 is not the date from which the Belgian party system and Belgian public opinion is split. And it is of course a bit early to really assess the dynamics created by the adding of the regional elections, especially since in 1995 and in 1999 the regional and federal elections were organized on the same day, producing close to identical results. The peak in 2007 can also partly be explained by the presence and sudden success (6.4 per cent of the Flemish votes) of the liberal breakaway party Lijst Dedecker.

A closer look at the figures in Table 5.6 reveals that the substance of the difference between north and south has been changing. The huge difference between the scores of the Christian democrats has been reduced, to a large extent because of the steep decline of the Christian democratic vote in Flanders. In the socialist family the difference has fluctuated a bit, but remains quite important. The Flemish socialist party is very small. It belongs among the smallest socialist parties of Europe. In Wallonia the PS has lost some votes, but has remained a large party. Since 1981 – elections at which Christian democrats lost heavily – the largest party in Wallonia is larger in its region than the largest Flemish party. The larger number of Flemish voters has however always placed a Flemish party in the number one position statewide.

In the liberal family the differences are generally low. Both parties have more or less the same size in their own region. The large difference between the two in 2007 is an exception, caused by the strong losses of the Flemish liberals, confronted with a breakaway party.

Regionalism is also a party family for which there are some differences between north and south. The regionalist parties first appear in Flanders, which explains the difference in 1965. Wallonia (and Brussels) followed, but the subsequent decline of regionalism in Wallonia was quite rapid. In Flanders the decline is much slower, with 2007 being so far the first election in which there was no regionalist party participating in the elections on its own.

The two green parties were never one party. They each developed on their side of the language border. Their electoral fate has been quite similar, at least if one looks at the ups and downs. They always win or lose together. Their size is however quite different. Ecolo is a very large green party. Since 1991 (except for 2003), it has been able to score more than 10 per cent of the Walloon votes. Its Flemish counterparty is smaller and only once reached the exceptional score of 11 per cent in Flanders.

The populist radical-right is another story of important differences between Flanders and Wallonia. Actually the story of the populist radical-right in Belgium is almost exclusively a Flemish story. The francophone FN can hardly be called a party, although it is able to attract some 5 per cent of the votes. In contrast, Vlaams Belang is a strong and well-oiled machine and its electoral successes have been the source of many debates and discussions in the Flemish political world and public opinion. For the francophones in Belgium, right-wing extremism is indeed a Flemish problem.

Long before the split of the parties and of the party competition, north and south thus returned quite different electoral results. With the split of the parties the two electoral competitions therefore just continued to be different on each side of the language border, which also means that the significance of electoral results can differ widely between north and south. The type of competition and the stakes are indeed not the same. Table 5.6 shows how for Flanders the competition has taken on a very different meaning since 1999. For the very first time the Christian democrats lost their leading position and saw the Liberal party take over. The liberal victory of 1999 was however a very narrow one and Flanders now has four parties that are quite close to each other. One of them is a populist radical-right party. Losing or winning a few percentages can make a major difference. The Liberal party has experienced that being number one is something that can no longer be taken for granted. Forming a coalition in Flanders – whether at the federal or at the substate level – requires at least three parties (see also Chapter 6). And all governing parties always know that they might pay for their participation in government cash at the next elections.

For the francophone parties the stakes of the electoral competition are different. For a long time the Socialist party was by far the dominant party in the south of the country. The Liberal party has however moved closer and has even overtaken the PS in 2007. The crucial and hard competition is thus one between two large parties only. The Christian democrats and the greens are potential coalition partners – of the PS in the first place – but cannot dream of playing a leading role in the near future.

Substate elections

Elections to the federal parliament involve a competition between two groups of parties each engaging in a race within their own language group only. The results of these federal elections are read and interpreted at that community level and not at the statewide level. The election of the Senate is even formally organized as an election of representatives of the language communities only. The two electoral results for House and Senate do however produce one single parliament.

Elections for the regional parliaments are thus not fundamentally different. In Brussels alone, the regional sections of the Flemish and francophone parties participate rather than the 'national' parties themselves. But in Brussels both language groups also organize their own competition for their own reserved seats.

The almost complete overlap in the meaning and stakes of federal and regional elections strongly limits the possibility that these elections develop a specific federal or regional flavour. Furthermore, the history of substate elections is still far too young to see a clear pattern emerging. In 1995 and in 1999 the two elections were organized on the same day, producing almost identical results. Only two federal elections and two regional elections have so far been organized separately. These last four elections do show differences between them, but it is impossible to tell whether they are (the beginning of) a reflection of different meanings for the two types of elections. The fluctuations between the elections seem rather the result of the high volatility of Belgian voters, who move easily from one party to another, irrespective of the type of elections.

For elections in multi-level systems a difference can be made between 'first order' and 'second order' elections (Reif & Schmitt, 1980). The second order elections are elections for which the voters actually send out a signal to the parties at the other level. It means that the stakes of that election are not seen as really important and that the opportunity to vote is used to say something about the level that is more important. European elections are typical second order elections, but regional elections in federal states can also be second order when voters try to say something about the federal government or parties when voting for a regional parliament. In Belgium though it is quite difficult to see which elections are first order and which are second order. Regional and federal elections are so similar because of the absence of statewide parties that actually both elections are first order. They are both always important and have consequences for both levels at the same time.

Only the European elections are really second order. They are organized on the same day as the regional elections, and that means that all the attention goes to the domestic election. The European elections are not only second order; they are completely hidden behind the regional elections and lose most of their significance.

All regional election results so far are presented in Table 5.7. They do not show many surprises. The general trends that could be seen for 'national' elections are nicely replicated in the regional elections. Only for Brussels does there seem to be a slightly specific dynamic. First there is the aggregate number of votes cast for the Flemish parties. It gives an idea of the strength (or weakness) of the Dutch-speaking population in the Brussels region. The total number of Flemish votes no longer affects the number of Flemish seats. Before the 2002 constitutional reform the seats were first distributed between the two language groups according to their total number of votes. On a total of (then) 75 seats only ten or eleven went to the Flemish parties. The 2002 agreement guarantees them 17 seats and has also increased the number of francophone seats to 72.

Table 5.7 *Results of the elections of the regional parliaments*

Flemish parliament				
	1995	1999	2004	2009
CD&V	26.8	22.1	26.1	22.9
Open VLD	20.2	22.0	19.8	15.0
SP.a	19.5	15.0	19.7	15.3
Vlaams Belang	12.3	15.5	24.2	15.3
Groen!	7.1	11.6	7.6	6.8
Volksunie/N-VA	9.0	9.3		13.1
LDD				7.6
SLP				1.1
UF	1.2	0.9	1.1	1.2

Walloon parliament				
	1995	1999	2004	2009
PS	35.2	29.4	36.9	32.8
MR	23.7	24.7	24.3	23.4
CDh	21.6	17.7	17.6	16.1
Ecolo	10.4	18.2	8.5	18.5
FN	5.1	4.0	8.1	2.9

Brussels parliament					
	1989	1995	1999	2004	2009
PS	22.0	21.4	16.0	28.8	23.3
MR	18.9	35.0	34.4	28.0	26.5
CDh	11.9	9.3	7.9	12.1	13.1
Ecolo	10.2	9.0	18.3	8.4	17.9
FN		7.5	2.6	4.7	1.7
CD&V	4.2	3.3	3.4	2.3	1.7
Open VLD	2.8	5.7		2.7	2.6
SP.a	2.7	2.4		2.4	2.2
VB	2.1	3.0	4.5	4.7	2.0
Groen	1.1	1.0		1.4	1.3
Volksunie/N-VA	2.1	1.4			0.6
LDD					0.4
VLD – VU			3.2		
SP.a – Groen!			3.1		
All francophone parties	85.1	86.2	85.8	86.5	88.8
All Flemish parties	14.9	13.8	14.2	13.5	11.2

The small number of available seats has also pushed the Flemish parties into the formation of electoral alliances that would not be easily formed at the federal level or at the level of the Flemish region. In 1999 the Volksunie presented a common list with VLD, while greens and socialists also put their candidates on a common list. With 17 seats available from the 2004 election all Flemish parties in Brussels went back to their 'normal national' presentation.

Local elections

Provinces

There are two further levels below the regions: provinces and municipalities. Provincial councils are directly elected every six years on the same day as the local elections. Until 1995 the provincial elections were organized simultaneously with federal (national) elections. That also meant that the provincial councils were dissolved whenever the national parliament was dissolved. Elections for the provinces were thus always completely overshadowed by the national elections. The new fixed six-year cycle has not however increased the relevance of provincial elections. The elections to the local councils are far more important. Local councils and local executives are much more visible for the citizens. The powers of the provinces are fairly limited and the type of government formed – normally a coalition between two or more parties – does not substantially influence the provincial policies.

The electoral system for the provincial elections is furthermore quite complex and thus not very transparent for the voters. Every province is divided into 'arrondissements' and further into 'districts'. The distribution of the seats is done in two steps. A first step at the district level allocates the seats by means of a simple quota (total number of votes cast divided by number of available seats). The remaining seats are allocated at the arrondissement level by using the D'Hondt divisors.

For the provincial elections the political parties all participate under their national name, and possibly with the electoral alliance that has been used for the federal elections. That turns the provincial elections into an interesting 'opinion poll', since all parties can use them to measure their potential strength for the next federal or regional elections. Results of provincial elections thus follow exactly the same general trends and evolutions as the other elections.

Local municipalities

The elections of the local councils – also organized every six years on the second Sunday of October – are much more salient than the provincial elections. They are important because they are important for each and every municipality. The powers of that level are indeed limited but quite relevant for the citizens. And since all local elections are organized on the same day the results can be aggregated (at the regional and/or community level) for the parties to measure the evolution of their electoral strength in the country.

The fusion operation of 1976, which reduced the number of local municipalities from 2,359 to 589, was an important turning point for the significance of elections. The larger size of the new municipalities drastically reduced the presence and importance of purely local lists. Local sections of the national parties became the crucial players in most places. These local sections could also use their national name and receive a national list number, which facilitates the centralization of the electoral campaigns. For the parties (and for political scientists) is has thus also become much easier to aggregate the local results into national results and trends.

The party offer at local elections is however not a perfect reflection of the national (community) party offer. There is quite some variation between the parties and between the regions and this fluctuates over time. Tables 5.8 and 5.9 give an overview of the presence of the national parties in local elections in Flanders and Wallonia. It shows the number of municipalities in which they are present on the ballot paper under their national name and acronym. It also shows which proportion of the voters in that region has the opportunity to cast a vote for that national party.

In Flanders the presence and reach of the Christian democrats is quite impressive. Except for 1994 (when many local alliances and common lists with the Volksunie were arranged, including in the largest city, Antwerp) CD&V reaches almost all voters in local elections. For 2006 this included the places where the 'national' alliance with N-VA was presented to the voters. The Socialist party used to have this wide reach, but it has gradually declined. It means that many local sections of SP.a do not participate in elections under that name (or in alliance with SPIRIT). It is interesting to note that in 2006 there were 43 municipalities where a common list of socialists and greens was on the ballot paper, even though the central level of the green party fiercely opposes this

Table 5.8 *Presence of national parties in local elections and percentage of voters reached per region in Flanders*

	CVP CD& V/N-VA	SP Sp.a- Spirit	PVV Open VLD	VU N-VA	Agalev Groen!	Vlaams Blok Vlaams Belang	Sp.a – Groen!
Number of municipalities (total = 308)							
1976	265	255	147	156			
1982	277	264	180	162	61	24	
1988	282	264	218	173	149	50	
1994	243	224	214	75	156	131	
2000	258	213	211	84	188	181	
2006	270	172	223	35	110	224	43
Percentage of the voters reached							
	CVP CD& V/N-VA	SP Sp.a- Spirit	PVV Open VLD	VU N-VA	Agalev Groen!	Vlaams Blok – Belang	Sp.a – Groen!
1976	92.93	91.47	64.81	67.45			
1982	95.36	91.79	72.27	72.29	35.96	28.88	
1988	96.33	94.01	83.90	74.83	68.44	40.64	
1994	78.68	83.15	82.43	36.87	70.98	64.90	
2000	90.73	79.28	78.07	43.92	76.93	78.75	
2006	94.21	63.74	83.56	11.65	51.52	87.43	14.78

combination for regional or federal elections. Another interesting pattern in Flanders is the gradual penetration of Vlaams Belang. It started off in Antwerp and surroundings, and in the other larger cities, but at each local election there were more local lists, always – without any exception – using the well-known national label of the party.

In Wallonia this aspect of 'nationalization' of local elections is less visible. Wallonia has a larger number of very small and rural municipalities. The fusion kept alive a number of entities with small numbers of inhabitants but covering a fairly large area. It is interesting that in Wallonia the green party is the one that is present in the largest number of municipalities, reaching almost

Table 5.9 *Presence of national parties in local elections and percentage of voters reached per region in Wallonia*

	PS	PSC CDh	PRL MR	RW	Ecolo	FN
Number of municipalities (total = 289)						
1976	172	104	63	44		
1982	176	82	72	14	73	
1988	173	71	67		84	
1994	166	74	79		131	37
2000	149	54	75		185	9
2006	139	85	97		147	15
Percentage of the voters reached						
	PS	PSC CDh	PRL MR	RW	Ecolo	FN
1976	82.9	64.1	44.3	43.7		
1982	74.9	47.0	45.3	11.4	51.7	
1988	83.9	52.1	52.4		59.5	
1994	81.9	55.7	53.2		75.3	34.4
2000	77.2	42.4	53.7		87.9	18.8
2006	73.4	56.6	61.0		78.4	25.1

80 per cent of the Walloon voters. Since that is realized by being present in just over half of the municipalities, it shows also to what extent Ecolo focuses on the cities and on the larger municipalities. That is also the case for the PS. The party is present and strong in urban and industrial Wallonia, but not in the smaller villages of the Ardennes (provinces of Namur and Luxembourg).

In Brussels the situation is very different and is impossible to grasp or present in a neat table. Unlike the regional elections, there are no reserved seats for the Flemish parties. To increase their chances of having representatives elected in one of the 19 local councils in Brussels, they can either form an electoral alliance of several Flemish parties (but of course never with Vlaams Belang) or run on the lists of the francophone parties of the same ideological family. The latter is actually the most frequent choice. These common lists can use the francophone party name but generally use another name to make clear that a particular alliance is presenting itself to the voters. Incumbent mayors also often present a list with candidates of more than one party, under the simple label of 'Mayor's list'. This also happens in Flanders and Wallonia, but then rather in smaller villages and not in the cities. The party offer in Brussels is thus very varied between the municipalities and changes a lot between elections. That makes it very difficult to analyse election results at the local level over time. The only figure that is clear and unambiguous is the number of Flemish candidates elected in the local councils in Brussels. Since 1976, that figure has always fluctuated around 10 per cent.

Conclusions

The split party system of Belgium has important consequences for the organization and significance of elections. There are actually two elections, whatever the level at which they are organized. At that single level of the language groups, there are thus many elections. In a very fragmented party system with quite volatile voters, this produces a lot of insecurity. Parties have no electoral certainties. A position won during one election can be lost soon at the next. And the next one always comes soon. That constant fear for the sanction of the voters is one of the factors that make the necessary formation of coalitions both at the federal and at the regional level quite difficult.

Chapter 6

The Government

There are a few basic rules that apply to any Belgian government. In the first place it is a coalition government. The last one-party government goes back to 1954. The absence since the 1970s of political parties covering the whole of Belgium obviously reduces dramatically the chances for one single party to win a majority. For the francophone parties it is even mathematically impossible.

The second basic rule is that a government needs to secure a majority of the seats in the parliament. While some European countries – such as the Scandinavian countries and Spain – have a tradition of forming minority governments that seek support from (varying) parties outside government, Belgium forms governments that are, from the very first day, absolutely sure that they will survive a confidence vote. One of the reasons for that is the constitutional requirement for a new government to receive the parliament's confidence before it can start work. These two rules – coalition and parliamentary majority – apply for governments at the federal and at the substate level.

A third basic rule applies at the federal level only. It refers to the obligation to have an equal number of Dutch-speaking and French-speaking ministers. This is a constitutional requirement that leads in practice to a government for which the support from both language groups in parliament is quite balanced. Although there is no formal obligation to be supported by an absolute majority in both language groups, a federal government usually controls this double majority.

In this chapter we first present the procedures and rules for coalition formation at the federal level and we explain why this is often a difficult and lengthy process. Next we look at the functioning of the government and at its chances for survival. It will become clear again how crucial and important the role of the political parties is.

The procedure at the federal level

Forming a coalition government is never an easy exercise. There are always at least two cleavages to be bridged. First one needs an agreement between political parties defending a different political ideology. And second one needs an agreement between parties of the north and parties of the south. Forming a federal government therefore often takes some time. The absolute record so far was set in 2007, when it took no fewer than 194 days to put together a (temporary) government. In second place comes the formation of Martens 8 (that is, the eighth government under Prime Minister Martens), which took 148 days (see Table 6.1).

The formation process follows a classic pattern. If the elections come at the end of the term of the parliament and the government has not resigned before the elections, the outgoing prime minister goes to the King on the Monday morning after the elections to offer the resignation of the cabinet. This is accepted by the King, who then has a series of meetings with the presidents of both houses of parliament and with the leaders of the political parties. Parties belonging to the populist radical-right family have, however, never been invited to the palace. The francophone FN is too irrelevant to play a role in coalition formation and the Flemish Vlaams Belang is not only a radical party but also a separatist party whose representatives would probably not even accept an invitation from the King.

After a few days of consultation the King appoints an 'informateur'. The role of the informateur is to inform the King about the possible coalitions. The informateur starts meeting with the party presidents, in order to see which parties are willing to engage in negotiations. Actually, the King's choice for an informateur is already inspired by the direction in which the negotiations will go. If for instance a coalition of liberals and socialists is the likely outcome, and a Flemish liberal is likely to become prime minister, the leader of the francophone socialists has the best chance to be appointed informateur.

The informateur takes a few weeks to become informed. He invites party leaders and leaders of all the major pressure groups to present their demands for the new government. The informateur period is a good time to take stock of these demands while at the same time the heated political atmosphere of the campaign can slowly cool down. The informateur writes a report for the

King, who subsequently appoints a 'formateur'. The formateur – which is again not a 'real' choice for the King – is asked to form a new government. The name of the formateur is the obvious consequence of the election results and of the willingness of a number of parties controlling a parliamentary majority to start the negotiations. The formateur is normally the future prime minister. The government formed in 1987–88 by Jean-Luc Dehaene was an exception to that rule. Wilfried Martens took the leadership of that coalition.

The formateur organizes and leads the negotiations between the parties. They will usually all send a core delegation of two or three persons, to which experts are added whenever needed. The party delegations discuss the programme of the future government and draft the extensive coalition agreement. In that agreement the plans of the government are written down in great detail, including the timing for each of the initiatives (see below). If everything goes well and an agreement can be concluded, the formation can be ended. That is however not always the case, and then a variety of possible scenarios can ensue. A formateur can fail and give back his task. A new informateur can be appointed to see what the remaining alternatives are. And then a new or the same formateur can be appointed. Instead of an informateur, the King sometimes asks one or a few persons to act as 'negotiator' or as 'go-between'. That is the case when the two language communities have problems finding a compromise. The politicians invited to build the bridges are then usually older and 'wiser' and, more importantly, bilingual politicians. They can try to clear the minefield and pave the way for the formateur to finally put together a coalition.

If that process has come to an end and a written coalition agreement – translated in both languages – is agreed on, the political parties planning to be part of the new government call for a meeting of their party congress. The party leaders defend the agreement and ask the members and militants to approve it. This is not necessarily an easy job: sometimes the majority is quite narrow. Only once has a party congress refused to accede to the coalition agreement. Ecolo did not enter the Brussels regional government in 1999 because its members found the agreement insufficient.

As soon as the parties have given their agreement, the party leaders of the new coalition meet again to discuss or to finalize the distribution of portfolios. That is another complex negotiation in which a number of subtle equilibria have to be respected. The basic rule is that ministerial posts are divided proportionally between the parties by using a system of 'points' (De Winter & Dumont, 2006). The position of prime minister is three points, while all other ministers, the presidency of both houses of parliament and the membership of the European Commission count as two points. The number of seats of each party in the parliament is then used to compute how many points each party is allowed to claim. With only 15 ministers and with the obligation to have 7 francophones and 7 Dutch-speakers, this basic logic needs some adjustments. The normal means to correct the mathematical balance is by appointing a number of 'secretaries of state' to be used as 'small change'. These are junior ministers, and their number is not limited by the constitution. In the distribution of portfolios they count for one point. There will usually be a few more Dutch-speaking than French-speaking secretaries of state.

Within each party and within the government there is another important hierarchy. Each party of the government will have one 'vice prime minister'. These are actually the leaders of their party team in the government and the really senior ministers. The prime minister and the vice prime ministers together form a small core of the government that decides important issues and settles important discussions in the government (see below).

Once the numbers are agreed, the names have to be filled in. The selection of the ministers is done by the party president, who acts very independently. It is one of the important powers of a party president. The selection depends on a number of variables. In the first place the choice of ministers is related to the policy domains for which the party expressed its preference. No party has real experts in all fields. Second, each party tries to keep a regional balance: that is, every province should have at least one person in a leading position. Since there are five provinces for each of the parties to be taken into consideration, this balance can never be perfect. Yet the existence of coalition governments for the regions and communities does allow parties to better respect this unwritten rule. And when a province appears to be left empty handed, it knows that compensation will have to follow soon.

The ministers of the federal government do not have to be elected members of the federal parliament. In fact, a minister is not allowed to be a member of parliament. If he or she holds a

Table 6.1 *Composition of Belgian governments since 1945 (De Winter &*
Dumont, 2006a)

Date	Parties in coalition (party of PM first)	Prime Minister	Days to form	Duration (days)
12/02/45	BSP/PSB – CVP/PSC – PL/LP – KPB/PCB	Van Acker	5	174
2/08/45	BSP/PSB – CVP/PSC – PL/LP – KPB/PCB – UDB	Van Acker	6	225
13/03/46	BSP/PSB	Spaak	23	7
31/03/46	BSP/PSB – PL/LP – KPB/PCB	Van Acker	11	100
3/08/46	BSP/PSB – PL/LP – KPB/PCB	Huysmans	25	222
20/03/47	BSP/PSB – CVP/PSC	Spaak	7	610
26/11/48	BSP/PSB – CVP/PSC	Spaak	7	213
11/08/49	CVP/PSC – PL/LP	Eyskens (Gaston)	45	219
8/06/50	CVP/PSC	Duvieusart	1	64
16/08/50	CVP/PSC	Pholien	5	511
15/01/52	CVP/PSC	Van Houtte	6	818
22/04/54	BSP/PSB – LP/PL	Van Acker	10	1502
23/06/58	CVP/PSC	Eyskens	21	134
6/11/58	CVP/PSC – LP/PL	Eyskens	2	872
25/04/61	CVP/PSC – BSP/PSB	Lefèvre	29	1490
27/07/65	CVP/PSC – BSP/PSB	Harmel	64	199
19/03/66	CVP/PSC – PVV/PLP	Vanden Boeynants	36	690
17/06/68	CVP – PSC – BSP/PSB	Eyskens	77	1239
20/01/72	CVP – PSC – BSP/PSB	Eyskens	74	307
26/01/73	BSP/PSB – CVP – PSC – PVV – PLP	Leburton	64	358
25/04/77	CVP – PSC – PVV – PLP	Tindemans	45	47
11/06/74	CVP – PSC – PVV – PLP – RW	Tindemans	1	957
4/03/77	CVP – PSC – PVV – PRLW	Tindemans	2	43
3/06/77	CVP – PSC – BSP/PSB – VU – FDF	Tindemans	46	495
20/10/78	CVP – PSC – BSP/PSB – VU – FDF	Vanden Boeynants	9	59

cont'd

3/04/79	PSC – CVP – SP – PS – FDF	Martens	106	288
23/01/80	CVP – PSC – SP – PS	Martens	7	77
18/05/80	CVP – PSC – SP – PS – PVV – PRL	Martens	39	142
22/10/80	CVP – PSC – SP – PS	Martens	15	162
6/04/81	CVP – PSC – SP – PS	Eyskens (Mark)	4	168
17/12/81	CVP – PSC – PVV – PRL	Martens	39	1397
28/11/85	CVP – PSC – PVV – PRL	Martens	45	690
21/10/87	CVP – PSC – PVV – PRL	Martens	2	54
9/05/88	CVP – PSC – SP – PS – VU	Martens	148	1238
4/10/91	CVP – PSC – SP – PS	Martens	0	57
7/03/92	CVP – PSC – SP – PS	Dehaene	103	1170
23/06/95	CVP – PSC – SP – PS	Dehaene	33	1452
13/07/99	VLD – MR – SPa – PS – Ecolo – Agalev	Verhofstadt	29	1407
12/07/03	VLD – MR – Spa/Spirit – PS	Verhofstadt	52	1490
21/12/07	Open VLD – MR – CD&V – CDh – PS	Verhofstadt	194	90
21/03/08	CD&V – CDh – Open VLD – MR — PS	Leterme	1	275
31/12/08	CD&V – CDh – Open VLD – MR — PS	Van Rompuy	10	

parliamentary seat, it has to be left to the first available successor on the party list (see Chapter 5). A party can also choose to select somebody who was elected in a regional parliament, or reshuffle a regional government in order to solve the puzzle. Presidents of other parties or the future prime minister may voice some discontent about the choices made by their colleagues, but the basic rule is that one respects the choice made by each of the party leaders.

The persons selected to become ministers are normally elected politicians. It is rather exceptional for a party to search for a minister outside parliament, but it does happen once in a while. The most common pool for non-elected members of government are the major pressure groups. In 2004 CD&V asked Kris Peeters – the former leader of the smallholders' organization

UNIZO (always close to Christian democracy) – to become a minister in the Flemish government. He became Flemish prime minister in 2007. Paul Magnette, professor of political science at the Université Libre de Bruxelles, was asked in 2007 by the PS to become a minister in the Walloon government and later in the federal government.

When all the names have been filled in, the selected ministers and secretaries of state go together to the royal palace. The outgoing prime minister co-signs with the King the appointment of the new prime minister, and the new prime minister co-signs the appointment of all members of the new government. They all take the oath at the hands of the King, after which an official photograph of the new coalition is taken on the steps of the palace.

The final phase in the process of government formation is the presentation of the government's programme in parliament. After a first meeting of the Council of Ministers the prime minister reads his 'governmental declaration' in the House of Representatives. This is followed by a debate after which a – very predictable – vote of confidence is given to the new government. According to the constitution, only the House of Representatives needs to approve the new government. Yet in practice the governmental declaration is also read in the Senate and the Senate also organizes a debate and a vote.

The role of the King

The King appears at several moments in the process of coalition formation at the federal level. That does not mean however that the King can make real choices. The choices are made by the parties. In general, the Belgian constitution has actually given a very limited role to the head of state, which most kings have accepted only reluctantly. Leopold I was very active in the early days of the Belgian state and used his diplomatic skills to finalize the independence and international recognition of Belgium. Leopold II found himself a new country – the Congo – over which he could reign as a real and powerful monarch. Albert I went way beyond his ceremonial role by actively leading the Belgian army during the First World War. Leopold III tried to form a government during the German occupation of Belgium and faced a major conflict with the post-war government. He had to resign in 1950 (see below). Beaudoin was head of state from 1950 until his death in 1993. He was able to build a strong moral stance, but could not bear as much influence on political decisions as he would have liked. He had to accept the devolution process that gave far-reaching autonomy to regions and communities. In 1990 he was involved in a major incident that quite clearly showed that the role of the monarch is not to govern but to be a ceremonial head of state.

In 1990 both houses of parliament had adopted a new and liberal abortion law. The King had already announced openly that he did not approve of this, but then was confronted with the obligation to sign the bill. He refused, and asked the government to find a solution. This was found by the creative use of Article 93 of the constitution, which says that when the King is unable to govern, the function of head of state is taken over by the Council of Ministers. Although this article is meant to guarantee continuity in case the monarch is severely ill, the houses of parliament took a vote that confirmed that the King was unable to govern. All ministers of the government – including the Christian democrats who had also opposed the abortion law – then signed the bill. One day later parliament declared the King able to govern again. He had literally been 'suspended' for a while to allow the majority of parliament to pass a new abortion law.

King Albert II became king when he was 59 years old. He was actually chosen by the politicians. It had been generally accepted that his son Philip would succeed Beaudoin, yet the government of Prime Minister Dehaene believed that it would be better not to skip Albert and therefore asked him formally to take up his duty. He accepted, and has played his role in a very modest way. He is the first really 'low key' monarch. Beaudoin had often tried to influence decision-making, not only in the abortion case, but also for the Congo policy and even for the choice of ministers.

The King has thus no major role to play, since he only co-signs the acts and thus the decisions of the ministers. The prime minister gives a weekly report to keep the King well informed about what is going on. The King also regularly meets the other ministers and invites people to the palace to discuss public life in the country. He can make suggestions to the government, but the government decides whether the suggestion will be followed up. The 'low key' profile of Albert II actually means that he very seldom tries to interfere, contrary to all his predecessors.

During the formation of a government the King does however appear centre stage. As explained above, this role is also not a substantial one. The King appoints the informateur and the formateur, but these decisions are only the consequence of agreements between the political parties. When a government formation is very difficult, there is a bit more room for the King. Yet while Beaudoin in 1981 invited all party leaders to the palace to hear a severe speech about the need to be responsible and to overcome the differences between north and south, Albert II appeared to be quite helpless during his first difficult government formation in 2007. All he could try to do was buy some time and wait for sound advice on the next step to take. The fact that his advice and questions were hardly kept secret by the political actors also undermines his capacity to be an active player on the political scene (Brinckman et al., 2008). The Belgian king reigns but he does not govern.

The procedure at the regional level

Forming a government for a region or community follows a slightly different path, although the basic mechanisms are the same. The major difference is the absence of the King. After regional elections, the initiative to start the process of government formation is given to the leader of the largest party. He or she takes the first steps by inviting the other party leaders to see what is possible and then begins the real negotiations. These are easier than at the federal level, since the north–south division does not have to be bridged (except in Brussels – see below). When a coalition agreement is reached and written down, the parties call their congresses to approve it. And then comes the distribution of the portfolios. The same rules apply here. The party leaders decide who can become a minister and the number of ministers per party is proportional to the number of seats of each governing party in the regional or community parliament. Contrary to the federal level, there is no 'small change' available here. There are no junior ministers. In Flanders that is not a real problem, since the Flemish government (of both the Region and the Community) can have up to 11 ministers. With the president of the Flemish parliament also included in the deal, that creates enough 'points' to be divided between the parties.

In the Walloon Region and in the French Community the number of ministers available appeared to be too small when a three-party coalition was formed in 1999. The French Community raised the number of ministers from 4 to 8 and the Walloon Region raised it from 7 to 9. The Walloon Region and French Community have so far always had exactly the same coalition. That is not an accident, but a deliberate choice. It has allowed the parties to be very creative with the distribution of portfolios. Indeed, the same person can be a minister in both governments (which is actually also the case in Flanders, where regional and community governments simply function as one single government). In 2007 the PS even decided to select the same person to be prime minister of the Walloon Region and of the French Community.

After a regional or community government is formed, its members are formally elected by the parliament. Here also there is no need to have been first elected to that parliament. And if a minister was holding a seat in the parliament, he or she has to resign and be replaced by the first available successor on the party's electoral list. When the government is elected and has taken the oath in the regional or community parliament, the regional or community prime minister goes to the King to be sworn in. That is the only, and purely ceremonial, role played by the King in government formation at the substate level.

The formation of a regional government in Brussels follows a few special rules and logics. It is actually a two-step procedure. First a coalition is formed in each language group. Parties will attempt to keep these symmetric, but that is not necessarily the case. The presence of a strong Vlaams Belang in the Flemish language group and the exclusion of the VB from power by the other parties reduce the possibilities and, for instance, led in 1999 to an all-party grand coalition on the Flemish side, while liberals and socialists joined forces on the francophone side. Both also form the government of the Community Commissions in Brussels (see Chapter 3). The two unilingual coalitions then join to negotiate a coalition agreement for the region as a whole. This agreement needs to be approved by the congresses of the Brussels' sections of the parties, after which the portfolios are distributed. The numbers here are very small: on the francophone side there are two ministers, two secretaries of state and the prime minister; on the Flemish side there are two ministers and a secretary of state. The presidency of the Community Commissions is also part of the deal on the distribution of positions between parties.

Table 6.2 *Composition of Flemish governments*

	Prime Minister	Parties (party of prime minister first) *
1995–1999	Van den Brande	CVP – SP
1999–2003	Dewael	VLD – SP – VU – Agalev
2003–2004	Somers	VLD – SP – Spirit – Agalev
2004–2007	Leterme	CD&V – N-VA – VLD – SP.a – Spirit
2007	Peeters	CD&V – N-VA – Open VLD – SP.a – Spirit
2008	Peeters	CD&V – VLD – SP.a – Vl.Pro

NOTE: * Name of the parties as they were at the start of the coalition.

Table 6.3 *Composition of Walloon governments*

	Prime Minister	Parties (party of prime minister first) *
1995–1999	Collignon	PS – PSC
1999–2004	Van Cauwenberghe	PS – MR – Ecolo
2004–2005	Van Cauwenberghe	PS – CDh
2005–2007	Di Rupo	PS – CDh
2007	Demotte	PS – CDh

NOTE: * Name of the parties as they were at the start of the coalition.

Table 6.4 *Composition of the French Community governments*

	Prime Minister	Parties (party of prime minister first) *
1995–1999	Onkelincx	PS – PSC
1999–2004	Hasquin	PRL – PS – Ecolo
2004–2008	Arena	PS – CDh
2008	Demotte	PS – CDh

NOTE: * Name of the parties as they were at the start of the coalition.

Table 6.5 *Composition of Brussels regional governments*

	Prime Minister	Parties (party of prime minister first) *
1989–1995	Picqué	PS – PSC – CVP – SP
1995–1999	Picqué	PS – PSC – CVP – SP
1999–2000	Simonet	MR – PS – VLD – SP – CVP – Agalev
2000–2003	De Donnéa	MR – PS – VLD – SP – CVP – Agalev
2003–2004	Ducarme	MR – PS – VLD – SP – CVP – Agalev
2004–2004	Simonet	MR – PS – VLD – SP – CVP – Agalev
2004	Picqué	PS – CDh – SP.a /Spirit – VLD – CD&V

NOTE: * Name of the parties as they were at the start of the coalition.

For the allocation of portfolios in Brussels there is a special procedure, guaranteeing that the Dutch-speaking ministers receive substantial powers. There are a number of fixed packages for the ministers and secretaries of state and a set order in which a member of each language group can make a choice.

The mechanics of coalition formation

The formation of coalition governments is generally a quite predictable process. Political science theory has identified patterns related to the size of parties and to their ideological position that allow us to understand why some coalitions are more likely to form (De Winter, 2002). These theories and insights tell us that oversized coalitions with surplus partners or coalitions between parties with very different policy proposals are less frequent. Yet these general principles are disturbed by requirements belonging to the institutional environment in which the coalitions have to be formed. These institutional elements explain why the classic patterns of coalition formation are more likely in some countries and less likely in others.

In order to understand the mechanics of coalition formation in Belgium, a number of both formal and informal institutional rules have to be brought into the picture. First there is the rule to form coalitions that are from the outset sure that they control a majority of the votes in the House of Representatives. The formation of minority governments that need to rely on the support of non-governing parties – a very normal feature in Norway, Sweden, Denmark or Spain – is almost excluded in Belgium. The major reason for that is the formal obligation for a new government to ask for the confidence of the parliament. And for this confidence an absolute majority of the votes is needed. Only two governments were ever formed without a majority. The first was a homogeneous socialist government led by Paul-Henri Spaak in 1946. It did not survive its first confidence vote and disappeared seven days after it had been formed. The second was the Tindemans 1 government in 1974. It could rely on the support of the Walloon regionalist RW, because it was clear that RW would soon join the government as a full partner, which indeed happened after 47 days. When the RW ministers left the government in 1977, it became a minority coalition again, but only to dissolve parliament and to resign the day after the elections.

While minority governments do not belong to the Belgian political culture, oversized governments certainly do. There are two reasons why a coalition often has at least one surplus partner. The first is the constant desire for constitutional change since the 1960s. The Lefevre government (1961–1965) was composed of the two largest parties at that time – Christian democrats and socialists – and secured a clear two-thirds majority. The plan was to build further on the 'Val Duchesse' agreements of 1963 and to amend the constitution in the direction of more autonomy for regions and communities (Witte, 1988). Yet this coalition of the two largest parties, comprising also the largest political force in both the north and the south, lost its two-thirds majority in 1965. After that a combination of two parties was never able to control a two-thirds majority, which is no surprise since all parties had split, thus reducing their electorate to only one of the two language communities.

Amending the constitution thus required either the formation of larger coalitions or the seeking of support from outside government to deliver the extra votes. Broad two-thirds coalitions were formed in 1978, in 1980, in 1988 and in 2007. Only in 1980 however was the government itself able to change the constitution. All other constitutional amendments were accepted by the parties of the coalition government with the external support of one or more non-governing parties.

Another feature leading to the creation of coalitions with a surplus partner is the split of the old national political parties and the unwritten rule or habit of keeping the members of the same party family together in government or in opposition. There have been very few minor exceptions to that rule: in 1974 the Walloon regionalist RW governed without a Flemish counterpart, in 1980 the Brussels FDF governed without Volksunie or RW and in 1987 Volksunie governed without FDF or RW. These exceptions are not too surprising. The regionalist parties do belong to a same party family, but in the Belgian context they support quite different views on the structure of the state (see Chapter 3). Populist radical-right parties have never governed, and thus remained together in opposition. The three traditional party families always stayed together (until 2007), and the greens – who form one single group in the parliament – have a clear agreement to stay together. That brought both parties into the 1999 government, while only one of them would have been enough to provide the coalition with a parliamentary majority.

That symmetry of the federal government had been a hard and fast rule until 2007, when for the very first time only one member of a major party family – the francophone PS – joined the coalition while the Flemish SP.a remained in opposition. To understand why this happened, we need to take into account the multi-level context in which coalitions in Belgium are formed (Swenden, 2002). Since there are no statewide parties, the parties forming a federal and a regional or community government are exactly the same. Only in the Brussels Region are the coalitions formed by the Brussels regional sections of the parties. That means that the composition of a coalition at one level has important consequences for the way in which a government at another level can be formed.

After the first direct election of the regional parliament in 1995 the guiding rule in this respect was *congruence:* parties tried to form coalitions with the same partners at all levels (Deschouwer & Buelens, 2007; Deschouwer, 2009c). In 1995, as all parliaments were elected on the same day, that was an easy thing to do. All governments – including the German Community government – were composed of Christian democrats and socialists (see Figure 6.1). They were all congruent and the federal coalition was symmetric. The Flemish Christian democrats secured the position of prime minister in Belgium and in Flanders, while the francophone socialists took the lead in the governments of the French Community, German Community, Walloon Region and Brussels Region. By doing so, intergovernmental relations could all be organized between the same parties. Within the parties the internal hierarchy was also quite clear: the federal level was the core where everything was tied together. With only four party presidents all matters related to all the governments could be dealt with.

In contrast, the 1999 elections led to coalitions that were not at all minimal, mainly because they were formed with the rules of symmetry and congruence in mind. The major event of the 1999 election was the loss of the number one position of the Christian democrats in Flanders and thus in Belgium. The Flemish liberals had taken over and wanted to form a coalition without the Christian democrats, which was exactly what the francophone liberals and socialists had already agreed to do before the elections. Forming a winning coalition without the Christian democrats for the Flemish government did, however, require not only the liberals and the socialists, but also the greens and the Volksunie. In the

Figure 6.1 *Structure of the coalitions in 1995 and number of seats in the federal and regional parliaments (party of prime minister in bold italic)*

BELGIUM (150)			
CD&V (29)	SP.a (20)	PS (21)	CDh (12)
CD&V (37)	SP.a (26)	*PS* (30)	CDh (16)
FLANDERS (124)		WALLONIA (75)	

French Community and Walloon Region liberals and socialists did not need an extra partner. At the federal level the liberals and socialists needed at least one extra party. And that led to the coalition structure shown in Figure 6.2.

The federal coalition was oversized, since one of the two green parties could be left out. Yet the green parties firmly stuck to the rule of symmetry and wanted to govern together. Not taking them would kill the plans for forming the Flemish coalition, and thus both green parties were taken on board. The francophone green party Ecolo joined the Walloon Region and French Community government, although, mathematically, they were not needed. And in Flanders a minimal winning coalition of no fewer than four parties was formed. The picture then was one of almost perfect congruence and symmetry. Only the Volksunie found itself in a rather awkward position, being part of the Flemish government but not of the federal coalition. The party could have requested its presence in the federal government since it was mathematically needed for the Flemish

Figure 6.2 *Structure of coalitions 1999–2003 and number of seats in the federal and regional parliaments (party of prime minister in bold italic)*

BELGIUM (150)						
Open VLD (23)	SP (14)	Groen (9)		MR (19)	PS (18)	Ecolo (11)
Open VLD (27)	SP (19)	Groen (12)	VU (11)	MR (25)	*PS* (21)	Ecolo (14)
FLANDERS (124)				WALLONIA (75)		

government. It decided however to opt for the double role and for the incongruent position. That would allow it to put pressure on the other parties to realize constitutional reforms at the federal level, without having to engage in difficult negotiations itself.

From 2003 on the elections at the regional and federal level have been organized on a different day: federal in 2003, regional in 2004, federal in 2007 and regional again in 2009. Sticking to the principle of congruence has since then proved to be much more difficult. Governments have become incongruent and asymmetric. Figure 6.3 shows the multi-level structure of the coalitions formed and in place after the 2007 federal elections. An attempt to form a federal coalition without the socialists failed for two reasons. The first was the willingness of the government to introduce further reforms of the state for which a two-thirds majority is needed. Second, the small CDh was very unhappy about governing with MR and against PS at the federal level while it was part of a coalition with PS against MR at the regional level. The result is a new combination of parties in government.

Coalitions that bring together in power a new combination of parties are not a peculiar but a fairly normal feature of Belgian politics. The party system is indeed quire 'open' (Mair, 2006), in the sense that the competition for power does not follow a rigid and predictable structure. Although there are a few basic combinations of the three traditional parties or families, the new parties have always been able to join a coalition as soon as they became electorally relevant. Table 6.6 shows a list of all coalitions that were 'new', either because a new party entered government for the first time or because a new combination of parties was put together. The 2007 coalition only adds a new dimension – asymmetry – to the newness of coalition combinations.

Figure 6.3 *Structure of the government formed in March 2008 (party of prime minister in bold italic)*

BELGIUM (150)					
	CD&V-NVA (30)	Open VLD (18)	CDh (10)	MR (23)	PS (20)
SP.a-Vl.Pro (25)	*CD&V-NVA* (35)	Open VLD (25)	CDh (14)		*PS* (34)
FLANDERS (124)			WALLONIA (75)		

Table 6.6 *Innovations in the composition of Belgian coalition governments* *

Year	Parties in the coalition	New party	New formula
1914	Catholics – Liberals – Socialists	Socialists	+
1925	Catholics – Socialists		+
1944	CVP/PSC – BSP:PSB – PL/LP – KPB/PCB	KPB/PCB	+
1946	BSP/PSB		+
1946	BSP/PSB – PL/LP – KPB/PCB		+
1954	BSP/PSB – PL/LP		+
1974	CVP – PSC – PVV – PLP – RW	RW	+
1977	CVP – PSC – BSP/PSB – FDF – VU	FDF – VU	+
1980	CVP – PSC – SP – PS – FDF		+
1999	VLD – MR – SP – PS – Agalev – Ecolo	Agalev – Ecolo	+
2007	CD&V – CDh – Open VLD – MR – PS		+

NOTE: * Names of the parties at the time the government was formed.

Table 6.6 shows how new parties could quite easily and quite early move from opposition to government. The Socialist party entered governed in 1914, and the strength of the Communist party after the Second World War brought them immediately into power. In the 1970s the regionalist parties that had by then reached their electoral peak were allowed into power and in 1999 the greens entered government. There is only one, but important, exception to this principle of openness in Belgian coalition formation: the exclusion of Vlaams Belang. Unlike its francophone counterpart, which is electorally small and irrelevant, Vlaams Belang is a large party by Belgian standards. After the regional elections of 2004 it even formed the largest group in the Flemish parliament. Yet its entry into government is stopped by a formal agreement between the other parties. For the francophone parties, it is obvious that they will not govern with a party wanting the end of the Belgian state. For the Flemish parties, the origin of the so-called 'cordon sanitaire' around VB is the very radical position that the party took on issues of migration, asylum seekers and security in the late 1980s and early 1990s. After its first success at the local elections in Antwerp in 1988 and again after its sudden growth at the national elections of 1991, all Flemish parties promised each other that they would never even engage in coalition talks with VB.

The exclusion of VB from power does however not mean that the party has no role to play in the process of coalition formation. To the contrary: Vlaams Belang is a typical example of a party with a strong *blackmail potential* (Sartori, 1976). Its very presence and size and its exclusion from power affect the way in which the other parties can form a government. The best example of this was seen at the regional level in 2004, when VB had polled no less than 24 per cent of the votes. Since the green party had clearly announced that it was not available for the next coalition, no other combination of two parties could secure a majority in the Flemish parliament. A large coalition of Christian democrats, liberals and socialists was put together, including the smaller regionalist parties N-VA and Spirit which had presented common lists with CD&V and SP.a respectively.

A difficult and lengthy process

Clearly coalition formation in Belgium is a difficult process that has in the past few decades become even more difficult and therefore time-consuming. Four coalition formations since 1978 took more than 100 days (see Table 6.1). These are unsurprisingly all coalition formations during which the cleavage between north and south was quite deep and new agreements about the structure of the state had to be found before the new government could start its work. That is however not the only reason for the longer formation processes. Until 1968 the average time needed to put together a coalition was 28 days (De Winter & Dumont, 2006a: 294). After 1968 there was not one single coalition formation that took fewer than 29 days. That was the formation of the 'rainbow' coalition of liberals, socialists and greens in 1999. The eagerness to govern without the Christian democrats produced enough enthusiasm for rapidly concluding the talks. The continuation of the coalition without the greens in 2003 took 52 days to finalize.

Four more reasons – besides the language cleavage – explain the long duration. First is the number of parties involved. The split of the national parties brought into the formation process not only the obligation to first bridge the gap between north and south but also an increased complexity of the negotiations. The last two-party coalition died in 1968, and after the split of the national parties the lowest number of parties in a government is four.

Second is the increased volatility of the voters. That actually increases the potential 'cost of ruling' (Paldam, 1986). The normal pattern is that the parties that have governed lose votes at the next elections. There are in Belgium only very few examples of an outgoing coalition winning votes, and the highest gain is 0.45 per cent for the Verhofstadt 1 government. There is not one single example of all outgoing parties winning votes (after Verhofstadt 1 the two green parties lost heavily). If the price of power is indeed that high, all parties involved in the process of coalition formation are likely to play a fierce game (De Winter & Dumont, 2006a).

The third reason for the longer duration is the absence of a clear market leader on either side of the language border. Until 1999 the Christian democrats were (and for a long time by far) the largest party in Flanders. They could afford to lose, until they lost their leading position to the Liberal party. At the regional elections of 2004 and thanks to the electoral alliance with N-VA the Christian democrats reconquered the leadership. They know however that nothing is certain for the next election. The liberals took the lead in 1999, but know that it can be lost again quite easily. The three traditional parties have more or less the same size and an increasingly volatile electorate, which means that any compromise risks costly payback at the polls.

On the francophone side the competition is also quite keen, after a very long period of evident dominance by the Socialist party. In 1999 the liberals overtook the socialists in the French Community and in 2007 they became even stronger in the Walloon Region. But the electoral differences between these two major francophone parties are minimal. Both thus need to go back to their voters with promises kept. All this produces an environment in which forming a coalition can never be easy.

The fourth reason for the increased insecurity of the parties is the timing of elections. Since 2004 the regional and federal elections have been organized on different days. They have their own rhythm. Yet the parties participating in the federal and regional elections and the voters to whom they have to present themselves are exactly the same. Every coalition is thus confronted with the fact that there will be elections during the term. After the federal elections of 2003 a liberal–socialist government was formed almost at the beginning of the campaign for the 2004 federal elections (at which both liberals and socialists lost votes). The 2004 regional governments had three years of peace, until the federal elections of 2007. And the extremely long formation process that followed can also be explained by the fear of all parties for the opinion of the voters at the regional elections of 2009. And these could be followed by federal elections in 2011 and again regional elections in 2014. The absence of statewide parties therefore obliges Belgian parties to engage in coalition negotiations for which the sanction always comes before the end of the normal term.

The functioning of the government

Bringing together at least four parties belonging to the two language groups is an extremely difficult job. Keeping them together in a functioning government that will have to face crucial mid-term elections (at the other level of government) is therefore a constant equilibrium exercise, and is the most important reason for drawing up a detailed coalition agreement. The drafting of this document is indeed an integral and important part of the negotiation process. Usually the formateur produces a first draft, on which all the parties engaged in the negotiations can suggest additions and amendments. The negotiations are considered finished when all the parties have agreed to the same text, translated carefully in both languages.

The coalition agreement contains a long list of general policy principles and aims of the new government, and a long and detailed list of concrete actions that will be undertaken by the government. This also includes a timetable that must guarantee each of the participating parties that its demands will not be postponed until it is too late. This written coalition agreement is the 'bible' of the government. That refers first to its length: the last five agreements had a length of 17,000 words (Dehaene 2), 14,500 words (Verhofstadt 1), 24,000 words (Verhofstadt 2) and 14,000 words (Leterme 1). It is also the bible of the coalition because it is a 'holy' text. It has been accepted solemnly and approved by the congresses of each of the coalition partners. It is a contract. It can be referred to and invoked whenever one of the parties tries to realize more than it was able to get accepted in the coalition agreement (De Winter & Dumont, 2006a).

Actually the existence of a coalition agreement precisely avoids these attempts to keep on trying. It is therefore a device that has the important function of creating a minimal level of stability in a coalition between parties engaged in fierce electoral conflict. It does so by providing a catalogue of what can be done and of what can be discussed. Equally important, therefore, is what is *not* written in the agreement. These are the matters for which no common ground could be found. This non-agreement can also be made explicit, by mentioning that the government will not deal with certain issues, or that it will only deal with them if in a later phase a compromise can be found.

Governmental agreements are one of the factors that drastically reduce the power and room for manoeuvring of the parliament (see also Chapter 7). Individual MPs are indeed not expected to try to raise issues on which the governmental agreement has clearly stipulated how and when it will be dealt with. The initiative to do so belongs to the government. The government can possibly ask MPs of the majority to introduce the issues in parliament, but that will then be done with texts provided by the government. Since the 1990s most governmental agreements have even explicitly stated that members of parliament of the majority parties have to refrain from taking initiatives on certain issues. This follows the experience in the early 1990s of the Christian democrats, who saw their socialist partner and the liberal opposition join forces to drastically change the abortion law.

Flemish liberals also had a bad experience in 2003. They had agreed during the formation of the federal government that the issue of local voting rights for non-Europeans could be left to the parliament, since no agreement appeared possible between VLD and the other parties (francophone liberals and the two socialist parties). These other parties rapidly introduced a proposal in parliament and could – with the help of the green parties – have had it accepted against the will of the VLD. Since VLD had promised its voters not to accept the granting of voting rights, it faced a severe defeat at the (*regional*) elections of 2004. These examples only increase the awareness that one had better also agree formally on what will be done and on what will not be done. This is all written down in the 'bible' of the government. Formally it is not a legally binding document, but it is essential for the good functioning of the government.

The parties that have committed themselves to govern together thus need to keep in close touch. Entering government does not mean that a party or its ministers can do whatever they want.

Ministers in the Belgian government can therefore not be considered to be *policy dictators* (De Winter, 2002). All important decisions – including important personnel decisions in their public administration – need to be discussed collectively. There are several mechanisms for organizing the permanent negotiation between governing parties. First there are the meetings between the heads of the 'ministerial cabinets'. This is a team of ministers' personal collaborators and advisers (see below). The 'chef de cabinet' is very close to the minister and negotiates with his or her colleagues. When an agreement is found at this level, it can easily be approved by the government.

Every Friday all ministers and – if needed – one or more secretaries of state meet as the Council of Ministers. This is the place where the actions of the government are discussed and agreed on. Points prepared and approved by the heads of the cabinets can be dealt with easily and rapidly. Other and more important matters are left to the ministers themselves. The prime minister chairs the meeting, which has also been prepared by his head of cabinet. The Council of Ministers discusses issues until there is consensus. A government never votes. If no consensus can be reached, the point is postponed until it is ready to be decided on.

For really difficult or for urgent matters, a smaller core of the government can meet more often than once a week. This is called the Kern (core) of the government. It is composed of the prime minister and the vice prime ministers. This Kern has no formal status, but it is the heart and soul of the coalition. Since all parties are represented in the Kern with their most important minister, the Kern can in fact take decisions. If needed, and depending on the topic under discussion, one or more other ministers can be present during the debates. When the Kern has reached an agreement, the other ministers are not supposed to raise new questions; they have to follow whatever has been decided by the parties. In the Kern the leading and steering role of the prime minister is absolutely crucial (Plavsic, 1989; Fiers & Krouwel, 2005).

There is an alternative to a meeting of the Kern. When the matter is really crucial and might endanger the survival of the government, the prime minister can also engage in talks with the party presidents. This is actually not too different from a meeting of the Kern. Most parties have a rule saying that a party president who becomes a minister in the government (and the federal or regional level) should resign and be replaced. This rule is however not always respected and party presidents then simply become a vice prime minister while keeping the party mandate.

It is clear though that all parties in a coalition government constantly keep a direct link with what is happening in the government. All parties in government have a weekly meeting at which they prepare the Council of Ministers and if needed coordinate their actions between the federal and the regional governments. The composition of these groups is not fixed by the party statutes. They will usually involve the party president, ministers in the government and group leaders in the parliaments, but the group can also be smaller. Most important is that they decide on the way in which the party will behave in the governments in which it participates. A Belgian government is thus in many ways very clearly a *party government* (De Winter, 1996; De Winter & Dumont, 2006b). The government is hardly ever an independent body that develops its own dynamics. And if it does, this is the result of a small group of ministers – the Kern – getting to know and to respect each other. And the Kern is nothing more than the parties in government.

The internal functioning of the governments of the regions and communities does not differ from the way in which it works at the federal level. The mechanics of the federal level were simply replicated when coalition governments had to be formed and had to survive at the regional level. Ministers of the regions and the communities also have their personal ministerial cabinet and a head of the cabinet who can constantly monitor the functioning of the government and who keeps in touch with his or her colleagues. Since the governments of the regions and communities are smaller than at the federal government, there is less need for a restricted Kern to decide on important matters. All parties in the coalition have a vice prime minister though and he or she can speak on behalf of the party, since he or she will be in permanent contact with the party leadership. Government at all levels in Belgium is clearly party government.

The survival of the government

Like all coalition governments, the Belgian government has a high potential for internal conflict. That is especially the case at the federal level, where at least four parties are needed to reach a winning majority and where the north–south cleavage has to be bridged. A solid and detailed coalition agreement and permanent inter-party negotiations help to keep the conflict at an acceptable level. Yet governments do face the threat of collapsing before the end of the term.

The average duration of all governments between 1946 and 2007 is only 565 days or 18 months. That is very low. Yet the average is misleading, since it is the result of a large number of extremely short-lived governments, during a few periods of high instability (see Table 6.1). The first was 1946–1958 with initially the difficult post-war period and then a number of changes of prime minister in the Christian democratic party. There were no fewer than 9 governments in 12 years. The second period of high instability was the late 1970s and the 1980s. The short duration of many governments was then due to the difficult and regularly failing attempts to reform the state and to give autonomy to the regions and communities. Prime Minister Wilfried Martens played an important role at that time and led nine governments between 1979 and 1991 (Heylen & Van Hecke, 2008). After 1991, and thus also after the direct election of regional and community parliaments, a new period of stability followed with four governments going to the end of their four-year mandate. After the 2007 elections the topic of state reform was high on the agenda again, leading to record long negotiations and the formation of a transition government that was explicitly meant to last no longer than three months. Its successor collapsed after eight months.

Whether a government lives until the end of its term or collapses earlier is not a decision taken by the parliament. Belgian governments are party governments and parties decide whether it is time to stop. A prime minister might go to the parliament to check formally whether the government still has a majority, but generally that is not the way in which one proceeds. The normal routine is for the prime minister to call for a Council of Ministers or a meeting of the Kern, and if no agreement can be found he goes to the King to offer the resignation of the government. The King does not have to accept the resignation though, and most often the King's first reaction is to ask the prime minister to try one more time to keep the government alive. If that works, the resignation is never accepted and the government simply goes on. Actually a resignation can also be a deliberate and tactical move by the prime minister or by his party. It is a way in which he can show the partners that the conflict is serious and that the consequences of a non-agreement might be dramatic.

At the regional level the stability of the coalitions is – so far – quite high. The major element disturbing that stability is the frequent change of prime ministers, which results from the fact that the parties use their political personnel as one single pool from which they can choose ministers at the federal and at the substate level. Ministers thus hop from one level to the other. Regional elections and the formation of new substate governments always involve reshuffles at the federal level and vice versa.

Individual ministers can resign without their party leaving the government. This happens when governments are reshuffled, but also when one minister is forced to resign. This happens regularly, but it is difficult to describe the rules that define when a minister has to go. That is a matter of interpretation. The unwritten rule says that a minister should resign when he or she feels that it has become impossible to function normally. That can be an individual decision of the minister, or one in which the party feels that the pressure is too high to keep the minister in place. Some ministers have resigned because of errors and mistakes made by their collaborators or by their public administration. If a minister and his or her party decide that they want to remain in place, they can do so. Only when the prime minister explicitly asks them to go, and the survival of the coalition is at stake, will the minister have to resign. But in that case again the party will have accepted that this is better than ending the life of the government. The personal life of ministers is never a reason for resignation. In Belgian political culture this fully belongs to the private sphere.

Governing at the local level

Provinces

Belgium is divided into ten provinces. Originally the provinces were the territorial building blocks of the country. The introduction of new meso-levels of government has however reduced their importance and relevance. One might even wonder why this intermediate level is still needed. But the provinces are traditional structures, and that usually means that it is not easy to abolish them. The provinces fulfil a number of functions in federal Belgium and, for the political parties, they are one extra level where elected and executive mandates can be conquered and controlled.

Probably the most important consequence of the reform of the state has been the disappearance of the central province of Brabant. The fixing of the language border and the coming to life of the three regions meant that the geography of Brabant was no longer adapted to the new organization of the state. The constructional reform of 1993 thus created two new provinces: Walloon Brabant and Flemish Brabant. Brussels is not a province and does not belong to a province (see Figure 6.4).

The provinces deal with matters of provincial importance, unless the federal, the regional or the community level has the right to deal with them. That is at the same time a very broad and a very narrow set of powers. Provinces typically act as partners in the policies controlled by the other levels. They can promote tourism in the province (a community competence) or stimulate cultural activities

Figure 6.4 *The Belgian provinces*

(*idem*). They also play a role – but do not have the final say – in overseeing the activities and decisions of the municipalities.

The provinces have a directly elected council with a six-year mandate that coincides with the term of the local municipalities. The number of councillors ranges between 47 (Luxembourg) and 89 (Antwerp), depending on the population size. The council elects a Permanent Deputation that acts as the executive power of the province. This Permanent Deputation is composed on a party political basis, like governing coalitions at the other levels. It is composed of six members who need to be elected in the provincial council and who remain a member of the council.

The council elects its chair, but the Permanent Deputation is chaired by the governor of the province. The governor is not elected but appointed by the regional government. The appointment is for an unlimited duration, which means that the governor does not change when the coalition changes. The governor is also a party politician. The political parties carefully balance the positions of governor between them on the basis of their electoral strength.

The governor has a double role to play. He or she chairs the executive and represents the province but he or she is also the representative of the higher levels of government in the province. The governor needs to make sure that the province complies with the rules of the higher levels. He/she is also responsible for the order and security in the province and takes the lead whenever a 'disaster plan' needs to be activated in case of floods, industrial accidents, major fires and so on.

Local municipalities

Belgium is further divided into 589 municipalities. Until 1976 there were 2,359 of them, but by merging smaller units into larger entities the number was drastically reduced. In Brussels though there has been no fusion. The central region is and remains divided into 19 local municipalities. One of these is the city of Brussels. It is actually the city of Brussels and not the region (although it is formally called capital region) that is the capital city of the country.

The local level can deal with all matters related to local life, unless other levels have the power to deal with them. Like the provinces, that can mean a lot but is in practice very much limited to a role of co-producer of public goods. The way in which the local level organizes that has however a real and visible impact on the daily life of the citizens. The municipalities are (co)responsible for important things like the local public infrastructure (roads, parking lots, theatres, sport facilities), waste removal and treatment, and the local area management (within the limits set by the regions) and many have municipal schools. Some of the tasks – like providing a public library – are however simply imposed by the higher level. Municipalities receive a part of the taxes levied by the federal or the regional level, but they also have the capacity to decide on specific local taxes and can claim a proportion of the income tax paid by their citizens to the federal state.

All municipalities have a directly elected local council. Only inhabitants of the municipality can be elected and whenever an elected member moves to a different place he or she has to be replaced. The number of members of the council varies between 7 and 55, depending on the number of inhabitants.

The executive is composed of the mayor and a College of Aldermen. Forming such a local executive is rather easy when one party or one list has secured an absolute majority of the seats in the local council. This is actually the case in 50 per cent of the local municipalities. In Wallonia 65 per cent of the local councils have one party holding a majority, in Flanders 39 per cent and in Brussels 42 per cent (Ackaert et al., 2007: 440). In the other councils a coalition needs to be formed. Local party sections are quite autonomous in this respect, although in the larger cities the central party leadership keeps an eye on what is happening. It is also interesting to note that local coalitions are often formed before the elections. Local party leaders often negotiate a full agreement on policies and personnel, with the formal promise that they will implement it if the electoral results provide them with a majority in the council (Dumont et al., 2008).

The mayor is not directly elected but is appointed for a six-year period by the regional government. The aldermen are elected by the council, and this election is the result of a coalition agreement between parties that control at least half the votes in the council. Meetings of the council are public (except when dealing with individual files) and are held at least ten times per year.

The role of the mayor is important and also dual like that of the provincial governor. He or she is the head of the municipality and represents it, but also represents the higher levels of government.

The mayor is for instance a member of the inter-municipality council (bringing together several smaller municipalities) that leads and organizes the local police force (Ackaert, 2006).

In each local municipality there is a public centre for social welfare (OCMW – Openbaar Centrum voor Maatschappelijk Welzijn/CPAS – Centre Public d'Action Sociale). It organizes help – financial and other – for persons living in a precarious situation. They can receive money if they are not entitled to receive any from the social security system (see also Chapter 8). This OCMW/CPAS has a council that is elected by the municipality council, and one third of the local councillors can combine both functions if they want. The OCMW/CPAS elects a chair. These local centres play a crucial role as first and final help and assistance to people, and in larger municipalities they run an important network of hospitals and homes for the elderly.

All these basic rules for the functioning of local municipalities are the same in the three regions. Yet since the regions are now empowered to control the organization and functioning of the local level, a number of variations can be seen between the regions. In Wallonia the president of the OCMW/CPAS automatically becomes a member of the local executive, that is, he or she becomes one of the aldermen. In Flanders the municipalities can decide themselves whether the OCMW/CPAS chair is added to the College. In Flanders the mayor is not automatically the chair of the local council. The council can decide to elect a chair that is not a member of the College. In Wallonia the mayor is appointed by the regional government but the candidate who receives the highest number of preference votes in the largest party that forms the coalition is automatically selected to become the next mayor. And also in Wallonia the local executive can be replaced, while elsewhere the elected College (and appointed mayor) are in power for a fixed period of six years. A Walloon local council can adopt a constructive vote of no confidence, suggesting a new executive to the council (Dandoy & Fournier, 2008).

Conclusions

Governing in Belgium means coalition government. And with a split party system and lots of electoral movements and swings, this is never an easy task. Forming a government often takes a lot of time, and the survival rate of coalitions is not very high. At the regional level the formation of coalitions is easier, since the language divide does not have to be crossed (except of course in Brussels). But in all cases a government is put together after negotiations between party leaders and after the approval of a quite detailed coalition agreement. This is the contract and the 'bible' of the coalition and therefore all the partners are expected to respect it. That also goes for the members of the parliamentary assemblies. When a government is formed and if it wants to survive, it does not need active and critical members of parliament. Members of parliament are – as will be discussed in the next chapter – very docile and loyal party soldiers.

Chapter 7

The Parliament

The House of Representatives and the Senate are both located in the same building, right opposite the royal palace. King Leopold III, who in the 1930s was not too fond of the increasing powers of the parliament and especially of the political parties therein, is said to have referred to the parliament building as 'la baraque d'en face' (the barracks across the road). The offices of the prime minister are a few blocks down the road, as part of one large complex hosting the formal powers of the Belgian state. This physical proximity also nicely symbolizes the extent to which government and parliament are closely related. Both the government and the parliament form together the legislative power. Without cooperation between government and parliament no policy can be decided on.

In this chapter we first describe how the parliamentary system works. We present the two houses of the federal parliament and the way in which they make laws and control the government. By looking at the members of the parliament and at the way in which they fulfil their representative tasks, we can conclude that the parliament loses power vis-à-vis the government and that individual MPs have little room to play a very active role.

Two houses of the parliament

The bicameral system installed in 1830 was one in which a second house – the Senate – was meant to be a higher house. Voting rights were (even) more restricted for the Senate and the minimal age to be a senator was set at 40, while it was 25 for the House of Representatives. The idea was that the Senate could have a moderating power, like other first chambers in parliamentary democracies. Whenever access to the House was broadened by changes in the electoral law, some changes were also added to allow the Senate to remain different, that is, not elected directly by all citizens. In 1893 a new category of provincial senators was introduced, who

were elected by the councils of the provinces. In 1919 the introduction of universal male suffrage for the House introduced the
category of co-opted senators. These were to be added to the
assembly by the already elected members. The idea was to attract
experts who would not feel the pressure of re-election.

In the course of history however, the House and the Senate
gradually became much more similar to each other. Elections to
both houses (and to the provincial councils) were controlled by
the same political parties, who simply divided their strong candidates between the lists for one of both assemblies. The co-opted
senators were frequently just candidates who had failed to be
elected on one of these lists. The party composition of both houses
was therefore almost identical. Since both houses had equal
powers, all bills had to be accepted twice by the same governing
coalition of the same political parties.

The Senate

The state reform of 1993, finalizing the federal logic of Belgium,
included a thorough reform of the Senate. Like other aspects of the
state reform though, the new Senate was the outcome of a difficult
compromise between several principles. And that has produced a
quite complex assembly that ever since the reform has been in search
of a clear identity and a meaningful place in the Belgian institutions.

There are four categories of senators. The first is the group of 40
directly elected senators. These are elected by the two language
communities. The francophones – actually the inhabitants of Wallonia and of the district of Brussels-Halle-Vilvoorde (see Chapter 5)
– elect 15 senators. The Flemish can elect 25. These are elected by
the inhabitants of Flanders and Brussels. Inhabitants of the central

Figure 7.1 *Composition of the Senate*

Flemish Community	French Community	German Community	Royal princes
25 directly elected	25 directly elected		
10 elected by Flemish Community parliament	10 elected by French Community parliament	1 elected by German Community parliament	Currently 3
6 co-opted	4 co-opted		
Total = 41	Total = 29	Total = 1	Total = 3

BHV district thus have the free choice between the lists of both communities. The election of the senators is organized on the same day as the election to the House of Representatives. Both houses are also dissolved together.

The results per list of the direct election are also important for two of the other categories. The numbers of these per party are further allocated according to the D'Hondt system.

The second group are the *community senators*. They are selected from the community parliaments. The Flemish and the French Community each send ten community senators and the German Community parliament one. It is actually the only place in the federal institutions where the German Community has a reserved seat. The party groups in the community parliaments decide who they will send to the Senate. These community senators thus have a double mandate. They have a seat both in their community parliament and in the Senate.

To these 61 senators – 40 directly elected and 21 indirectly elected – a group of ten *co-opted senators* is added. Four of these are francophones and six are Flemish. Here also the number of seats per party is computed by further distributing seats on the basis of the results of the direct election. As in the case above, the co-opted senators are usually party members who were not elected to the House or to the Senate (or to one of the regional parliaments if elections were on the same day). This brings the number of senators to 71, and actually this is the real political composition of the Senate.

The fourth category is another remainder of the old system: the children of the King have the right to become a senator. All three children of Albert II – Crown Prince Philip, Princess Astrid, and Prince Laurent – have taken the oath as a senator. They do have the right to vote (from the age of 21), but they actually never vote. They only participate in meetings when these are ceremonial. Whenever real discussions take place or real decisions have to be taken, the royal senators are not present and do not voice an opinion. And, of course, they do not belong to one of the language groups.

The new Senate meets in the same room as the old Senate. Unlike the House where members sit on benches, the senators sit on velvet-covered chairs. They have more room, since the old Senate had more than 100 members. The colour of the seats is red, which has always been the colour of the Senate. In the houses of parliament, the carpets on the floor indicate in which part of the building one is. The colour of the House is green.

As can be seen – more or less – from the composition of the Senate, it is meant to be a house of the language communities. Like in most other federal states, the desire was to have a second house in which not the people but the substates would be represented. The problem is though that Belgium has two types of substates: regions and communities. The Senate thus only reflects the division in communities. The constitution does state that at least one member of each of the language groups must be an inhabitant of Brussels. If nobody has been elected directly, the next two categories can be used to make sure somebody from Brussels is present. Yet this rule is not always respected on the Flemish side, without any formal consequences though.

The House of Representatives

The House of Representatives has 150 members, directly elected by the population. Until the state reform of 1993 the number of members of the House was 212. The number of MPs in both House and Senate was reduced because new representatives would be elected in the three regional parliaments. The division of tasks between House and Senate is now also different. The Belgian bicameral system has become asymmetric, with specific tasks for each assembly. Actually the House is by far the most important assembly. The Senate has received specific powers. It is only needed – always together with the House – for a revision of the constitution, for legislation changing the basic structure of the Belgian state, for the ratification of international treaties and for laws organizing the structure of the judicial power. In all other matters the Senate has the right to discuss any legislation accepted in the House and it can suggest amendments. But the House does not need to accept the Senate's suggestions. The House finally decides.

The House of Representatives is explicitly the only assembly that has the right to vote the budget and to decide on confidence in the government. The House of Representatives is the place to be for politicians wanting to play a substantial role. But because of its election in two very large districts the top candidates tend to go to the Senate. Indeed, the large district offers candidates the opportunity to test their popularity in their language community as a whole. For those who subsequently become a minister in one of the governments this is not a problem; they are replaced by a candidate from the successor list. For the leaders of the opposition though, the Senate is the wrong assembly to be elected to.

This perverse effect of the electoral system for the Senate is one of the elements of the ongoing debate about its structure and use. The idea of simply abolishing the Senate is heard once in a while, but since the Senate has to approve its own abolishment that is not very likely to happen. It all depends on the role that a second house could play in Belgian politics.

It is the house where the communities are represented, but the senators do not especially act as representatives of their community: that is, all federal MPs – also those elected in the House – represent their community since all parties limit their electoral participation to one community only. The Senate cannot add something extra to this by being elected and further composed per language community. The Senate is also not the place where the federal level needs to seek the approval of the communities. That is done elsewhere. Actually no government can function without the approval of the communities. There are thus other institutions where the language communities are really visible and represented. The Senate cannot add anything extra to that.

Since 1995, the Senate is also supposed to be a house for reflection, for debates about long-term developments. That is a role that has slowly developed. The Senate organizes more hearings and symposia to reflect about issues without the need to produce immediate legislative initiatives. The role of house of reflection has also been enlarged with a few 'investigation commissions' (see also below). There has been one analysing organized crime in 1995, one investigating the Rwandese genocide in 1997 and one dealing with legal and illegal trade and the role of Belgium therein in the natural resources of the Great Lakes area in central Africa. It is clear though that the current role of the Senate remains one that can be, and indeed often is, questioned. Further reforms in both composition and role of the Senate can be expected.

The legislative function

Making laws is one of the major tasks of the parliament. It does so in close cooperation with the government. Members of parliament – both House and Senate – have the right to introduce private member bills, which they can do alone or together with other members of their own group or of other groups. This is however not the most important source or origin of laws. A vast majority – 85 per cent – of the laws that are finally accepted by the parliament have been initiated by the government. The making of a law requires a number of formal steps between initiative and final vote. We will describe this process below for a proposal that is introduced in the House of Representatives (see Figure 7.2)

For government bills the advice of the Council of State is needed. This judicial body checks whether the proposal respects the constitution and international treaties and whether it is clearly formulated. The advice of the Council is not binding, but if substantial remarks are formulated they will generally be accepted. For private member bills, the advice of the Council of State is not required. It can however be requested by one-third of the members of an assembly or by a majority of one of the language groups. But even then the remarks of the Council of State are still only suggestions.

Figure 7.2 *The legislative procedure*

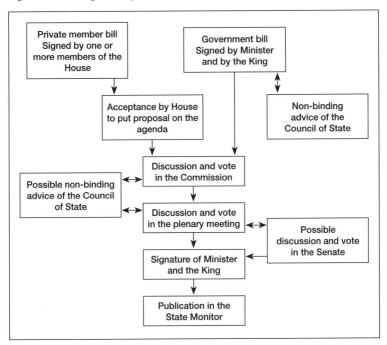

For private member bills, the House first needs to decide whether the proposal can be taken into consideration. This is not a major hurdle. All proposals are in principle accepted. It is just a matter of fair play. For government bills, the House cannot decide whether it will take it into consideration. To the contrary, a government bill will almost automatically end up on top of the agenda. This agenda of the House is set weekly by a meeting of the speaker of the House and the group leaders. In practice this means that the government – always controlling a majority in the House – decides on what will be done first.

The proposal is then sent to one of the commissions of the House. These commissions roughly reflect the competences of the federal state. There are the important commissions for Finance and Budget, Defence, Social Affairs, Justice, Foreign Policy, Infrastructure and Public Health, Home Affairs, and many more very specific and ad hoc commissions. The composition of the commissions reflects the strength of the party groups in the parliament. The D'Hondt divisors are used to allocate the seats in the commissions between the party groups. Each commission has a chairperson and here again the distribution of the chairs is done according to the strength of the party groups. While the speaker of the House is always a member of one of the governing parties, the chairs of the commissions can thus be members of opposition parties.

In the commission the text is thoroughly analysed. If it is a government bill, the responsible minister is present to introduce the proposal and to give explanations if needed. All members of the commission can suggest amendments, as well as the government if it is the author of the proposal. After the discussion the commission votes on each amendment and decides by simple majority whether it can be accepted. The commission votes on every article of the proposal and finally also on the text as a whole. Since the composition of the commissions reflects the composition of the House as a whole, a government bill never fails to be backed by a majority of the commission, although amendments – rather technical than substantial – suggested by members of the opposition can also be accepted.

The next step is bringing the proposal to the plenary sessions. Indeed, only the plenary meeting can accept or reject a proposal. For that reason the whole procedure – discussion, amendments, votes – is replicated. This, however, is not an important phase. It has to be gone through for legal reasons, but the real work is done in the commission where each party sends its specialists on the matter. The end of the work for the House is the final vote on the proposal as a whole.

For some issues the Senate must also have its say – in that case, the same procedure is repeated in the Senate until a final vote is taken. If the text accepted differs from the one accepted in the House, a negotiation between the two houses is needed. An inter-parliamentary commission with members of both houses needs to find an agreement. If both houses in fact agree on the same text, the work is done. For matters in which the Senate is not needed, the Senate can still ask to have another look at the proposal. In that case a disagreement between the two houses does not require negotiations. The final word is for the House. In practice, the government is in control of the legislation process from beginning to end, and disagreement between the two houses is not expected. So far a coalition government has always controlled a majority in both houses. The fact that both houses are elected on the same day strongly reduces the chances that both houses have a different majority, but the possibility cannot be excluded.

When the parliamentary procedure is finished, the proposal needs to be published in the State Monitor. It is signed by the responsible minister and by the King. If the proposal is a government bill, the proposal itself also carries the signature of both the minister and the King.

Majorities and special majorities

Decisions by the House of Representatives and by the Senate are normally taken with a simple majority. That means that at least half of the members of the assembly have to be present and that half of these must support the proposal. The election of the speaker of the assemblies also requires this simple majority. Both positions are actually part of the coalition agreement and are counted as the equivalent of a ministerial position for the party able to choose the speaker. The majority of the parliament accepting or rejecting proposals is then normally the majority of the coalition government.

In some cases though a simple majority is not enough. That is the case for revisions of the constitution. Since 1970 the Belgian constitution has been changed and amended quite often, and this always had to be done according to a quite lengthy procedure.

First the articles of the constitution that could be amended have to be identified. A list of these articles is drafted, normally on the initiative of the government. As soon as the government and both houses of parliament have approved the same list, the parliament is automatically dissolved and new elections have to be called within 40 days. The newly elected parliament then has the power to amend the articles that were identified before the elections. For a change to be accepted, a two-thirds majority is needed. That means that two-thirds of the members have to be present and that two-thirds of that number have to approve the proposal.

Special majority laws also require more than a simple majority. This is a type of law that was also introduced in 1971. A special majority law comes quite close to a constitutional rule. Special majority laws are used for spelling out details of the process of regionalization. The list of competences given to the regions and communities or the rules for the financing of regions and communities are all described in special majority laws. These do not require the long preparation of a constitutional change, but need to be accepted by a two-thirds majority in both houses and by a majority in each language group in both houses. They actually offer an extra protection for the smaller French language group.

These devices and special majorities thus require a clear distinction between two language groups in both houses of the parliament. For the Senate this is quite straightforward, since its very composition is built on the distinction between two language groups. All members are elected or selected within either the French or the Flemish community. For the House, extra rules for the MPs who are elected in mixed districts are required. This, for instance, is the case for the province of Liège, which comprises the German-speakers. All members of the House elected in Liège do however belong to the French language group. For the central district of Brussels-Halle-Vilvoorde, the first language in which an elected candidate takes his or her oath defines the language group. An MP is free to repeat the oath in the other languages, but needs to make a choice for the first one.

The language groups also allow for the activation of the alarm-bell procedure, another device for protecting the French minority in Belgium (and the Flemish minority in the Brussels regional parliament). Whenever three-quarters of the members of a language group support a motion explaining that the acceptance and implementation of a proposal might harm the interests of that language group, the discussion in parliament is stopped for 30 days. During that time the government – with an equal number of francophone and Flemish ministers – needs to find a compromise. This procedure can be used only once for each private or government bill. The very existence of the procedure is actually enough to ensure that no actions are taken that clearly go against the interests of one language group. And when that happens, it is with the knowledge that at the end of the day a compromise will be needed anyway.

Controlling the government

Interpellations and questions

A second major task for the parliament is controlling the government; overseeing the actions of the executive power. For doing so, there are several instruments at its disposal. The first is the right of *interpellation*. An interpellation is a question for explanation voiced by a member of parliament and aimed at a minister of the government. The minister is asked to explain and defend the government policies for which the member of parliament is criticizing him or her. After the interpellation the minister has an opportunity to answer and the debate is closed with a vote. The vote can be on a motion of no confidence in the government or – most often – on a 'simple motion' agreeing that normal activities can be continued. The latter is actually an implicit vote of confidence. An interpellation can be held in the plenary session but is normally put on the agenda of one of the parliamentary commissions. An interpellation is used for serious and important matters. It is mainly an instrument of the opposition. A member of a majority party can of course also table an interpellation, but that would be a major incident.

Members of the majority and members of the opposition can also ask *questions*. These are meant less to criticize directly the actions of the government than to ask for information. In practice, interpellations and questions can be of a very similar kind, but the debate after a question is not closed with a vote. A question is therefore more a routine activity. Members of both houses can ask questions, but only members of the House of Representatives can table interpellations.

Questions can be oral or written. Oral questions have to be put onto the agenda of the House, which means there is no possibility for the minister to delay answering the question. The government has more freedom in terms of timing when written questions are asked. These are published in a 'Bulletin of Questions and Answers'. And here not all questions are answered swiftly and many questions simply remain unanswered. One of the reasons for that is the very large number of questions being asked. During the 2003–2007 session there were no fewer than 11,820 written questions. There were 32 interpellations in the plenary sessions and 816 interpellations in commissions.

The government needs the confidence of the parliament. It must however not necessarily resign if that confidence is refused. Only when a *constructive motion of no confidence* is accepted, does the government have to go. Such a constructive motion not only refuses the confidence to the incumbent government, but also suggests the name of a new prime minister. If such a motion is accepted, the political parties have already agreed on a new coalition. The device was introduced in 1995 and is meant to guarantee a greater stability of federal government. So far a constructive motion of no confidence has never been proposed. Government formation is indeed not a game that is played in the parliamentary arena.

Investigation commissions

One very strong instrument in the hands of the parliament is the investigation commission. The parliament can decide that it wants to dig deeper into a matter in which the government or its public administration has not functioned correctly (Fijnaut et al., 1998). A majority of the assembly needs to approve the creation of such a commission, which means again that the incumbent government almost certainly needs to agree with it. The party composition of the commission follows the same principle as for the usual and permanent commissions: it reflects the strength of the party groups. Each group can decide freely who will be sent to the commission.

The powers of an investigation commission are important. It can actually function like a judge. It can summon witnesses to be present and to respond to questions under oath. It can search private houses and offices and confiscate documents if needed. There are also some weaknesses of investigation commissions though. The first is the fact that it is and remains a commission of members of parliament who are neatly divided into governing and opposition parties (Deschouwer, 1998). If the investigation risks bringing the incumbent government into trouble, it will not function or even not be installed. The second risk is its vague boundary with a purely judicial investigation. By organizing public hearings and interrogating witnesses, it risks undermining the possibility of a real judicial investigation in the future by bringing the files fully into the open. Persons under accusation can then easily claim that it has become impossible to have a fair trial.

There have however been a number of quite successful investigation commissions. In 1996–97 the so-called 'Dutroux commission' tried to analyse why the police forces had failed to identify and to arrest Marc Dutroux. This man had kidnapped and abused several children whom he held imprisoned in his cellar. Apparently the different components of the police had not collaborated properly and competition between them had allowed Marc Dutroux to keep his appalling business going. The country had been shocked when the truth about Dutroux was revealed after his arrest in August 2006 and the meetings of the investigation commission were broadcast integrally on television. Its final report criticized the functioning of the police forces and formulated important suggestions for a thorough reform. That reform was indeed implemented a few years later, basically integrating all the smaller police forces into one single body.

In 1997 the Senate decided to set up a commission to investigate the murder of 10 Belgian paratroops – members of a UN mission – in Rwanda on the eve of the genocide in 1994. The speaker of the Senate chaired the commission and the later Prime Minister Guy Verhofstadt was a very active member of it. The commission discussed and researched the conditions in which the Belgian troops had been put into danger, the way in which the Belgian and other governments had reacted to the first signs of the conflict in Rwanda and to the development of the genocide. It identified shortcomings in both the Belgian military management and in the decisions taken by the UN (like retreating as soon as the conflict escalated). It advised the Belgian government not to send troops for peacekeeping missions to Congo, Rwanda or Burundi, because of the close relation between these countries and Belgium. In 2000, Prime Minister Verhofstadt referred to the report of the commission when he apologized in the name of Belgium to both the families of the Belgian troops murdered and to the Rwandese government for not having reacted properly.

Another commission looked further back into history and tried to identify the possible responsibility of the Belgian government in the murder of the Congolese prime minister Patrice Lumumba in 1961. Its conclusions in 2002 were that the Belgian government of that time did not formally order the physical elimination of Lumumba, but that it carried at least part of the responsibility by having indicated that he'd better disappear from the scene (see also Chapter 9).

The use of language

Both houses of the Belgian parliament now function fully in both languages. That has of course not always been the case. The use of Dutch was only very slowly introduced into the practices of the parliament. After the introduction of universal male suffrage in 1918 an increasing number of MPs who were elected in Flanders no longer belonged to the francophone elite. Yet between the two World Wars 70 per cent of all the interventions in the House of Representatives were still in French. The official reports of the debates were always first published in French, and the translation into Dutch was often criticized for its very poor quality (Van Dyck, 1992).

In 1936 simultaneous translation was introduced both in the House of Representatives and in the Senate. That was a major step that actually suited both language groups. The Dutch-speakers could use Dutch and be sure that they would be understood, and the francophones were not obliged to use or to understand Dutch. Until the early 1960s some Dutch-speakers still preferred to use French once in a while (mainly ministers responding to questions in the language they had been posed), but since then everybody uses his or her own language, thanks to the simultaneous translation that is always available, even in very small committee meetings. All documents produced in and distributed by the parliament are in both languages. That includes all legislative proposals, all amendments, all written questions and the responses to them and all reports of all meetings. The State Monitor in which the decisions of the public authorities are published is also in both languages. Text is always presented in two columns, one for each language.

The members of parliament

Parliaments and their members in all parliamentary democracies face a decline in the importance of the assemblies and thus a decline in their power and impact. Governments have become more important. Governments take the lead in the legislative process. Governments are better equipped to deal with rapid developments. Governments have easier access to the technical expertise needed and modern communication technologies allow members of governments to keep in touch with each other on a permanent basis. This evolution towards a strengthening of the executive power is also very visible in Belgium. There are however a number of elements that have sped up the weakening of the parliament in Belgium. Most of them are related to the creation of a federal political system (Fiers, 2001).

The direct election of regional parliaments since 1995 has in the first place augmented the number of parliamentary mandates. Before the reform the House of Representatives and the Senate had together 369 seats. The size of both houses was reduced to 190 directly elected members, but to these no fewer than 313 new positions were created in the regional councils. This should as such not cause a decline in the power and prestige of the members of parliament. All federal countries have large numbers of representatives at the substate level. In Belgium though the difference between federal and regional MPs has remained unclear. In 1995 and in 1999 federal and regional parliaments were elected on the same day. The federal elections of 2003 and 2007 and the regional elections of 2004 were for that level only, but the parties still did little to mark the specific role and importance of federal and regional elections (Deschouwer, 2000; De Winter, 2006b). The same small group of top candidates lead the electoral lists for both regional and federal elections. Whether they take up their seat when elected depends on the personnel policy of the party. The elected candidates can also remain at the level where they had been elected before. In both cases a seat will be filled by a successor candidate. These successor candidates are not very likely to play an active role. They are extremely dependent on their party for reselection and possible re-election. They are the anonymous loyal soldiers of their parties in an immature multi-layered system of political representation. The absence of statewide political parties further exacerbates the lack of specific implications and stakes for regional and federal elections. All elections are a competition between the same parties in their part of the country. And by the way in which they select the candidates, the parties themselves do not make any effort to clarify the distinction.

And as a consequence all members of parliament – whether they are at the federal level or in the new regional parliaments – are perceived as belonging to one large political class. There are simply more than 500 elected members of parliament. And many of them are followers who do not have the opportunity or the time to develop expertise or prestige. Only a few top politicians in each party remain very visible, but many of these are in government or become a member of government as soon as they can. And governments to move into are available at both the federal level and in the regions and communities. In the House of Representatives, of the 150 members elected in 2007 there are (at the end of 2008) 22 who were not elected directly but who replace a member of one of the governments. Of the 150 members elected in 2003, 27 were replaced. There were 13 members of the federal House who left to become a minister in a government of the regions and communities (www.dekamer.be/www.lachambre.be).

The coming of age of the federal state has thus strongly devalued the role and strength of both the federal and the regional assemblies. It has put members of parliament in a position of high insecurity and instability. Meanwhile other and older developments further strengthen this insecurity and instability. Increasing voter volatility and the fragmentation of the political landscape are making it very difficult to plan and to build a long and stable parliamentary career (Fiers, 2006). Again only a small number of politicians can be sure that there will be a seat somewhere that guarantees their survival. For many candidates every election might be the last one, and the only way to get into parliament again is by being and remaining a loyal follower of the party.

And loyal followers are what the parties want and need. Coalition formation is a difficult process in a volatile electoral environment. Agreements between the parties are therefore written down in detail, making sure that there is a clear contract in which each of the parties in government is guaranteed a number of policies with which they can score. During the life of the government the party leaders in and outside of government keep an eye on the agreement and make sure that the government can survive. If needed, they renegotiate or refine the agreement. In such a system the party in parliament has very little room to manoeuvre. The parliament is not expected to discuss or to question the deals made between the parties in government. Members of the majority groups in the parliament thus have no other option but to accept what has been agreed by the parties in government. Group discipline is therefore absolutely needed and is indeed also well respected (Depauw, 2002). Voting against a government bill is not done. Critical questioning of members of government is only possible for the (few) well-known and experienced MPs.

Controlling the government is thus not the real core task of the parliament. The Belgian parliaments at all levels are reactive, uncritical and accommodating. Individual members of parliament thus need to be inventive to make sure that their presence in the assembly is picked up by the media. They very actively use two instruments to do so. The first is taking legislative initiatives. During the 1993–2003 session members of the House of Representatives launched 1,224 legislative initiatives. During the 2003–2007 session there were no fewer than 1,614 individual members' bills. Only a very small fraction of these are eventually accepted (6 per cent during the 2003–2007 session), but many of them allow MPs to communicate their ability to pick up questions and demands from society.

The second instrument is asking questions. Here, this is also an opportunity to relay rapidly an issue that has been raised in the public debate. Reponses to written questions, which often ask the minister to provide statistics on activities of the public administration, provide MPs with pieces of information that can easily be communicated to the press. The parliament thus fulfils a 'fire alarm function' (Depauw, 2002). It listens to the signals of pressure groups and individual citizens and tries to publicize issues related to the functioning of the public authorities. Yet this does

Table 7.1 *Number of initiatives taken by members of the House of Representatives*

	1999–2003	*2003–2007*
Legislative initiatives	1,224	1,614
Oral questions	1,731	1,827
Written questions	7,481	11,820

Source: www.lachambre.be/www.dekamer.be

not bring the government into danger. As far as governing is concerned, the members of parliament only rubber stamp what has been decided elsewhere.

The parliament has during the last few decades clearly changed in its composition. There are more young members, more female members and more inexperienced members. That is in the first place a consequence of the expansion of the number of available mandates. Political parties have had to find more and new candidates to send to the different parliaments. And that has meant that the parliamentary experience in each of them is lower than ever before. The average length of a parliamentary mandate is between five and six years (Fiers, 2006; Fiers & Reynaert, 2006), which is roughly one and a half terms. The easy change from one level to another obviously reduces the length of stay in one of them.

The search for new political personnel has been directed to younger candidates. This is the result of the creation of new positions but also of the electoral volatility and severe losses that each party faces once in a while. The electoral defeat of the Christian democrats in 1999 caused a number of older and experienced MPs to disappear and the party deliberately opted for a younger generation to bring the party back into power. The heavy losses of the greens in 2003 also marked a generation change. The parties generally believe that young candidates can embody the demand for change and renewal. For the federal elections of 2007, the average age of the candidates was 42.8 years. Only 6 per cent of the candidates were older than 60, and only 2 per cent of the candidates on a more or less secure place on the list were older than 60 (Weekers et al., 2007).

Among these younger candidates the presence of women is striking. The introduction of gender quota for electoral lists (see Chapter 5) has obliged parties to find a large number of new female candidates. And by doing so the profile of the parliament has also changed. Table 7.2 shows the evolution of female members of the different assemblies since 1995. For all of them the percentage of female MPs has clearly increased.

There are however large differences between the assemblies, while the same quota rules apply to all of them. This marks a difference in the 'party magnitude', that is, in the number of seats per party per district. When parties have a larger number of seats available, they are less reluctant to put new (and female) candi-

Table 7.2 *Percentage of female members elected to the federal and substate assemblies*

	1995 %	1999 %	2003 %	2004 %	2007 %
House of Representatives	12	23	33		35
Senate	24	28	38		30
Flemish parliament	17	20		32	
Walloon parliament	12	11		21	
Brussels parliament	30	36		42	
German Community parliament	20	32		28	

dates on the list. For the election of the Senate there are 25 seats available for the Flemish parties and 15 for the francophone parties. For the francophone parties in the Brussels regional parliament there are no fewer than 72 seats available in one single district. The electoral reform of 2003 and the introduction of provincial districts also increased the party magnitude and thus the number of female candidates elected in the House of Representatives and in the Flemish parliament. The Walloon parliament is elected in small districts, and that strongly reduces the effects of the gender quota (Meier, 2005a).

The regional parliaments

The functioning of the regional and community parliaments does not differ significantly from that of the federal parliament. The descriptions above about the role of the parliament in political decision-making and about the evolutions in the composition of the parliaments are also valid for the substate parliaments. The regional MPs have the same instruments to control the government, and they can also set up investigation commissions. The only major difference between the federal and the substate parliaments is the absence of a second house for the regions and communities.

The Flemish parliament functions in Dutch only. The Walloon parliament and the French Community parliament function in French only and the German Community parliament functions in

German only. In the Flemish parliament there has always been since its first direct election in 1995 one member of the list Union Francophone, defending the rights of the francophone inhabitants in the Brussels periphery. That one candidate must however also function fully in Dutch, both for oral and for written activities.

The use of languages in the Brussels regional parliament is exactly the same as for the federal parliament. All documents are available in both languages, and like the federal parliament the Brussels parliament thus has a well-staffed translation service. For all oral debates, simultaneous translation is available.

The rule for accepting a decree or an ordinance in the regional and community parliaments is simple majority. That is also the case for the Brussels parliament. No double majorities are needed for its legislative activities. But here also – like at the federal level – the composition of the government ensures that the governing majority is a double majority. At the federal level it is possible – and it happens exceptionally – that a governing majority is not supported by a majority in each language group. In Brussels it is impossible. The formation of the Brussels government is a two-step procedure, in which first each language group forms a coalition able to secure the majority of the votes in its respective Community Commissions (see Chapter 3). And these two unilingual coalitions are then brought together to produce the Brussels regional government. That guarantees a double majority, even if the Dutch-speakers are a small minority in Brussels.

Conclusions

The Belgian parliament is not a strong parliament. It is the victim of the subtle equilibrium that is constantly needed for governing a divided society. At both levels of government the very fragmented party system and the electoral volatility require firm and clear agreements between the parties and thus loyal members of the parliamentary groups. At the federal level the linguistic divide adds one layer to that complexity and one more reason for keeping the control at the level of the governing parties' leadership rather than in the parliamentary party.

Chapter 8

Policymaking

Policymaking in a federal state is a complex matter. Policy competences are indeed spread over different levels of government. For many policy domains, the centrifugal dynamics of the state reform and thus the willingness of the substates to acquire their own powers have produced a quite clear and unambiguous distribution of powers. Important policies like public transport, public works, education, arts and culture, area development planning and housing are fully reserved for the substate level.

For economic and social policy however, the distribution of powers is less clear-cut. Basically the regions can conduct their own economic policy and their own employment policy. But the federal state has kept control of labour market policy, wage policy, price policy and the financing and organization of social security. Unsurprisingly Flanders would like more say in the matters that have so far not been devolved. The different type and speed of the economy in north and south require policies adapted to these differences. Francophones however fear that the solidarity mechanisms – especially in social security – might be eroded and that would not favour the Walloon Region (Cantillon & De Maesschalck, 2006; Béland & Lecours, 2008).

In this chapter we first look at economic and social policy. We again find the parties and related organizations at the centre of decision-making and implementation. For policymaking at the federal level, the very high public debt is a problem that has been around for a few decades and is not likely to disappear soon. We further discuss the economic structure of Belgium and its strengths and weaknesses. We conclude by looking at the economy in north and south. The economic differences between north and south are indeed to be added to their cultural differences, making the governing of the country once again a difficult enterprise.

189

Once again the political parties

Whether matters are dealt with at the federal or at the substate level does however not make much of a difference if one looks at the way in which policies are prepared, decided and implemented. At all levels a classic pattern is and remains visible: the political parties sit at the steering wheel (De Winter, 1996; De Winter & Dumont, 2006b). Government formation is fully controlled by the political parties and the coalition agreements fix the policies for the years to come. The parliamentary groups are not supposed to question these agreements.

But the party grip on the policymaking process also goes deeper into the preparation and implementation of policies. Public administration has until recently been extremely 'politicized', meaning that recruitment and promotion were organized on a party-political base. What is usually referred to as 'political appointments' is the principle in which each governing political party receives an agreed share of the personnel in a given administration. Whenever new appointments need to be made – either recruitment or promotion – these are chosen from the pool of 'own' people. Civil servants wanting to make a career thus had to openly declare themselves as supporters of one of the major parties. This means that the public administration has been divided and colonized by the Christian democratic, the socialist and the liberal parties. The most obvious consequence is that the public administration can hardly be considered to be a neutral one, committed to the government of the day whatever its composition may be.

The government of the day therefore puts into place a supplement to the pubic administration. Each minister of the government has a personal 'cabinet', with a number of advisers and assistants and an administrative staff (Pelgrims, 2001; Brans et al., 2005; Pelgrims, 2006; Pelgrims & Dereu, 2006). The size of these cabinets is quite impressive, with some 60 collaborators per minister. Ministers with more than one portfolio and especially the vice prime ministers (in all governments at all levels) have more than one cabinet. The members of them can be chosen freely, making sure that the cabinet is composed of very loyal collaborators. Although minor exceptions are possible, these will all be loyal party members, from the top advisers to the secretaries and chauffeurs. Often a minister will recruit them from his or her own region.

Members of the ministerial cabinets can also be civil servants. They are then taken out of the existing pool of party members in the top positions. If their party is removed from government or the minister with whom they had a personal tie is not in office any more, they can return to their old position. Chiefs of cabinets though usually end up being promoted to a better position. Together with the subsidies given to the party groups and to the central party organization (see Chapter 4) the ministerial cabinets are another source from which collaborators of the party can be recruited. A party that is removed from power, often also after having lost votes, is then confronted with the need to find jobs for large numbers of loyal party members.

The role of the ministerial cabinets is quite important. They are directly involved in the permanent negotiations between the governing parties. They also prepare and write the text of government bills and closely follow parliamentary procedure. When a minister attends a parliamentary commission to defend initiatives or to answer questions, a close collaborator from the cabinet sits at his or her side.

The extreme politicization of the public administration has gradually declined. Today more open and objective procedures are used for the recruitment and promotion of civil servants. The need for a loyal top administration should therefore also become less pressing. Yet the practice of having ministerial cabinets has by no means disappeared. At the federal level a reform plan of the civil service – called 'Copernicus' to make it clear that it was a major turnaround – was implemented from the year 2000 on (Brans & Steen, 2006; Brans et al., 2006). It reorganized the administrations that have remained federal into ten 'Federal Public Services' (Federale Overheidsdienst – Service Public Fédéral). It also introduced a more managerial style for recruitment and assessment. The top manager of each Federal Public Service has a mandate of six years, and thus no permanent position any more. The plan also abolished the ministerial cabinets, but introduced a new 'Policy Preparation Cell', for which the minister can choose personal collaborators. In practice this has simply continued the habit of having a personal and party-political cabinet for each minister (Vancoppenolle & Legrain, 2003; De Visscher, 2003).

The public administration linked to the competences of the regions and communities has gradually been transferred to these new authorities. Each of them has to a greater or lesser extent reorganized and reshuffled the old structures. Flanders especially went quite far in the introduction of principles of 'new public management', with a greater autonomy for important parts of the administration, with public–private cooperation and with recruitment and assessment techniques inspired by the private sector (Brans et al., 2006). None of the regions and communities has however done away with the ministerial cabinets. They remain in place and fulfil the same function as before. At all levels there is thus a spoils system, in which the real top of the administration is replaced with every change of government. It is normal practice to clean out the drawers of a ministerial cabinet when the keys are handed over to the new minister. The new minister can indeed start from scratch and build his or her own ministerial cabinet on which he or she will rely.

Segmental autonomy or pillarization

The way in which public policy is prepared, organized and implemented thus reveals a state that allows a far-reaching encroachment of private organizations into its core processes. As far as parliament and government are concerned, this is a quite normal feature of party democracy. The intrusion into the public administration is less common. It is however only one dimension of a phenomenon that is typically present in consociational democracies, in which societal segments receive the right to organize the lives of their members according to their own principles. Rather than trying to find a 'one size fits all' policy, the policies and their implementation are delegated to the segments of society. And their organizations then become fully involved in the production and implementation of state policies and services (Jones, 2002).

This situation has actually also secured their survival. Indeed, the pillar organizations reflect a societal segmentation along religious and socio-economic lines. These have today lost the sharpness and salience that they used to have. The coming of age of the welfare state and the introduction of the social partnership (see below) has reduced the tension along the economic cleavage. The School Pact of 1958 also symbolically put an end to the division between the Catholic and the anti-clerical groups that had been standing on both sides of the religious cleavage since the early days of Belgian history. Yet both the introduction of social partnership and the

School Pact institutionalized the existence of the pillar organizations. Since the 1950s Belgian society has changed a lot as a result of both economic growth and secularization. There has been a process that can be labelled 'depillarization of the minds' (Huyse, 1971; 1987; Dobbelaere, 1979; Billiet, 1981). Society is no longer segmented in terms of identity of the population. The hard lines between the segmental groups have faded away.

But the structures have survived. The two separate school networks are still there. But it is in social and economic policy that the insitutionalized presence of pillar organizations is especially striking. The trade unions play a very important role. And that also goes for the pillarized health insurance companies or so-called 'mutualities' (see below).

The social partnership

The Belgian welfare state came into being immediately after the Second World War. Even during the German occupation, political leaders of the three traditional parties and leaders of the most important social organizations – linked to these parties – had been discussing and preparing the post-war system (Luyten, 1995; 2006). The 'Social Pact' concluded in 1944 laid out the basis of a well-organized cooperation between the state and the social and economic pillar organizations. It turned Belgium into a copybook example of a *neo-corporatist* system (Schmitter & Lehmbruch, 1979). A solid and institutional triangle has been created between the state and the representatives of labour and capital. The latter do not only represent their interests, but are permanently present in a number of institutions where policies are discussed, prepared, decided and implemented. In this triangle the state does not play the most important role. The state is the facilitator of the permanent social partnership. Only if needed the state intervenes. Since the Second World War this system has not fundamentally changed, although there has been an increase in the role of the state that either decides in the case of a non-agreement or that defines and controls the limits within which the social partnership can decide on policies involving state expenses.

Agreements between workers' and employers' organizations can be reached at three levels: the national level, the sector level and the company level. In all cases the concluded agreement – a Collective Labour Agreement (Collectieve Arbeidsovereenkomst/

Accord Collectif de Travail) – can be declared 'binding' by the government. In that case it becomes a binding set of rules that applies to all companies and all workers, irrespective of their membership of the trade union. A binding Collective Labour Agreement is a law-like text that has however not been put before or agreed by the parliament. The social partners actually decide themselves on the rules that they will impose on themselves.

At the national or inter-sector level the negotiations take place in the National Labour Council (Conseil National du Travail/Nationale Arbeidsraad). It has 24 members, appointed by the federal government for a four-year mandate. The seats are equally divided between the organizations of the workers and of the employers. In the National Labour Council their national peak organizations are present (and actually decide on who will be appointed by the government as a member of the council). These peak organizations are:

- The Christian Labour Union: Algemeen Christelijk Vakverbond (ACV)/Confédération générale des Syndicats chrétiens et libres de Belgique (CSC)
- The Socialist Labour Union: Algemeen Belgisch Vakverbond (ABVV), Fédération Générale des Travailleurs Belges (FGTB)
- The Liberal Trade Union: Algemene Centrale der Liberale Vakbonden van België (ACLVB)/Centrale Générale des Syndicats Libéraux de Belgique (CGSLB)
- The Belgian Employers' Union: Verbond van Belgische Ondernemingen (VBO)/Fédération des Entreprises Belges (FEB)
- The Smallholders' Organizations: Unie van Zelfstandige Ondernemers (UNIZO) and Union des Classes Moyennes (UCM)
- The Farmers' Organzations: Boerenbond and Fédération Wallonne de l'Agriculture.

These are not the only organizations representing workers or employers. They are however the 'representative' organizations, that is, those having enough members to obtain the right to represent them in the institutionalized social partnership. For farmers and smallholders, there are two organizations, each representing only one language group. The large trade unions and the employers have one national organization (along with regional branches – see below).

At the level of economic sectors, there are 'Parity Committees', the parity referring again to the equal representation of labour and capital. Here the peak organizations are not directly present, but only the trade unions and employers active in that sector. They discuss and decide on agreements that can be made binding for that sector only.

This system of permanent negotiation and cooperation works relatively smoothly as long as economic growth is guaranteed. From the 1970s on though the tensions between employers and trade unions have increased. It appears impossible to find full agreements at the national level. The sector level and even more the enterprise level then become more important. At that lowest level the presence of the trade unions is also quite well organized and regulated. In all enterprises with at least 50 employees there is an 'Enterprise Council' and a 'Committee for Security and Hygiene'. They enable the representatives of the trade unions to be kept informed about the prospects of the enterprise and to have a say in the way in which the work is organized.

The representatives of the trade unions are elected every four years in 'social elections'. These are organized countrywide by the Federal Public Service of Labour (Federale Overheidsdienst Werkgelegenheid, Arbeid en Sociaal Overleg/SPF Emploi, Travail et Concertation Sociale). In 2008 social elections were organized in 6,500 companies. The results given in Table 8.1 show a clear dominance of the Christian ACV/CSC, even in Wallonia. It is much larger than membership figures would suggest. This reflects the strength of ACV/CSC in smaller enterprises (of which there are a larger number) and especially in the not-for-profit sector. The socialist trade union is strong in larger and traditional industrial enterprises.

The number of agreements reached at the enterprise level has grown, but at the same time the federal state has put important limits to what the sectors and companies can agree on. From the 1980s on, the federal state has tried to control the development of salaries espe-

Table 8.1 *Results of the social elections of 2008 for representation in the 'Enterprise Councils' (percentage of the votes)*

	ACV CSC	ABVV FGTB	ACLVB CGSLB	Others
Belgium	52.4	36.2	9.7	1.7
Flanders	57.1	32.2	9.8	0.9
Wallonia	48.3	43.7	6.1	1.0
Brussels	45.5	38.7	12.7	3.1

Source: Federal Public Service of Labour (www.werk.belgie.be)

cially and to avoid their growing too easily beyond the inflation rate. Wages in Belgium are automatically adapted to inflation. This is done by linking salaries to the 'index of consumption goods', which is an index based on the monthly evolution of a basket of goods representing the spending necessities of average households. It is agreed on in the 'Index Commission', in which members of the employers' organizations and trade unions are equally represented.

Employers (and to a certain extent the state) are not too happy with that mechanism, which is however fiercely defended by the trade unions. By rapidly adapting wages to the inflation rate, the salary costs for companies go up. Belgian labour becomes systematically more expensive than labour in neighbouring countries. That is why mechanisms have been put in place that must keep any further rise of wages and thus of the cost of labour within limits that do not reduce the competitiveness of the Belgian economy. They are important too for the Belgian state and for the other public authorities, because they are the largest employer in the country, with 32 per cent of the labour force working for the state (Albrecht, 2008): that includes all schools and universities, since the state pays the salaries of all educational institutions, both state and private (mainly Catholic) institutions.

A law agreed in 1989 attempts to protect the competitive power of the Belgian economy by keeping the cost of labour under control. The extent to which salaries can be raised beyond the automatic 'indexation' is based on the evolution of the cost of labour in the most important trade partners of the country (the neighbouring Germany, France and the Netherlands). The 'wage norm' is set after negotiations in the Central Council of Business (Centrale Raad voor het Bedrijfsleven/Conseil Central de l'Economie). This organ was set up to give advice on the economic situation of the country, and in 1996 was given the extra task of setting the wage norm for the next two years. If it can find no agreement, the norm is set by the government. The Central Council of Business is of course composed of representatives of interest groups of workers and employers.

The social security system

The Social Pact of 1944 also contained the agreement to introduce a full and generous system of social security. The first law for the organization of Belgian social security was agreed by the parliament in December 1944, even before the end of the war. It has since then been expanded and improved several times, but, like in other European countries, today it faces the problem of matching increasing expenses to a shrinking basis from which the income can be generated. Because the system is based on compulsory payment of dues by the people participating in the labour process, it therefore needs a good balance between the dues-paying working population and the different categories of receivers of social benefits.

There are three sources of income for the social security system. The first are the dues paid by the employees. These are deducted directly from the gross salary and transferred to the State Service for Social Security. On all salaries paid the employers also pay dues to the system. They amount to 34 per cent of the total income, while the employers generate 13 per cent of the income. The remaining part is covered by the state, which means that all taxpayers also contribute to the social security system. For the self-employed and for civil servants, the system is slightly different, and for the self-employed particularly, it is less generous than for employees and civil servants.

The State Service for Social Security (Rijksdienst voor Sociale Zekerheid/Office National de la Sécurité Sociale) receives the money and redistributes it to the different subsectors of the system (see below). The leadership of the State Service is in the hands of – once more – an equal number of representatives from workers' and employers' interest groups. Two members represent the government: one for the Minister of the Budget and one for the Minister of Social Affairs.

Health insurance

The system of health insurance is one more illustration of the way in which the pillar organizations that were involved in the early days in private health insurance have remained an integral part of the system and thus of the state. Every citizen has to join a health insurance organization or *mutuality*. The citizens are free to choose between the Christian, the Socialist, the Liberal, the Neutral or the Independent mutuality. The larger ones are obviously the Christian and the Socialist. These mutual help organizations have a large network of local offices, and offer a wide range of services (including centres for family holidays or rental services for wheelchairs or crutches).

Their most important service is the reimbursement of health insurance money to their members. The mutualities actually distribute the public money to their members. The normal procedure is for the patient to pay the doctor, and then have the larger part of that reimbursed. For the payment of hospital costs or for the reimbursement of medicines, the patient does not have to pay first. The part that is reimbursed by the state is paid directly to the hospital or to the pharmacist.

Tariffs and principles – like the selection of medicines that can be reimbursed – are typically set by a negotiated agreement between representatives of the mutualities and of the medical doctors' interest groups, within the limits set by the federal state.

Health insurance is one of the sectors of social security that is facing important financial challenges. Expenses are constantly increasing and growing much faster than inflation and economic growth. The ageing of the population makes it very difficult to keep expenses under control while keeping intact the generous reimbursement of medical costs.

Unemployment

Unemployment is another old sector of social security that was integrated in the modern system after the Second World War. The trade unions that originally set up the unemployment insurance are still very much present. The unemployment allowance is paid to all workers who have lost their job involuntarily. The amount of money is calculated on the basis of the last salary, but also adapted to the family situation. Heads of households receive up to 60 per cent of their last salary, with a maximum of 1,800 euro per month. People who live on their own receive that amount for one year, after which it goes down to 50 per cent of the last salary.

The right to receive unemployment money is not limited in time. One can in principle receive it as long as needed, that is, as long as one remains unemployed. The unemployed are however closely monitored and receive job proposals that fit their profile. If they do not accept a suitable job, they can lose the unemployment money.

For members of a trade union it is the trade union that pays the money. The trade union also takes care of all the administrative procedures. It receives the money from the state and a subsidy to pay the personnel needed for organizing and monitoring this task. In fact the trade unions thus function as a part of the federal state administration. The unemployed who are not affiliated to a trade union receive their unemployment money directly from the state.

Pensions

For both men and women the retirement age is 65 years. It used to be 60 for women, but this difference has gradually been abolished during the past few years. At the end of their career Belgian workers receive a so-called 'legal pension'. The amount of it depends on a number of parameters, such as the number of years that one has worked and the size of salaries earned during one's career. Heads of households receive roughly 75 per cent of their average salary, others more or less 60 per cent. There is however a maximum amount of 40,000 euro per year, and a minimum of 950 euro per month.

For the payment of these legal pensions, the Belgian state spends yearly more than 10 per cent of the GDP, and that proportion is constantly growing. It puts the legal pension under great pressure. Workers and the self-employed are therefore increasingly encouraged to make sure that they also receive a pension from what is called the second and the third pillar of the pension scheme. The second pillar is composed of collective pension plans per enterprise or per sector, for which employers receive fiscal stimuli. The third sector is composed of individual insurances for which the yearly dues can be deduced from taxes for up to 830 euro per year (as in 2008).

For older workers who lose their job, there is a system of 'bridge pension'. It is actually an amount of money that is added to the unemployment allowance. Originally the system was meant to allow employers to hire younger workers, but has become just a cheap way to fire older employees and a not too uncomfortable way to opt for early retirement. It has become a very costly system that furthermore encourages people to leave the workforce far too early. A much debated 'Generation Pact' adopted in 2005 has tried to reduce the use of bridge pensions by raising the age from which it can be obtained to 60, but still with several exceptions. Bridge pensions are often used when large companies want to downsize. For the older workers who lose their job, the bridge pension is a more acceptable way to go than just becoming unemployed at an age when finding a new job is not very easy.

Other social benefits

The Belgian social security system offers more than these three large sectors. It also includes child allowances, paid per child to the parents. Maternity leave is also paid by the social security system. Mothers receive 82 per cent of their salary for one month and 75 per cent after that for a maximum of 15 weeks. Fathers can take up to seven days that are paid by the social security. If one is not able to work as the result of occupational related diseases or after an accident at work the social security offers an allowance. And for all those who for some reason fall through the fine mesh of the net, help can be offered by the local agencies of social welfare (Openbaar Centrum voor Maatschappelijk Welzijn OCMW/Centre Public d'Action Sociale CPAS).

Tensions

The Belgian social security system was set up as a very complete and very generous system. It is therefore also very expensive. Today it is facing a number of serious challenges. Probably the most important are for the pension scheme. It is a repartition system, which means that for paying the pensions of today there has to be enough money coming in. There are some reserves, but these will absolutely not suffice to face increasing numbers of pensioners who also live much longer than before. There is a growing imbalance between those who are active in the workforce and who can provide for the income on the one hand and those who have the right to receive a legal pension on the other.

For Belgium this general problem of an ageing population is further exacerbated by the fact that levels of employment are substantially lower than in most other European countries. Table 8.2 shows the employment rate – the percentage of the working age population effectively at work – for both the age group 15–64 and for the age group 55–64. It compares Belgian employment rates with the average for the 27 EU countries and with the average for the group of 15 countries of the pre-2004 EU. The differences are quite striking. In 2007 only 62 per cent of the active population was working in Belgium. In Sweden it was 74 per cent, in the Netherlands 76 per cent and in Denmark 77 per cent. Of the 15 pre-enlargement EU countries only Greece (61 per cent) and Italy (59 per cent) remain below Belgium.

Table 8.2 *Employment rates as proportion of the working age population*

	Age group 15–64			Age group 55–64		
	Belgium	EU 27	EU 15	Belgium	EU 27	EU 15
2002	59.9	62.3	64.2	26.6	38.5	40.2
2003	59.6	62.6	64.3	28.1	40.0	41.7
2004	60.3	62.9	64.8	30.0	40.7	42.5
2005	61.1	63.5	65.4	31.8	42.4	44.2
2006	61.0	64.5	66.2	32.0	43.5	45.3
2007	62.0	65.4	66.9	34.4	44.7	46.6

Source: Eurostat (epp.eurostat.ec.europa.eu)

The figures for the age group 55 to 64 are even more dramatic. The employment rate of this group is quite important. People of that age who are no longer active in the workforce have to be taken in charge by the social security system (unemployment, early retirement, bridge pension in Belgium). This age group also generally earns higher salaries, and if they remain at work they can provide the much needed income for the social security system. The numbers in Belgium are quite far below those of its neighbouring countries. In 2007 only 34 per cent of the 55–64 age group was at work, while it is as high as 51 per cent in the Netherlands and in Germany, and up to 70 per cent in Sweden.

The members of the European Union are well aware of this problem. At the 2000 summit in Lisbon they agreed that the European economy had to become the most dynamic and competitive knowledge-based economy in the world. One of the so-called Lisbon criteria by which this can be measured is the employment rate. It should reach 70 per cent by 2010, but Belgium is still quite far away from that goal.

Another reason why the expenses for social security are a heavy burden for the Belgian state is the problematic situation of the state finances. In the 1970s and 1980s Belgium had rapidly built up an impressive public debt by having a number of seriously unbalanced budgets. This deficit spending was partly a deliberate choice to face the economic crisis of the 1970s, but also the result of the high instability of governments during these two decades. Lots of energy went into the discussions and negotiations about the reform of the state (see Chapters 2 and 3), and the budget policy was not as orthodox as it should have been.

The public debt reached no less than 138 per cent of the yearly GDP in 1993. The ambition to participate in the euro after the ratification of the Maastricht Treaty forced the Belgian governments to reduce that debt as much and as soon as possible. The limit of 60 per cent of GDP set in the convergence criteria for the euro were not met in 2000, but Belgium was accepted to the euro because the evolution of the public debt was going in the right direction. In 2003 it finally dropped under 100 per cent of GDP and it has since then gone down further (see Figure 8.1). Extra investments to secure the survival of the banks will however slow down the reduction of the debt or even increase it again after 2008.

In any case Belgium is still facing an enormous debt of more than 80 per cent of its GDP and that means that there is hardly any room for raising the expenses of the state. Budgets have to be balanced and should actually show a surplus for many years to come. With an ageing population needing more social security expenses for pensions and for healthcare, and with a fairly low employment rate, this budgetary situation makes the pressure on the social security system even greater.

Social security is a federal competence. And that means that the federal state needs to be able to collect the income for the social

Figure 8.1 *The evolution of the Belgian public debt (all public authorities) in percentage of GDP*

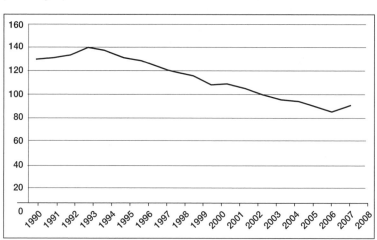

Source: Federal Public Service of the Budget

expenses. The federal state has however agreed to transfer an increasing amount of money to the regions and communities.

Parts of the social security could be taken over by the regions or communities. That is actually what Flanders would like to see. The Flemish parliament passed resolutions in 1999 asking for the transfer of the system of child allowances and health insurance to the Flemish Community. Francophone parties are however very much opposed to the idea of a de-federalization of social security. They fear that this would endanger the basic principle of solidarity. The Flemish counterargument is that regions and communities – which already have the competences for health prevention policy and for family policy – could conduct a more coherent and cheaper policy (Béland & Lecours, 2008).

The redistribution through the social security system is today clearly transferring money from north to south. Employment is higher in Flanders (see below) and wages are higher. The fiscal capacity of the north is therefore higher while social needs are higher in the south. Discussions about the future and financing of Belgian social security are therefore always also discussions between the Flemish and the francophones.

The economic structure

Belgium is a small country with no natural resources. That makes the Belgian economy quite vulnerable and very much dependent on the world economy and trade. It also means that the Belgian government and the governments of its regions have very limited power to really steer the Belgian economy. Many decision centres, including those of the financial markets, of distribution of commodities and of multinational enterprises, are abroad.

The position of the Belgian economy in the world today has changed profoundly since the Second World War. The flagships of the Belgian economy were in the sectors of coal and steel, glass production and textiles. The Société Générale de Belgique (SG), an investment company created in the times of the short-lived Kingdom of the Low Countries, played an important role for a very long time. In the early days of Belgium it invested in the transport infrastructure and later in heavy industry in the south of the country. The links between the SG and the Belgian government have always been very close, precisely because of its crucial position for the Belgian economy. When Belgium acquired its colony in Congo the SG expanded its activities and played a key role in the financing and exploitation of the rich Congolese resources.

The Europeanization and internationalization of economic activities have however severely undermined the powers of a purely national investment company in a small country. In 1988 the ownership of the SG passed to the French company Suez. Its banking activities remained in Belgian hands and became the core element of the Fortis Bank. The financial crisis of 2008 proved it unable to survive and the Belgian parts of Fortis were sold to the French bank BNP Paribas. The Belgian government was unable to offer enough financial backup for a bank of this size and preferred to let it go into foreign hands.

The story of the Société Générale and of its bank is not the only example of flagships of the old Belgian economy – closely linked to the state and the government – that have disappeared. Another example is the national airline company SABENA. It went bankrupt in 2001. Interestingly the government asked prominent investors and bankers of the old SG – Maurice Lippens and Etienne Davignon – to convince the members of their economic network to invest in a new Belgian company. They succeeded and created Brussels Airlines. But Brussels Airlines was too small to survive alone on the European market and merged with Virgin Airlines in 2007. It will in the near future be taken over by Lufthansa.

There is however also one Belgian company that has been able to survive and to become a world player itself: the Leuven-based brewer of Stella Artois. Its expansion policy has transformed it into the largest beer producing and trading company in the world, first under the name Interbrew and then – after a merger with a Brazilian company – under the name Inbev. The merger with the American group Anheuser-Bush transformed it into AB Inbev. In 2009 though, the headquarters of AB Inbev started moving to the US.

Beer is of course one of the 'identity markers' of Belgium. More than 300 different (often very local) beers are being produced, and many of these are now controlled by AB Inbev. One could also expect Belgium to be a leader in the chocolate business, but here the story is again one of large foreign companies taking over Belgian brands: Côte D'Or belongs to Kraft Foods, Godiva belongs to Campbell, Callebaut belongs to Suchard.

For beer and chocolate, the Belgian domestic market is important, but far too small. And that goes for other products too.

Belgium needs to export its economic production. And that is indeed what happens: more than two-thirds of the GDP is exported, and 75 per cent of these exports go to member states of the European Union. The closest neighbours are the most important partners: 20 per cent of the Belgian export goes to Germany, 17 per cent to France and 12 per cent to the Netherlands (www.mineco.fgov.be). The most important export products are textiles, petroleum products, diamonds and metal products.

Belgium imports raw materials or semi-finished products and exports the finished products. For this type of activity the transport infrastructure is extremely important. The port of Antwerp especially is crucial for the Belgian economy. After Rotterdam, it is the second largest port in Europe and the fourth worldwide. The presence of the port with its easy access to the sea has attracted a strong concentration of petrochemical industries since the 1950s. For the diamond industry also, Antwerp is the vital centre.

The port of Antwerp is also important for the export of cars. Belgium has important centres of car assembly – a situation that is fairly typical for modern Belgian industry. The plants are located in Belgium (in Brussels and Flanders) because of the availability of a well-skilled and very productive labour force. Volvo Cars, Ford Motor Company, Opel and Audi are all present in Belgium. But the decision centres are not in Belgium and the fate of these assembly lines depends on worldwide cost–benefit analyses where the high cost of Belgian labour – linked to the strong system of social security – can be a serious handicap. In 1997 Renault decided to terminate its activities in Belgium, closing a company of more than 3,000 workers, but also affecting the employment of several other local companies providing the car parts for Renault. In 2007 Volkswagen drastically reduced its activities in Brussels, leaving only one type of Audi to be assembled there.

The major part of employment in Belgium is however not in industry. Almost 75 per cent of the working population is active in the service sector and 3 per cent in agriculture. Except for the (large) public sector, these services are also very much linked to international activities. Brussels is – together with Antwerp – an important centre in this respect. The presence of the European Union and of NATO has attracted many services in the financial sector, hotels and restaurants, transport and communication. Many companies have an important administrative seat in the Brussels area.

Brussels has nevertheless the highest unemployment rate of the three Belgian regions (see Figure 8.2). The overall unemployment rate in Belgium fluctuates around 7–8 per cent. The lowest unemployment is in Flanders, where there is less than 5 per cent unemployment. That means that in some sectors – like the building industry – there is a structural shortage of workers. Wallonia has an unemployment rate that is roughly twice the Flemish one. Walloon unemployment is structural. It is the result of the decline of those industries that used to be the very motor of the Belgian economy: coal and steel. The decline of these old industries has made the economic activity move to the north of the country, where new industrial activities (especially petrochemical activities) and services were developed. The Brussels unemployment rate is strikingly high at more than 17 per cent. That is the consequence of a serious mismatch between the type of employment offered in the capital city and the available workforce. Brussels has far more

Figure 8.2 *Evolution of the unemployment rates in Belgium and in its three regions*

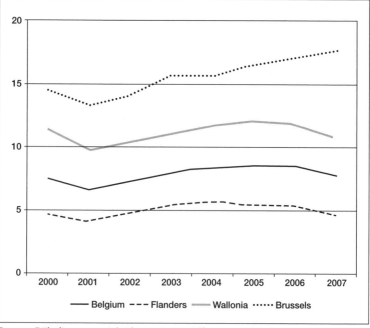

Sources: Rijksdienst voor Arbeidsvoorziening/Office National de l'Emploi

jobs than needed for the inhabitants of the region, but some 350,000 commuters from Flanders and Wallonia work in Brussels. Brussels has many jobs available in the public sector, since the administrations of Belgium, the European Union, NATO, Flanders and the French Community are located in Brussels. Other jobs are in service activities. An important requirement for many of these jobs is the knowledge of languages. Workers need to be bilingual French-Dutch and preferably also able to function in English. And that is exactly where the local labour force is under-skilled. Traditionally the education of the French Community has been weak in teaching the Dutch language. But for many pupils in the Brussels schools whose parents are of foreign origin the mother tongue is not even French. The type of education chosen by the parents of the migrant populations in Brussels also prepares pupils for manual skills rather than for the intellectual skills needed in the service economy. And that leaves large numbers of young people with foreign roots under-skilled and unemployed.

The economic policies of the regions

The unemployment figures and their evolution reflect quite important differences in the economic structures and capacities of the three regions. Table 8.3 shows the gross domestic product per inhabitant in each of them. The weight of Brussels here is very visible. The small central region is the economic motor of the country. That does however not mean that its inhabitants are better off than those of the other regions. As said above, some 350,000 jobs are filled by people living in Flanders and Wallonia. Figures on the individual income taxes (Table 8.4) therefore indicate that Brussels is, together with Wallonia, the poorer region and Flanders the richest. The evolution for Brussels is also quite negative. In 1990 its inhabitants were still earning more money than the inhabitants of the other regions. But migration of the middle classes to the periphery (one of the sources of linguistic pressure on that Flemish area) and the rising unemployment of the inhabitants of Brussels put it in a quite difficult position.

Brussels has received a number of competences that allow it to govern its own economy. But like Belgium in the world, it is very much dependent on what happens elsewhere. That also goes for the other two regions, but they have increasingly developed a

Table 8.3 *GDP per capita in the three Belgian regions*

	1977	2006
Brussels	45.653	58.277
Flanders	21.440	29.992
Wallonia	15.852	21.559

Source: www.belgostat.be

Table 8.4 *Individual income tax return index per region (Belgium = 100)*

	1990	2007
Brussels	112	87
Flanders	104	109
Wallonia	90	86

Source: www.belgostat.be

deliberate regional economic policy. The Flemish economy is very strong. More than 55 per cent of the Belgian GDP is produced in Flanders, against 25 per cent in Wallonia and 20 per cent in Brussels. In 1955 Flanders' share in the Belgian GDP was only 45 per cent, which illustrates clearly to what extent the economic weight of the country has shifted from the south to the north. Of all Belgian exports more than 80 per cent are today manufactured in Flanders. But that makes the Flemish economy very dependent on the world markets, on the willingness of international companies to invest in Flanders. Foreign trade is a regional competence and Flanders tries hard to market itself in the world. It pursues an economic policy that is generally quite liberal. The state and thus also the regional authority should be a facilitator, creating the conditions for a strong economy (Keating et al., 2003).

The Walloon economic policy, so far always led by the Parti Socialiste, places greater emphasis on the role of the state as an active economic player and as an employer. The Walloon economy is of course confronted with quite different needs. It no longer has a strong economy but must attract investments to develop new economic activities. The regional airport of Charleroi – calling itself Brussels South – has been able to develop, but is extremely dependent on the presence and strength of Ryanair. If that company decides to move its activities, Charleroi airport would be in deep trouble.

The difference in economic policy and philosophy between Flanders and Wallonia was nicely illustrated when the federal government asked the regions to participate in the new airline company that had to replace Sabena. Wallonia agreed to invest money in the new Brussels Airlines, but Flanders refused. It said that investing in an airline company does not belong to the core activities of the state. It was however willing to participate in the airport infrastructure to increase economic activities by private companies in the airport area. The national airport of Brussels is indeed located outside the city and on the territory of the Flemish Region.

The Flemish economic strength also explains why most political forces support an increase in the level of autonomy. With increased powers in fiscal and financial matters the region could make itself even more attractive. It could lower taxes to make sure that foreign investors keep coming to Flanders. It would like more say in the investments of the railroad company and can actually afford to build part of the infrastructure itself. Wallonia is very reluctant to see these competences move out of the federal level. It fears fiscal competition between the two regions and lacks the financial means to spend on new competences.

But the difference is also an ideological difference in policy choices. Wallonia spends more money than Flanders in direct subsidies to enterprises, to keep economic activity going and to guarantee the employment of workers in (old industrial areas) where new investments are not very likely to arrive. This social-democratic policy is heavily criticized by the Walloon liberals, but they have so far not convinced the Walloon voters to give them the leadership of the region.

The regions have received large economic powers and have actually copied much of the old Belgian techniques of policy-making in economic and especially social matters. The strongly developed social partnership at the federal level, with the guaranteed participation of the traditional interest groups of workers and employers, has been neatly replicated at the regional level. Each region has its own institution for negotiations between the regional actors.

Flanders has its 'Sociaal-Economische Raad van Vlaanderen' (SERV). It is composed of representatives of the regional branches of the three trade unions, and of the regional branches of the employers: Boerenbond (farmers), Unizo (self-employed) and

VOKA (employers). There are an equal number of representatives of the trade unions and of the employers' organizations.

Wallonia has its 'Conseil Economique et Social de la Région Wallonne' (CESRW). Here the regional branches of the trade unions hold discussions with the 'Union wallonne des Entreprises' (UWE), the 'Entente wallonne des Classes moyennes', the 'Fédération wallonne de l'Agriculture' and the 'Union francophone des Entreprises non-marchandes'.

For Brussels, the talks are organized in the Economic and Social Council of the Brussels Region, with the regional branches of the interest groups. The powers of these regional organizations are however limited. They are a meeting place to discuss regional politics and they give advice to the regional government. But the conclusion of Collective Labour Agreements is a strictly federal matter, since prices and wages are a federal and not a regional power. Here also Flanders would like to have full control over all aspects of labour policy and it demands the capacity to conclude regional and binding agreements between the social and economic partners. Wallonia fears that this will create agreements on higher wages that it will not be able to match.

Conclusions

In the previous chapters we have seen at many places and in many different ways how the governing of the country is built on a consociational logic giving both language communities a secure place in the decision-making processes. The social and economic policy though reflects the 'old' consociational and corporatist tradition in which the major pressure groups that are closely linked to the traditional political parties have a secure place in the decision-making processes. This old social partnership still functions quite smoothly and has actually been copied by the regions. The pressure on the system does not come in the first place from the territorial divide, but from the problematic financial situation of the federal state and from a far too low employment rate. That reduces the margins for finding agreements that are satisfactory for all the pressure groups and for the state.

When economic policy is being discussed, the north–south divide is however never far away. The three regions have a very different economic structure and Brussels is in a very peculiar situation with a strong service economy that generates a lot of jobs but with at the same time very high unemployment. The jobs go to the inhabitants of the other regions. This important role of Brussels in the Belgian economy is one of the elements – and not the least – that complicate all discussions about a possible post-Belgian alternative for the often difficult governing of this divided society.

Chapter 9

Belgium in the World

Belgium is not a country showing high ambitions of playing a key role in world politics. It is far too small for that. It cannot mobilize the people and means for competing beyond the category of small states. World politics is thus something that happens in Belgium, not something that Belgium can make happen. The fate of the country during the two World Wars is the perfect illustration of this lack of significance on the international scene. In both cases Belgium tried to stay out, to avoid choosing sides in the hope that the European and world powers would pay it no attention. This choice for a neutral stance failed twice and the impact of both wars on Belgian politics and society was quite important.

In this chapter Belgium is presented as part of world politics. We focus on two places where Belgium does play a role. The first is Africa, where the former colony Congo and the former UN trust territories Rwanda and Burundi are and remain the part of the world where most of the development aid and most of the diplomatic effort are spent. Next we look at the European Union and at the way in which Belgium not only takes the EU for granted but also supports a deeply integrated Europe. In the last part we look at how the new regional powers try to find some way of putting themselves on the world map.

The world in Belgium

The First World War is to a large extent associated with the Belgian territory. Belgium was one of the important places where it all happened. The western corner of the country, a flat land between the river Yser, the North Sea and the French border, was one of the crucial and brutal scenes of the war. It is still remembered in many countries that sent soldiers who died in high numbers on the battlefields of Flanders. The 'West Corner' (Westhoek) remains a place of remembrance and shows to what extent Belgium was the scene for something that it wanted to avoid by staying out.

Strict neutrality was indeed the position of Belgian diplomacy on the eve of the First World War. Yet on August 1, 1914 Germany asked Belgium to give its troops a free passage to France. It refused and a few days later the German army entered the territory. The non-respect for Belgian neutrality was for Great Britain one of the reasons for entering the war. By mid October the German troops had conquered almost the whole territory. The deliberate flooding of the area behind the Yser River froze the front line that from there ran further east into the north of France. It remained more or less frozen for four years, although several attempts to move in one or the other direction caused the death of millions of soldiers. There were several battles in and around the city of Ieper (Ypres). The last one culminated in the tragic battle of Passchendaele with more than 600,000 victims. These had come from all parts of the British Empire. Soldiers from the UK, Canada, Australia, South Africa and New Zealand came to die on the Western front in Belgium. The many graveyards with their endless rows of crosses remain landmarks of the 'Westhoek'. They have also been eternalized in the touching poem by John McCrae 'In Flanders Fields', written during the second battle of Ypres.

In Flanders fields the poppies blow
Between the crosses, row on row
That mark our place; and in the sky
The larks, still bravely singing, fly
Scarce heard amid the guns below.

We are the dead. Short days ago
We lived, felt dawn, saw sunset glow
Loved, and were loved, and now we lie
In Flanders fields.

Take up our quarrel with the foe:
To you from failing hands we throw
The torch; be yours to hold it high.
If ye break faith with us who die
We shall not sleep, though poppies grow
In Flanders fields.

For Belgium the war was a military but also a political shock. Its impact was considerable. First there were the tensions between

King Albert I and the government. The constitution states that the King is the head of the armed forces, but this role has to be played according to the central principle that the King cannot act without the approval of the government. In times of war this is not an easy construction, as would be proved again during the Second World War. King Albert tried to maintain Belgium's neutrality, because he feared that the conflict between Great Britain and Germany would last for many decades into the 20th century and he thought that it would be best for Belgium not to take sides. He believed that the war could be ended through negotiation and, indeed, engaged in talks with Germany. These failed and towards the end of the war the King accepted a more active position for Belgium on the international scene (Coolsaet, 2001).

Important fractions of the Belgian government seized the opportunity to voice quite radical requests for territorial changes. They claimed the left bank of the Scheldt and the south of Limburg from the Netherlands, the Grand Duchy of Luxembourg, and German border cities such as Eupen, Malmédy and Sankt-Vith. Claims were made for the Portuguese Cabinda (now an Angolan enclave in Congo), which would give Congo an easier access to the sea. At the end of the war though the Treaty of Versailles reduced Belgium to its real small size in world politics again. Only the claims for the German territories were accepted and hence a German-speaking minority living in the 'East Cantons' became part of Belgium. In Africa Belgium received control over the former German colonies Rwanda and Burundi.

Belgian domestic politics were drastically changed as a result of the war. First the socialist leader Vandevelde was co-opted into the government immediately after the German invasion. This was the very first government of 'national unity'. The end of the war also marked the beginning of consociational practices in Belgian politics. Belgium thus tried to stay out of the war, but became one of its centres and was deeply affected by it. It was – if needed – a clear signal that Belgium has no leading role to play when the great powers enter the scene.

For the Second World War the conclusion is very similar. After having first chosen to side with France and against Germany for close military and economic cooperation in the 1920s, Belgium returned to a more neutral position. That was a very pragmatic choice inspired in the first place by the need to keep good relations with potential trade partners. But at the end of the day

Belgium was again facing military aggression from Germany. As in 1914, this led to disagreements between King and government, and this time the conflict was going to last for a full decade (Stengers, 1980; Velaers & Van Goethem, 1994; Dumoulin et al., 2007). The war again brought together the three traditional political parties who used the wartime to discuss – together with the major interest groups closely linked to the parties – the social and economic future of the country. The war was also the time during which the Belgian system of social security was conceived. And, again, the war had a marked effect on the relations between north and south.

The Second World War greatly strengthened the belief that the country can only fare well if it keeps open relations with its neighbours. Yet while both pre-war periods had shown a Belgium trying not to make fundamental choices, Belgian diplomacy after 1945 adopted a much more active position. Belgium rapidly became one of the forces espousing the need for the creation of a large European market. It was in fact not primarily security concerns but economic goals that inspired the support for a multilateral foreign policy (Coolsaet, 2001). The small Belgian economy needs markets for export and a European Economic Community is an interesting strategy for securing them. 'Little' Belgium is well aware of the consequences of its size and therefore opts for an active European policy. The European level also offers many more opportunities for having a real impact on what is going on in the outside world and how it affects life in Belgium.

Belgium big in Africa

In Europe and in the world Belgium is a small country that has more than once experienced the consequences of its size. Yet at the same time Belgium has been a colonial power. In 1908 it acquired Congo, an area 80 times the size of Belgium. This was not the result of an active policy by the Belgian government. It was King Leopold II who had been able to gain control over the Freestate of Congo (*Etat Indépendent du Congo*) in 1885. He could rule as an absolute monarch over his new country and freely extract and trade its natural resources (which was primarily rubber at that time). The Belgian political elites had no clear colonial ambitions and were even reluctant to see the King engage in these kinds of activities. Heavy international criticism of the cruel way in which Congo was ruled by Leopold brought the Belgian parliament to take over Congo as a Belgian colony in 1908 (Hochschild, 1998). This more or less put an end to the most extreme excesses, but the large area in central Africa remained, primarily, a source of income for investors (Vangroenweghe, 1985; Ewans, 2002). The Belgian state did not develop a very active colonial policy, but made sure that the area was available for Belgian entrepreneurs and for Catholic missionaries. The Société Générale gradually developed more and more activities in Congo and turned it into an important economic force. Congo became a major supplier of copper, gold, cobalt, cotton, coffee, palm oil and uranium. The latter especially turned Congo into more than just one of the many colonies in Africa. And it made Belgium much bigger than its size on the European continent could justify. Antwerp harbour fared well as the place where goods were further distributed throughout the world (Vanthemsche, 2006; 2007).

During the Second World War the availability of resources in Congo made Belgium an important ally. Although the government at first did not agree with the King's decision to capitulate, the rapid crumbling of France made many members of the government hesitate about what to do. The importance of Congo for the continuation of the war on the side of Great Britain finally brought the Belgian government back together in London from where the resistance and final integration of Belgium into the allied forces was organized. The presence of uranium was of crucial strategic importance. The 'Union Miniére du Haut-Katanga', a mining company in the hands of the Société Générale struck a deal with the USA to ensure the delivery of uranium. The USA's first nuclear bombs were produced with Congolese uranium (Vanthemsche, 2006: 517).

This clearly illustrates the most important meaning of the colony for Belgium: it was an economic asset. Belgium had never shown any coherent ambition to mould Congolese society. That was a matter left to the missions. The Belgian presence in Congo was limited to a number of state administrators and the leading personnel of the companies doing business in Congo. The territories of Rwanda and Burundi, which were given to Belgium after the First World War, do not contain the same important resources as Congo and were therefore rather used as a possible workforce reservoir for Congolese industry.

The economic and strategic importance of Congo after 1945 reinforced the conviction that the colony was an important asset that needed to be kept under Belgian control. The idea of an independent Congo was out of the question, even if many other colonial powers (had perforce) granted their overseas territories a larger autonomy or full sovereignty. Belgium became a fierce and rapidly also quite isolated defender of colonialism, and felt increasing pressure from the United Nations to initiate the decolonization. Congo eventually became independent in 1960, but the transition was a drama. Belgium was badly prepared for it. During the last decades of the colonization it had invested heavily in Congo, but still with economic development as the primary goal. Political rights for the Congolese population were not on the agenda. Basic education was important, but the creation and formation of a Congolese elite was something for the future. The rise of Congolese nationalism and demands for independence therefore came more or less as a surprise. In only a few months, elections were organized and Congo became independent under the leadership of Prime Minister Patrice Lumumba and President Kasavubu. A very bitter speech by Lumumba during the independence ceremonies immediately set the tone for very troubled relationships between Congo and Belgium. Secessionist moves in the rich province of Katanga where lots of the mining activities were concentrated, mutiny in the Congolese army and direct interventions by Belgian troops forced Lumumba to ask for help from the UN. Blue helmets were sent to Congo, putting colonial power Belgium right into the middle of world politics (De Witte, 1999; Gondola, 2002; Nzongola-Ntalaja, 2002; Vanthemsche, 2007).

The new Congolese state was badly prepared for independence and the first years of independence were chaotic and full of violence. When the chief of staff Mobutu seized power in 1965 he brought stability, but at a very high price. The national wealth was systematically transferred to the family and followers of Mobutu, and mining activities were nationalized, although Belgian investors (Société Générale) remained active in the country. The clear anti-communist position of the Mobutu regime however ensured him the goodwill of the western powers. The relative stability offered by Mobutu allowed the economic activities in which Belgian investors and enterprises remained deeply involved to be continued. The bulk of Belgium's development aid also went to Congo, reflecting the awareness that Belgium was to a certain extent responsible for the life of the Congolese population. This feeling of responsibility was however not always appreciated by the Congolese regime, which wanted to move away from the paternalistic past. The relations between the Belgian government and Mobutu thus went up and down, always trying to balance economic interests, development aid and moral principles. Relations reached a turning point though in 1990. Killings on the university campus of Lumumbashi and the Belgian request to send an international commission to clarify the responsibility of the Congolese regime marked the end of relations between Belgium and Congo. Official development aid was stopped and only NGOs remained active in Congo.

The colonial legacy and the very troubled relations between Belgium and its former colony explain the way in which Belgium today conducts its foreign policy towards Africa in general and the Great Lakes area in particular. There is on the one hand a feeling of responsibility for the future of the area, a strong expertise about what exactly is going on and good relations with a number of key actors. On the other hand though the leaders of Congo, Rwanda and Burundi expect from Belgium that it should fully respect the sovereignty and autonomy of the former colony and trust territories, and not intervene in a patronizing way in its domestic politics. The dilemma was made dramatically clear during the Rwandan crisis and genocide in 1994. A UN force was present in Rwanda when, after the murder of the Rwandan and Burundian presidents in Kigali in April 1994, the mass killings started. Belgian troops were part of that UN force. Belgium had agreed to be part of it precisely because it felt responsible and wanted to make its expertise available. Yet Belgians were also held responsible for the internal divide between Hutu and Tutsi and ten of the Belgian UN blue helmets were trapped and brutally killed. Belgium then decided to withdraw. A Senate investigation commission in 1997 discussed Belgian policy in Rwanda (see Chapter 7) and issued the advice that Belgium should no longer participate in peacekeeping or peace-enforcing missions in the former colonies.

The Rwandan genocide is the origin of further tensions between Rwanda and Congo. And whenever these tensions build up again, Belgium tries to take the lead in the diplomatic moves to stop the violence. But at the same time it remains very reluctant to intervene too actively.

The Rwandan genocide and the tensions with Congo are also the origin of the regime change in Congo. Starting from East Congo, Laurent Kabila conquered Kinshasa and removed Mobutu from power. Kabila was murdered in 2001 after which his son Joseph Kabila took over. Here again, Belgian involvement in the stabilization and democratization of the new regime has been important. Belgian diplomats actively participated in the drafting of a new constitution, in the choice of an electoral system and in the organization of elections for president and parliament. These confirmed the power of Kabila. Belgium also helped the Congolese army – composed of many fractions of former warlords and different ethnic groups – to become a truly integrated Congolese army. The latter is however extremely difficult and the absence of a coherent and paid army is one of the reasons for the never-ending conflicts in the Great Lakes area. And here again Belgium finds itself torn between the role of active and reluctant participant.

The relations between Belgium and Congo remain quite tense. Belgium tries to put pressure on the new Congolese regime to ban corruption and to organize its public administration in a proper and transparent way. 'Good governance' is what Belgium asks and even demands from Congo as a prerequisite for further help. Transparency in the way the mining sector is organized and in the way the financial returns from mining are distributed and invested is a matter of great concern. But that regularly leads to crises and the almost full closure of contacts and diplomatic relations because the Congolese leaders do not want to receive lessons in good governance from the former colonizer. Yet while official relations go through ups and downs, Congo, Rwanda and Burundi remain the first countries to which Belgian development aid is transferred. That goes for the development aid financed directly by the state but also for the many NGOs that have old historic ties with Central Africa.

Belgium in Europe and Europe in Belgium

Belgium is one of the founding member states of the European Union. Yet Belgium is not only part of Europe. The European Union itself is part of Belgium. Although the European Union has no formal capital, and although its institutions are spread over several countries, the political and administrative heart of the

European Union beats in Brussels. That is the result of many incremental decisions, but they do reflect that for Belgium the membership of the European Union has always been more or less a matter of fact. Whether Belgium should be part of Europe, or not, has never been an issue. The idea of linking the Belgian economy into a larger market was easily accepted. And when the Treaty of Rome had to be ratified in the parliament, Prime Minister Gaston Eyskens complained that only a very small number of MPs had participated in the discussion.

Actually there is more than just acceptance of the European fact. Belgium has become – especially since the 1990s (Bursens, 2002) – a very active defender of the *communitarian* method, of the further supranational and federal integration of the Union. When Prime Minister Dehaene failed to become the president of the Commission in 1994 (because of a veto by the British prime minister John Major), one of the reasons for that was his far too obvious pro integration position. This might have been conspicuous on the international scene, but in Belgium he was never seen as having surprising views on this matter. He simply was an obvious supporter of the further integration of the Union, and this is considered to be the normal position. A Belgian prime minister or minister of Foreign Affairs can only be blamed at home for not having been European enough. When Belgium takes over the presidency of the Union, this is a major opportunity to try to make Europe move towards more integration.

During the 2001 presidency, Prime Minister Verhofstadt succeeded in having the so-called 'Declaration of Laeken' accepted and thus the organization of a convention that should lead to a new and preferably 'constitutional' treaty for the Union. Former Prime Minister Dehaene was appointed as vice-president of the convention and indeed tried hard to make the Union a more supranational organization (Dehaene, 2004; Norman, 2003). The Constitutional Treaty that was drafted during and after the Convention failed to be ratified after the rejection in a referendum by both France and the Netherlands. In Belgium, the treaty was ratified, without major discussion, by all the parliamentary assemblies.

Like all the earlier treaties, this was not a matter of heated debates and long discussions. All these debates were short and were held among a few EU-specialists in the parties. Not all parties always vote in favour. The governing parties vote in favour of the treaty, while opposition parties mostly vote against it. Yet the arguments to do so do not differ much from the arguments for a positive vote. Actually the debates show that the defenders of a new European treaty acknowledge that it could have been better, that more competences might have been transferred and that more matters might have been reserved for decision-making with qualified majorities. And these are the most important reasons why opposition parties then vote against the treaty. Only Vlaams Belang systematically votes against all European treaties and can therefore be considered as the only Eurosceptic party of the country (Deschouwer & Van Assche, 2008). It does however defend a strong Europe in matters of immigration, security and asylum. It greatly fears the transfer of competences related to culture and of course defends a Europe that should be based on the nations rather than on the state. Yet Vlaams Belang hardly stresses this (soft) Eurosceptic position in its communications. Only the possible membership of Turkey is a matter on which it takes a strong negative position, but then again this debate has never really been prominent in Belgium. Vlaams Belang never needed Europe to put itself outside the mainstream and to mobilize political discontent.

The elitist consensus on Europe is doubled by a very high acceptance of the European Union among the Belgian population. Europe is a good thing. That is what the Belgians believe. According to the Eurobarometer surveys, the percentage of Belgians thinking that European membership is a 'bad thing' for the country is usually below 10 per cent. The highest point ever was 19 per cent in 1996 (see Figure 9.1).

Yet one cannot say that Europe has had no visible effect on Belgian politics and policies. The convergence criteria for the participation in the single currency, in particular, have placed an extremely high pressure on the Belgian decision-makers. When the Maastricht Treaty was signed, the budgetary deficit was 7 per cent of GDP, while the public debt was at a peak of 135 per cent. When the decision about participation in the EMU had to be taken, the yearly deficit had been brought down to less than 3 per cent and the reduction of the public debt to 118 per cent of GDP (see Chapter 8). One would expect that such a harsh reduction of public spending had led to heated debates, and that one or more parties would have blamed the source of that policy. But nothing of the kind was heard (except from very marginal left-extremist movements and parties). Belgium was brought into the EMU by a

Figure 9.1 *Support for European Union membership in Belgium, 1981–2004*

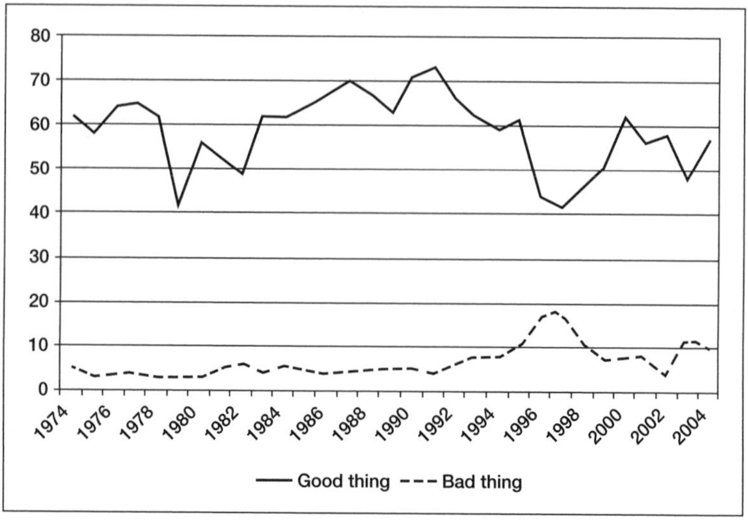

Source: Eurobarometer surveys (ec.europa.eu/public.opinion)

centre-left government, and the liberal opposition only blamed the government for being too slow, or for presenting figures that made the situation look better (that is, closer to the convergence criteria) than it was.

Europe is thus clearly not a crucial matter for discussion in Belgian politics. Europe is there and its effects on national policymaking are not perceived as disturbing. That is to some extent the consequence of early membership, although this cannot be the sole explanation. France is also an early member and has had much more heated debates about Europe and the place of France in Europe. The small size of Belgium – certainly compared with France – can also explain why themes like the loss of national sovereignty or the loss of power in the international context are not part of the daily political vocabulary. But then other small countries like Denmark – or the non-members Norway and Switzerland – also show reluctance to give away their state sovereignty.

An interesting anecdote is that the government that signed the Maastricht Treaty was actually a caretaker government, which had collapsed a few weeks earlier on a disagreement between the north and the south about exportation of weapons (produced in the south). The fact that this caretaker government signed the

Maastricht Treaty has never been seen as a problem. Europe is OK and Europe can always go on.

That does not mean however that elections to the European Parliament are treated as an important event. They are organized like the elections to the Senate, that is, with one list per language community (see Chapter 5). Popular politicians thus try to get onto the top of the lists and the lists are drafted at the highest party level. There is no need to involve provincial or even lower party levels in the drafting of the lists. European elections are a very centralized affair, offering possibilities for high-level personnel reshuffles. This is reinforced by the way in which elected candidates can be replaced when needed. Every party not only presents a list of 'effective candidates', but also a list of 'successors'. If one of the elected effective candidates needs to be replaced, it is not the next elected effective candidate but the first on the successors' list who enters the European Parliament (see also Chapter 5).

European elections are actually second order *substate* elections (Reif & Schmitt, 1980). European elections are always held simultaneously with the regional elections. That means that the campaign for the European level is completely obscured by the regional campaigns. The European election is just one extra element that allows for a personnel reshuffle if needed.

In contrast to the position of MEP, the position of member of the European Commission is very important. Belgium has one commissioner and it counts as the equivalent of one very heavy portfolio in the federal government. The choice of the Belgian commissioner is therefore always part of tough negotiations between the governing parties. Giving the job to an opposition party is out of the question. Being the European commissioner is actually close to being prime minister. Coming back to Belgian politics is therefore not an easy thing to do. Former members of the Commission have never come back 'down' to Belgian politics, but remained either at the European level (in the Parliament) or left politics altogether to move into the private sector.

The substate level abroad

Belgium readily accepts the transfer or pooling of national competences to the European level. Belgium participates in the euro, in the Schengen agreement on common control of the outer borders of the EU and in the creation of a common military defence. The building of the European level has however occurred at the same time as the internal devolution of the Belgian state. And this creates a potentially problematic and paradoxical situation. The matters transferred to the European level are competences that have increasingly been devolved to the regions and communities. A few characteristics of the Belgian federal system potentially aggravate this situation. First there is the principle '*in foro interno in foro externo*'. It means that in all matters for which the substates have received the internal competence, they also have the power for the external relations. The regions are for instance responsible for environmental policy, which means that the international relations for environmental policy are in the hands of the regions. Thus, when Europe deals with environmental policy, the Belgian regions should be involved and not the Belgian federal state (Bursens & Geeraerts, 2006).

The second characteristic is the centrifugal logic of the Belgian federation. Federalism in Belgium has not been put into place to stimulate or to facilitate cooperation between the substates. To the contrary: it tries to neatly divide the competences and to give each substate the capacity to conduct its own policies without interference from the others or from the federal level. That could then lead to a degree of competition between the substates when it comes to formulating, defending, and implementing decisions at the European level.

The European level itself allows an active presence of the substates. Regional ministers of decentralized European member states can be present at meetings of the European Council. They must however represent the state and its position as a whole. Splitting up the votes in the Council between the substates is not possible. The Belgian substates can thus participate at the European level for the competences that fall under their control, but they need to agree among themselves for their position to be heard effectively.

And this leads to an interesting and surprising European rescue of the Belgian federal level (Beyers & Bursens, 2006). The actual practice is indeed not one of constant competition, but of constant cooperation. In the Federal Ministry of Foreign Affairs there is a Directorate of European Affairs that makes sure that the necessary coordination between the federal level, the regions and the communities is organized. In the vast majority of cases, agreement is reached at the level of the civil servants. Only occasionally is a higher level – that is, meetings between the ministers or between their heads of cabinet – needed. What has been devolved to the substates is thus knit together again at the federal level through active intergovernmental cooperation (see also Franck et al., 2003; Kerremans, 2000; Kerremans & Beyers, 1996; Kerremans & Beyers, 2001; Kovziridze, 2002; Crombez & Lebbe, 2006).

For politics beyond Europe, the cooperation between the levels is however not always that smooth. Especially for international trade, the presentation and marketing of Belgium and its regions requires some creativity and sense of compromise. The National Institute for Foreign Trade used to be the single organization through which Belgium presented itself to the world. International missions to promote the Belgian economy and export were traditionally chaired by Prince Albert (the current King), accompanied by representatives of companies seeking to conclude agreements in foreign countries and representatives of the Belgian employers' organizations. The transfer of foreign trade to the regions has multiplied the number of institutions and organizations trying to present themselves abroad. Each region has its own Institute for Foreign Trade and sends permanent representatives to key countries, where they have to cooperate with the embassies in which only the federal level is represented. Flanders and Wallonia and to a lesser extent Brussels use their instruments and powers to secure themselves a visible place in the very competitive world economy.

Not only is there the issue of cooperation of policies and personnel abroad, the fragmentation of an already small country on the world markets makes it difficult to choose the right strategies and brand image. The regions especially need to brand themselves beyond and together with the existing brands 'Belgium' and 'Brussels' (or 'Antwerp' for international transport). When today international trade missions go to Singapore or China for instance, they are still led by a member of the royal family (the King's son Prince Philip), who carries the image of the old and recognizable Belgium. The mission is further populated with companies trying to invest abroad, with ministers for economy and trade of the federal and the regional levels and possibly representatives of the federal and regional employers' organizations.

Balancing regional autonomy and the need for coordination and keeping the advantages of still being (a united) Belgium on the international markets is thus a difficult exercise. The federal state has old and strong networks while the regions still need to build them. A similar tension has occurred for the development aid policy. In 2002 this policy was transferred to the regions. The transfer has however not really been implemented, mainly because the breaking up or splitting up of existing links controlled by the federal level might lead to inefficiency and thus to policies of development aid that produce less aid than before. The issue remains open for discussion and for heated debates about symbols and markers of identity.

Between principles and reality

For the 'high politics' of defence and security the federal level has remained fully in control. Membership of international organizations like the United Nations, the CVSE and NATO are a matter for the federal government and for the federal Minister of Foreign Affairs. During the past decade the focus of Belgium's international position has slightly changed, but is as always a subtle compromise between vital (economic) interests and basic values and norms (Coolsaet, 2001; 2004).

Under Minister of Foreign Affairs Louis Michel (1999–2004) and further under Karel De Gucht, Belgian foreign policy has announced and tried to follow a few clear and ethical principles. We have already mentioned the principle of 'good governance' that inspires the policies towards Central Africa. In the discussions about the creation of an International Criminal Court the Belgian government was a full supporter of the maximum option. Attempts to bring the former Chilean dictator Pinochet to trial were applauded by the Belgian government. The government did however also encounter the limits of what a small country can do. Belgium adopted a law in 1993 that gave the Belgian courts the ability to punish crimes against humanity. When the possible application of the law risked shaking relations between Belgium and important players on the international scene, it was gradually softened and eventually disappeared. There was an attempt to bring the Congolese Minister Yerodia to court, but that obviously risked disturbing the always difficult balance between Belgian diplomacy and the different groups and factions in the politics of Congo. Lebanese activists asked for former Prime Minister Ariel Sharon to be taken to court for his responsibility in the killings of Sabra and Shatila in 1982. Ariel Sharon was not amused to know that he might be arrested when coming to Belgium. Judicial actions were also started against the US general Franks and finally also against US President Bush. At a meeting of NATO in Brussels in 2003, US Secretary of Defense Donald Rumsfeld made clear that if US officials risked being arrested when visiting Belgium that might lead to the decision to take NATO headquarters away from Brussels. It was the beginning of the end of the brave Belgian genocide law.

Belgium has never been an important military force and has no ambition to become one. It substantially supports the attempts to create a European defence and has in the past decade opted for keeping its armed forces ready for humanitarian rather than for military actions. When Belgium is asked to participate in military interventions, it rather keeps an extremely low profile. During the first Gulf War in 1991 it even refused to deliver bullets for the British army. Sending soldiers for active duty is out of the question. Belgium usually sends a few ships for mine-sweeping (for which there is strong expertise) but preferably not too close to where the action is.

The Belgian army has increasingly been prepared and deployed for humanitarian actions. It participates readily in UN missions, but again preferably if they do not involve high risks. In 2003 the B-Fast service was put into place. It stands for Belgian First Aid and Support and is a cooperation between the federal services of Foreign Affairs, Foreign Trade and Development Aid, Internal Affairs, Budget and Defence. It is led by the Minister of Foreign Affairs and is meant to be activated whenever urgent help is needed somewhere in the world. As soon as help is asked for, an intervention team can be ready within 12 hours. There is one important restriction though: B-Fast never goes to areas where an armed conflict is going on.

Conclusions

Belgium is not a world power. It plays a very modest role in international politics and has no ambition for doing more. It is especially committed to the European Union. As one of the founding countries of the Union and as the host of many important EU institutions it sees the EU as part of the normal daily environment. Being part of the EU entirely fits into the basic logic of Belgian international relations. That logic is multilateral and always keeps an eye on the consequences for foreign trade. Easy access to world markets is absolutely crucial for the Belgian economy.

Chapter 10

Still Belgium?

Two stories

There are two stories that can be told about Belgium. The first is a positive and optimistic one. Belgium is a very good country to live in. Its GDP per capita of more than 40,000 dollars per year ranks it – according to the IMF – as number 17 of the wealthiest countries in the world. That is higher than Spain and Germany, but lower than the Netherlands (number 10) and Luxembourg (number 1). Belgium has a very generous and fine-meshed social security system. It does face a number of problems related to the low employment rate among older workers, but some tensions in a fifty-year-old social security system is not an exceptional feature. The generous welfare state is built on a strong economy and on the easy access of its products to the world markets. Belgium's capital city is also the political capital of the European Union and of NATO, which attracts lots of other services to Brussels and which makes Brussels and Belgium a visible and recognizable brand for the international community.

Belgium is also a country where cultural and territorial divisions have been settled in a peaceful way. There have certainly been moments of very high tension between the north and the south, but the conflict has never even come close to becoming a violent clash or a civil war. Whenever the tensions were really high, the political class found a way out. Political elites in Belgium have indeed displayed an incredible degree of creativity in crafting subtle compromises between demands that were at first sight fully incompatible. That is quite an achievement. In Canada, where a fairly similar territorial and language conflict is dividing the country, many attempts have been made to reform the political system, but half a century of discussions about the status of Québec has not led to significant constitutional changes (Jans, 2001). In Cyprus, where in contrast with Belgium and Canada the conflict between the two communities has not been limited to heated debates but has turned into violence and deep mutual hatred, the search for new political institutions for a reunification of the island looks actively and with great interest at the so-called 'Belgian model' (Emerson & Tocci, 2003). It means a territorial divide into homogeneous communities and power-sharing devices for the government of the matters kept in common. This is indeed the way in which Belgium has been able to ease and control the different views and demands of its two language communities.

But there is another story too. Belgium has been able to settle its territorial conflict in a peaceful way, but the arrangements are constantly questioned from the inside. Periods of high tension have been concluded with a compromise, but each compromise is only for the time being. It leads to a period of calm and stability that is always followed sooner or later by a new crisis. And every new crisis increases the awareness that the existing political institutions might not be able to contain the next one. Like the people of San Francisco who know that the city is built on a deep cleavage and who feel and realize once in a while that the foundations are not stable at all, one is waiting for the Belgian 'big one'. That does not stop the Belgians from living well and comfortably. After all, the territorial conflict is not that important or life-threatening. Health and financial security are more important concerns for the Belgians than the way in which the state is currently organized.

The double story and the ups and downs are also nicely reflected in the evolution of the trust Belgians have in their political system. Since 1975 the Eurobarometer has asked the inhabitants of member states to what extent they are satisfied with the way democracy works in their country. The responses for Belgium are displayed in Figure 10.1. The fluctuations are quite impressive.

The first serious dip occurred at the end of the 1970s and the early 1980s. Between 1978 and 1981 there were no fewer than eight governments, all struggling with the fact that the Flemish and francophones each wanted a very different reform of the state and a very different approach to the economic crisis. The over-concentration on these discussions led the short-lived governments to allow the situation of the public finances to get completely out of hand. It was at this time that the foundations were laid for a sky-rocketing public debt, reaching 130 per cent of GDP at the end of the 1980s. The consequences of this 'malgoverno' are still felt today and will be felt for at least one more generation (Heylen & Van Hecke, 2008).

Figure 10.1 *Percentage of Belgians who are 'satisfied' or 'very satisfied' with the way in which democracy works in Belgium*

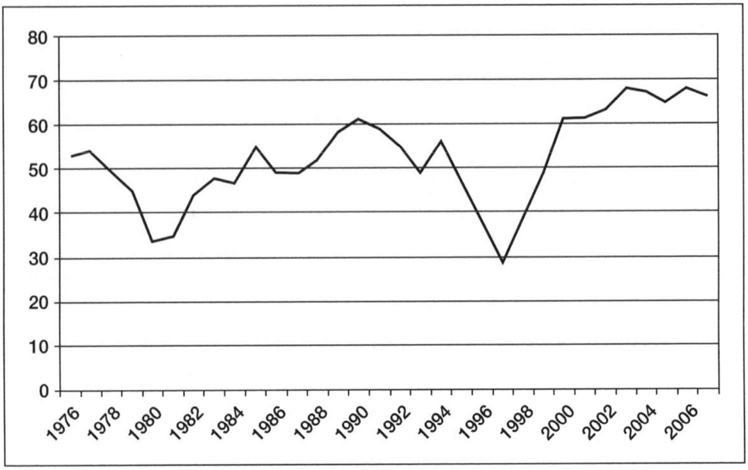

Source: Eurobarometer

Subsequent governments, however, were able after all to find a working compromise that was enshrined in constitutional reforms. And the confidence of the Belgians in their political system picked up again. The way up was however interrupted by a drop in confidence in 1985. This was the year in which Brussels hosted the final of the European Football Cup match between Liverpool and Juventus. The event turned into a drama in which 40 people were killed. It soon became clear – through the work of an investigation commission in the House of Representatives – that the poor organization of both federal and local authorities and the absence of proper communication between police forces was one of the reasons why so many people died. The capacity and performance of the public authorities appeared to be dramatically low (T'Hart & Pijnenburg, 1998). People at the top of the Belgian Football Association resigned, but the Minister of Internal Affairs refused to go. It marked the end of the government.

A second serious dip followed in 1991 and only ended in 1997 when less than 30 per cent of Belgians declared themselves satisfied with the functioning of their country. The way down is marked by a series of events that all reinforce the idea and perception that the Belgian state was not able to function properly. First there was the election result of November 24, 1991 or 'Black Sunday'. Unexpectedly, a populist radical-right party that was furthermore claiming the independence of Flanders polled 10 per cent of the Flemish votes. It took more than 100 days to form a new government. It was generally believed that the success of the radical-right was a vote of protest and discomfort, a rejection of the political class and a strong indicator of a 'gap' between citizens and politics. The core characteristics of the Belgian system were therefore called into question: the high degree of partitocracy, the widespread practice of clientelism, the solid grip of pillar organizations on the public services, the large number of parties and the opaque and difficult processes of coalition formation, the constant presence and return to power of the Christian democrats and the socialists while they lose at the polls, the cumulation of different mandates by politicians, and the backlog in the judicial system. As proof of a few of these points, a number of scandals related to dubious financing of political parties broke out. Top politicians of both socialist parties had to resign. And the final blow came in 1996, when during the summer Marc Dutroux was arrested and two girls were set free from his cellar where others had died before.

These horrible things unfortunately happen in many countries, but in Belgium it led once again to a questioning of the capacities of the state to do what is needed. The police had indeed been in the house before and had failed to discover the hidden part of the cellar where kidnapped girls were being imprisoned. Information held by the Gendarmerie had not been transferred to the local police and vice versa. And the consequences were dramatic (like the Heysel drama).

The Dutroux case – involving the fate of innocent children – lay at the origin of the largest public demonstration ever seen in the streets of Brussels, when 300,000 Belgians participated in the 'White March' (Hooghe, 1997; Rihoux & Walgrave, 1998). It was meant to show support for the parents of the children but also to tell the political elite that change was needed. The latter was however quite difficult to decode. Marchers in white clothing bore white balloons and umbrellas but no slogans formulating concrete requests. There was deep discontent and a desire for things to change. Among concrete reforms inspired by the White March was the creation of Child Focus, a now well-oiled and very performant organization that organizes the search whenever a person is reported missing. The judicial system was reformed to reduce the intervention of party politics in the nomination of judges and to give victims more protection and better access to information. And the different police forces were merged into one integrated Belgian force.

And trust in the Belgian political institutions went up again, reaching the highest point ever in 2003. By then a brand new coalition formula was in power, with liberals, socialists and greens, and the tensions between north and south were well under control. A constitutional reform was negotiated in 2001 without a real clash. A new-style Belgium was presented. Prime Minister Verhofstadt was quite confident that he could turn Belgium into a model state. He was convinced of the fact that his new and fresh approach would make the number of protest votes melt away. But in 2003 and once again in 2004 Vlaams Belang realized its highest score ever.

A reform of the electoral system introducing provincial districts brought the old issue of the Brussels-Halle-Vilvoorde district back onto the agenda in 2003. It also brought the issue of the boundaries of Brussels back onto the table. The Flemish Christian democrats, who had been the leading party of all state reforms so far, forged an electoral alliance with the separatist N-VA and promised that old Flemish demands would indeed be finally realized if they were to return to power. Francophones were horrified to see this gradual radicalization of Flemish positions. The francophone public television RTBf interrupted its regular programmes on December 13, 2006 to announce that the Flemish parliament had declared independence and that the King had fled the country. This hoax – in which several Flemish and francophone politicians had agreed to play a role – appeared to be believed as true by many viewers (according to polls by the RTBf itself). People panicked and went to the royal palace to express their support for Belgium and for the King. Suddenly the end of Belgium was not a strange demand by small or weird political parties from the north, but seemed to become a real possibility, even if the scenario of 'Bye bye Belgium' – including vehicles being stopped at the Flemish boundaries – was pure science fiction.

The 2007 elections for the federal parliament were heavily coloured by the Flemish parties' strong demands and by francophone fears for yet another further dismantling of Belgium. It was six months after the elections before a temporary government could be formed. The trust of the Belgians in their political class was on the way down again. After ten years of stability and high trust, the Belgian political foundations were shaking again. And this time the fear for the 'big one' was more openly voiced than even before.

Distrust at the top

Declining or strongly fluctuating trust in the political system by the citizens is a potential problem for democratic legitimacy. But what does it say about lack of trust at the elite level? Challenging a political system at its core is something to be expected from anti-establishment parties. One of the weaknesses and problems of Belgium though is that the system structurally lacks support at the elite level. The current Belgian state and its working principles are the results of many difficult but creatively crafted compromises. Its most important working principle is the sharing of power, the obligation to govern together at the central level. But for this to function adequately the decision-makers themselves need a minimal degree of belief in the system, an acceptance of the compromise that created it and an acceptance of the need for more compromises in the future.

Quite often however indicators to the contrary are given. Francophone parties have made several attempts to question the – in their eyes far too limited – way in which the francophone minority in Flanders is treated. They have convinced the Council of Europe to send a rapporteur to the Brussels periphery to witness that in Belgium the francophones of Flanders are not recognized as a national minority. Belgium has indeed not ratified the Framework Convention for the protection of national minorities, which states, in Articles 4 and 5, that the countries who have ratified it should:

> promote the conditions necessary for persons belonging to national minorities to maintain and develop their culture, and to preserve the essential elements of their identity, namely their religion, language, traditions and cultural heritage ... and refrain from policies or practices aimed at assimilation of persons belonging to national minorities against their will and shall protect these persons from any action aimed at such assimilation.

The arrangement for the francophones in the Brussels area – language facilities in six municipalities – is clearly much more limited, but it is the result of a compromise in which demands from both language groups about the use of language and the boundaries between the territories were combined.

On the Flemish side there have been several attempts to limit the use of language facilities as far as possible. While in the beginning inhabitants of the selected municipalities could register themselves as a francophone and automatically receive all information from the public authorities in French, the Flemish government has asked the local authorities to always send the information in Dutch, and only send translations to the citizens who explicitly ask for it. The normal discourse on the Flemish side is also to say that actually the facilities were meant as a transition mechanism and that they should be abolished in the near future. That was however never part of the compromise.

Francophone politicians perceive Flanders as a bulldozer that wants to homogenize its territory. In heated moments even terms like 'ethnic cleansing' can be heard. Flanders perceives the francophone demands as a never-ending attempt to use their language whenever and wherever they want, ignoring the fact that the use of language in Belgium has now been settled in a territorial way. Flanders thus behaves like a community that is threatened and that needs to protect its linguistic integrity. Neither community is able to accept the consequences of the compromise. And the most visible consequence of that is frustration.

Several countries have political tensions that can be labelled and understood as a conflict between the centre and a periphery (Lipset & Rokkan, 1967). A state-building elite is then challenged by groups belonging to a territory that is not and does not want to be fully integrated into the state and into its overall identity. In Belgium the periphery used to be Flanders, questioning the linguistic identity of Belgium. Today Belgium is composed of only two peripheries, and no centre. For each side, the centre is where the other community is also present, and where the other community is seen as the dominant one. The elite do not trust the system, because the system is perceived to be more in the advantage of the 'other' (Deschouwer, 2005b; 2006).

The uneasy consociation

The Belgian federal system is a consociational federation. Its central level requires power sharing and gives the participating partners a veto. This means that the Belgian federal level functions more like a confederation than like a federation. In the judicial meaning of the word, Belgium is of course not a confederation. That would assume a union of different sovereign states rather than one single state. But the rules and procedures of decision-making at the central level do not allow for anything other than a diplomatic agreement between the leaders of the two language communities. Of course the normal voting rule in the federal parliament is simple majority, but the way in which decisions are prepared and implemented makes sure that for anything that is of some importance a double majority is provided. A consensus is always needed in a paritary government to launch and to finalize legislative initiatives. And the situation in which a government is not supported by a double majority in the parliament is exceptional.

The Belgian federation is thus consociational and also bipolar. The unanimity rule applies to decision-making in which there are only two partners. And that is actually another reason why the rule can only be consensus. With only two partners there is no other choice. Yet that number is not conducive to the smooth functioning of power sharing:

> A multiple balance of power among the segments of a plural society is more conducive to consociational democracy than a dual balance of power or a hegemony by one of the segments, because if one segment has a clear majority its leaders may attempt to dominate rather than cooperate with the rival minority. And in a society with two segments of approximately equal size, the leaders of both may hope to win a majority and to achieve their aims by domination instead of cooperation. (Lijphart, 1977: 55)

When a consociational system with two partners has been put into practice, the bad conditions discussed by Lijphart remain present as powerful sources of frustration. Two is also an awkward number because the veto always comes from the same other partner.

The bipolarity of Belgium has been translated into almost all institutions and organizations. The most important and crucial in this respect is the party system. The schism in the national parties was the unavoidable consequence of the different views of north and south on the principles and building blocks of the Belgian state. Its consequences for the functioning and legitimacy of the system are tremendous, exactly because the split party system needs to function in a context of compulsory power sharing.

Overpromising is a normal feature of competitive democracies. And a delivery gap between promises made during the campaign and policies agreed during coalition formation are also a normal feature of multi-party systems. In the Belgian split party system the electoral promises are made to two different and entirely separate electorates. Being responsive to them is not an easy task. Elections are a good shortcut to read what is going on in society, to measure the importance and strength of alternative demands, to evaluate trends and exchanges of votes between parties making competing offers. Yet if all parties limit their presence to only half of the territory, it is hardly possible to read and interpret the election results and to be responsive to them. Results are therefore not read and evaluated at the Belgian level but at the substate level only. Elections produce two results. Government formation must then try to be responsive to these two different results and sometimes even different trends. For a very long time the almost natural response to the two different electorates was a coalition between the Christian democrats, strong in Flanders, and the socialists, strong in Wallonia. The liberal view on society – coming second or third in both language communities' level – was therefore kept out of power for a long time (Deschouwer, 1997).

The impact of the split party system on democratic legitimacy and accountability is also quite important when the political institutions themselves are the issue of the debate. Parties of each language community are quite easily seduced into promising to deliver a state structure that fits nicely into the dominant vision and perception of their own language community. There is nobody to contradict these proposals, except the parties of the other language community who communicate with the voters of their own community only. The split party system has removed most incentives for moderation. Yet at the end of the day the decisions on the state structure, on the distribution of competences, on the status of regions and communities, on the status and boundaries of Brussels, on the meaning and interpretation of language facilities, and on the extent of fiscal and financial autonomy and redistribution all have to be reached by consensus between the leaders of the two language communities. The gap between electoral pledges and promises kept is enormous. Compromising involves a loss of face that goes far beyond the normal double-role played by political parties in competitive democracies. In the bipolar Belgium, with its split party system and split public opinion, elected politicians wanting to govern at the federal level must first solve the problems that they have created themselves. Long and painstaking negotiations and incredibly complex compromises that allow for a different reading and understanding in north and south are the result of that.

This illusion of unilateralism is striking. It can also be seen in the attempts by both language groups to defend a more 'normal' functioning of democracy whenever they see the chance to do so. The consociational logic always blocks and excludes the use of majority power. Yet majority power is a much more straightforward technique and easier to explain than an obligation to compromise, especially when voters only receive one of the two party political offers. And there are clear and visible majorities in Belgium. The Flemish are a majority in Belgium and are therefore easily tempted to defend their claims by telling the voters that in a true democracy the will of the majority has to be respected. The francophones are a majority in the Brussels region, and are therefore easily tempted to say that the reserved seats for the Flemish in the Brussels parliament and the parity in the Brussels government are an unacceptable overrepresentation of the minority. Francophones are a majority in a number of Flemish municipalities around Brussels. That leads them to defending the principle that they have the full right to decide on – for instance – the way in which language facilities are to be offered to their inhabitants. Majoritarian democracy is much easier to defend and to explain than consociational democracy with its checks and balances and mutual vetoes that silence the majority. For populist protest parties, the Belgian consociational federation is therefore a very fertile ground, especially in the community that is not able to use its demographic majority.

New institutions and capacity for decision-making

The elements that make Belgium a country that is not easy to govern are far from new. In that difficult context the Belgian political institutions have proved after all that they have the capacity to contain the tensions when really necessary. That has often taken some time and the price paid for the time spent on solving the internal territorial and linguistic problems has been high in budgetary terms. But after all, the price paid might be worth it. Other divided societies have proved less capable of controlling tensions related to identity and territorial claims.

An important question is therefore to what extent the Belgian political system will in the future still be able to display this capacity to govern the divided Belgian society. The question is relevant because the context of today and tomorrow is not fully identical to the context of the 1970s and 1980s. The basic ingredients of the conflict remain the same and the basic rules for dealing with it – power sharing and mutual vetoes – have not changed. Yet there have been a number of developments that might render the management of Belgium more difficult in the future. There is some irony in this, because the developments that could stall the machine are exactly those institutions that have been put in place to deal with the divided society. The Belgium of the past that was able to find a way out of periods of gridlock was a unitary state. The Belgium of today and tomorrow is a federal state. And a few characteristics of that federal state are not improving the capacity to govern.

One of the crucial differences between the old Belgium and the new federal Belgium is that there is now more than one centre of power. In the unitary Belgium the centre of power and the place where all policies and all reforms had to be decided on was the national government. The formation and the survival of the national government needed a formal agreement between the two language groups. In the absence of it all the politics of Belgium slowly came to a total standstill. The longer it took to find a solution, the more dramatic the absence of it became. Lack of agreement between the two language groups thus led to a 'generalized policy paralysis' (Jans, 2001). That made the pressure so intense that politicians were obliged to find incredible compromises that put a temporary end to the gridlock.

In the current federal state power is of course not concentrated in one government. There are several substate governments and they have substantial powers and competences. The power to define and to change federal institutions has remained in the sole hands of the federal government and parliament. Yet if at this level a solution is not found, the consequences are far less dramatic. It does not imply a generalized policy paralysis but a 'single policy paralysis'. There is no solution for a constitutional problem, and that's it. All policies controlled by the substate level can be continued without any problem. Of course the absence of a working federal government is a problem in the long run, but the recent political history of Belgium has shown that it is indeed possible to survive for quite a long time with just a caretaker government. The pressure to form one is quite low, and a community really wanting to see a demand realized cannot use the danger of a generalized policy paralysis to force the other community to sit down and talk.

There is also an international dimension to this much lower sense of urgency to have a working government at the federal level. Belgium is a member state of the European Union, and that means that many powers – especially those defining the rules of economic and financial exchanges – have been transferred to a level above and outside the Belgian government. If in the 1970s or the 1980s the Belgian state showed signs of weakness and lack of capacity or willingness to keep its financial policies under control, speculative attacks on the Belgian national currency could provide an extreme pressure to find the next compromise that would allow the Belgian state to keep on functioning. The Belgian currency has now disappeared and has been replaced by the euro. And some domestic troubles in a small country of the eurozone are not enough to question the strength of the euro on the world's financial markets. Belgium is anchored in the safe European haven, but exactly that safe harbour reduces the need to solve the Belgian problems. Belgium can afford to have its periods of instability last much longer than before. Its capacity for decision-making in constitutional matters has therefore declined.

The presence of the substate level also allows for keeping the constitutional negotiations out of the central level and for transferring them to an intergovernmental forum. This is a good way to keep the pressure almost completely off the federal government, but does not at all increase the capacity to find a solution. First, there is never a clear agreement on exactly which governments have the right to sit around the negotiating table. Flanders will defend a dialogue between the two communities, while francophones will want the regions and thus also Brussels as a full partner at the table. Second, the rules of decision-making – whether there are two or three partners – do not change. Only consensus and the removal of the vetoes can lead to an agreement. And finally, if intergovernmental negotiations fail, there is no other consequence than this single failure and the frustration for those who wanted them to succeed. But nothing can put pressure on an intergovernmental forum to succeed at any price. Failure is – even more than when it occurs in the federal government – a single policy paralysis. The very fact that Belgium is a federal state – which is the result of attempts to contain and to pacify the tensions between the language communities – reduces tremendously its capacity to further deal with these tensions.

The presence of more than one locus of power is one consequence of the introduction of the federal logic into the Belgian state. The organization of elections for these new levels is another consequence that has also affected the capacity for decision-making. It interacts with the split party system. As explained in Chapter 6, the effect of elections at different levels was in a first phase kept under control by organizing all elections on the same day and especially also by forming congruent coalitions, by making sure that the same parties governed at all levels. This also meant that federal and regional elections could not develop a dynamic of their own.

The different timing of five years for the regions and four years for the federal parliament was indeed meant to give the elections their own flavour. There are however two related factors that have made this fail. The first is the choice of the parties to go to each of the elections with to a large extent the same political personnel. The top politicians always occupy a visible place on the list, but do not necessarily take up the seat for which they are elected. Parties then reshuffle their personnel in the governments in which they are present after every election, irrespective of the level at which it was organized. This choice is of course related to the absence of statewide parties. Even if the personnel were different and the campaign themes were nicely chosen to fit the competences of the level for which the assemblies are being elected, the voters would always have exactly the same party offer and the results would always be read and interpreted at the same level. For the francophone parties, there is some difference between elections for Wallonia and Brussels on the one hand and for the federal parliament (meaning for the federal MPs of the French community) on the other, but for Flanders there is hardly any difference between electing the members of the Flemish regional parliament or electing the Flemish members of the federal parliament.

The decoupling of the elections since 2003 has not further differentiated them, but has led to a further weakening of the capacity for decision-making. Government coalitions at the different levels have become increasingly incongruent. This has introduced a new type of conflict into the Belgian federation: conflicts between governments. Intergovernmental tensions are not new, but with congruent coalitions they were kept under control inside the governing parties. With incongruent coalitions the conflicts between governments are always also conflicts between parties. A party governing, for instance, only at the regional level and thus being in opposition at the federal level can use the relations between governments to put the federal government into a difficult position. Yet the parties governing at the federal level might be its partners in the regional government. This does not help to build trust between partners in a coalition.

The decoupling of federal and regional elections has thus introduced a sort of *permanent election campaign* into the system. Whenever elections are approaching, all parties call all hands on deck. Each election result has consequences for all the governments. All coalitions are constantly composed of parties that are getting ready to go to the voters. Forming a coalition and keeping it alive in a context where the next elections are just around the corner, can however never be an easy exercise.

For the federal level this has proved to be quite problematic. If all parties are afraid to move because they fear the sanction of the voters at the next regional elections, which will kick in somewhere during the term of the new coalition, the willingness to compromise – especially on constitutional matters – is reduced to almost nothing. Gridlock is the consequence. And again: the introduction and coming of age of a federal Belgium reduces the capacity of the state to further deal with the tensions between north and south.

One last element that reduces the capacity is not related to the federal institutions, but is a more general development of the societies in north and south. Both regions still return, as always, quite different election results, but both have become quite unpredictable. The two dominating forces in north and south – Christian democrats and socialists – have lost their leading position. That means that they have lost their almost secure position in the government of their region and in the federal government. Losing a few percentages of the votes can make a huge difference. The increased competition in each of the two Belgian party systems is another element adding to the reduced willingness to play the consociational game at the federal level. Compromising means accepting a settlement that is a long way from what was promised to the voters. The sanction of the voters always comes soon, because all elections mobilize the same voters for the same parties on each side. And since the absence of a solution is not dramatic enough to put pressure on the other side to find the necessary compromise, the periods of crisis and gridlock in the new federal Belgium might be longer and deeper than they ever were in the old unitary Belgium. The federal solution has become part of the problem.

Still Belgium?

There are two stories to be told about Belgium (Peters, 2006). The first one is the story of a prosperous European country that has been able to solve its identity conflicts by crafting institutions that accept the differences and allow them to be kept at the low tension level where they have always been. The second story is one of a country that often does not believe in itself. The attitude of the population in the political system alternates between high trust and deep distrust. Trust is also not very high at the elite level. The new Belgium is far from the ideal for both language groups. Both are frustrated by the strength – the veto power – of the other to bend the state structures in their direction. And furthermore the new federal institutions and increased competition in each of the two party systems offer few if any incentives to display a concessionary attitude.

Where can Belgium go? What can or will the future bring? Can this divided country survive (Swenden & Jans, 2006)? That question might at first sight not be really important. Belgium is too small to bother about. Who would invent it today if it did not already exist? The relevance of the question goes far beyond Belgium though. The question whether and how divided societies can build and sustain a democratic government is one of the grand questions of our time. Belgium is not the only multinational state in the world. And finding adequate institutions for governing the European Union also involves dealing with issues such as a divided and multilingual demos (see for example Chryssochoou, 1994; Lord, 2004; Hix, 2008; Kraus, 2008).

The Belgian institutional arrangements follow (albeit not on purpose) the prescriptions of consociational theory (Lijphart, 1977; 1979; Huyse, 1971; 1981; 1986; Seiler, 1997; Deschouwer,

2002; 2006). It suggests indeed that deep societal divisions should not be ignored but explicitly recognized and respected. Granting autonomy to the segments of a divided society offers those segments the capacity and institutional means to govern themselves, especially in matters that are or could be very divisive. The central government where common policies are decided on must then be based on the principle of power sharing between the elites of the various segments of society. And if these subgroups are territorially concentrated, federal-type arrangements combining the self-rule of the substates with the common rule of the central level are a well-known practice for organizing segmental autonomy and power sharing. This is indeed the Belgian solution.

There is however no consensus on the best way to organize the politics of divided societies.

The most outspoken opposing view has been voiced by Donald Horowitz (1985; 2002). He doubts whether the granting of autonomy suffices to make the elites of the subgroups become willing to participate in power-sharing devices at the central level. One should indeed take care that an attitude of compromise in the power-sharing institutions does not entail the risk of losing power or of being challenged by more radical forces within their own segment. Horowitz therefore defends institutions that foster *pre-electoral rather than post-electoral appeasement*. The consociational logic indeed expects that elites can combine the role of preacher in their own segment with the role of prudent leadership in the joint decision-making. They must be able to play that double role and to get away with it.

Political elites in the federal Belgium with its split party system are indeed confronted with the increasing difficulty of acting like this. That difficulty is however built on the assumption that the volatile voters are moving between parties – and punishing governing parties – because of their position on the constitutional issues. Electoral research does reveal though that these matters are not a top priority for the vast majority of voters (Swyngedouw, 2008). Only the voters of the regionalist parties are motivated primarily by identity issues. Even the voters of the separatist Vlaams Belang are more concerned with security, migration and law and order than with the demand to give Flanders its independence. Former prime ministers – who have obviously fulfilled a role in which prudent leadership had to be stressed above the good representation of their own (Flemish) identity – remain very popular in both language communities. The irony (and the democratic problem) is that this legitimacy cannot be conquered via the electoral channel, but only after having governed. But the interesting information is that defending the centre should not necessarily lead to the loss of votes and to the loss of power. Institutions that foster opportunities to also engage in a pre-electoral dialogue with voters of the other community might possibly offer more chances for reducing the gap between the identity language in the pre-electoral phase and the necessary accommodating language in the post-electoral phase (Deschouwer & Van Parijs, 2007).

So far the jury is still out on the question of which institutional arrangements are the best for governing divided societies. Debates about the best way to link a polity like the European Union to its variety of populations, identities and interests are also still very much open. The debate is important though, and all attempts to deal with the governing of a divided society can provide it with interesting examples and arguments. That might be a good – be it pure theoretical reason – to keep Belgium on the map.

But is it worth the while? Is it really necessary to go through all these pains if a much easier solution is readily available? Every political crisis increases the fears and the hopes that it will be the last one; that the regime will not be able to contain this one; that Belgium will have to call it a day. This assumes that if no agreement is found, there is still another possibility to resolve once and for all the difficult quest for constitutional reform. It assumes that there is an easy way out. That belief or the fear that the country might be split up, is an interesting illustration of the illusion of unilateralism that is being fostered by the federal institutions. It is the belief that since Belgium cannot be as one would like it to be, the post-Belgium will take away the sources of frustration. It assumes that ending the life of Belgium can be done without having to find an agreement on the components and on the way to draw the territorial lines between them. Can Belgium be split into the two language communities, with Brussels as part of Flanders? That is quite unlikely because it would mean that the Brussels population prefers – at times of high tension – to side with Flanders rather than with Wallonia. Can Belgium be split into a Flanders without Brussels and a Wallonia plus Brussels? That is unlikely. If Flanders were not to claim or need Brussels, the structures of Belgium could be much less complicated. Both communities see Brussels as their (capital) city and that is what has created the double federation of regions and communities. One can think of many different varieties of the territorial organization of the post-Belgium, including Brussels as a European 'District of Columbia', but all assume that the existing regions and communities would lose something that they have claimed and defended and – be it partially – secured in Belgium.

Of course the end of a country is a real possibility. History has taught that territories can be divided, that substates can break away. The very creation of Belgium was the result of a separation from the Kingdom of the Netherlands. But breaking it up, dividing the territory and the economy and the public debt among newly created entities is certainly not an easy way out. It requires a compromise that cannot have the merits of being vague and ambiguous to allow both sides to call it some sort of victory. There is no simple way to govern Belgium and there is no simple way out. What more is needed for a political class to voice its distrust of a system in which it finds itself entrapped?

Governing Belgium will thus never be easy. Governing a divided society is a messy affair, always balancing between conflict and compromise, between fear and hope, between great leadership and dirty moves, between satisfaction and frustration, between populism and prudence. One must be brave to survive all that. But maybe the Belgians are the bravest of the Gauls after all.

Bibliography

Ackaert, J. (2006), *Politiek in mijn gemeente*, Leuven: Davidsfonds

Ackaert, J., Reynaert, H., De Ceuninck, K., Steyvers, K. & Valcke, T. (2007), De gemeenteraadsverkiezingen van 8 oktober 2006, *Res Publica*, 49(2–3): 413–42

Albrecht, J. (2008), *Slank, zwaarlijvig of onbegrensd? Een analyse van de publieke tewerkstelling in België tussen 2001 en 2007*, Brussels: Itinera Institute

Andeweg, R. (2000), Consociational democracy, *Annual Review of Political Science*, 3: 509–36

Andeweg R. & Irwin G. (2005), *Governance and politics of the Netherlands*, Basingstoke: Palgrave Macmillan

Beaufays, J. (1998), Petite histoire d'un jeune état binational, in M. Martiniello & M. Swyngedouw (eds), *Où va la Belgique? Les soubresauts d'une petite démocratie européenne*, Paris: L'Harmattan, pp. 15–30

Beke, W. (2005), *De Christelijke Volkspartij. De ziel van een zuil*, Leuven: Universitaire Pers

Béland, D. & Lecours, A. (2008), *Nationalism and social policy. The politics of territorial solidarity*, Oxford: Oxford University Press

Beyers, J. & Bursens, P. (2006), The European rescue of the federal state: how Europeanization shapes the Belgian state, *West European Politics*, 29(5): 1057–78

Billiet, J. (1981), Kenmerken en grondslagen van het sociaal-cultureel katholicisme, in J. Servaes (ed.), *Van ideologie tot macht*, Leuven: Kritak, pp. 29–61

Billiet, J. (1982), Verzuiling en politiek: theoretische beschouwingen over België na 1945, *Belgisch Tijdschrift voor Nieuwste Geschiedenis*, 13: 85–118

Blondel, J. (1968), Party systems and patterns of government in Western democracies, *Canadian Journal of Political Science*, 1: 180–203

Boudens, R. (1975), *Kardinaal Mercier en de Vlaamse Beweging*, Leuven: Davidsfonds

Bouveroux, J. (1996), *Van zwarte zondag tot zwarte zondag*, Antwerp: Icarus

Bouveroux, J. (2003), *Van zwarte zondag tot paarsgroen*, Antwerp: Icarus

Brans, M. & Steen, T. (2006), From incremental to Copernican reform? Changes to the position and role of senior civil servants in the Belgian federal administration, in E.C. Page & V. Wright (eds), *From the active to the enabling state*, Basingstoke: Palgrave Macmillan

Brans, M., Pelgrims, C. & Hoet, D. (2005), Politico-administrative relations under coalition governments. The case of Belgium, in G. Peters, T.

Verheijen & L. Vass (eds), *Coalitions of the unwilling? Politicians and civil servants in coalition governments*, Bratislava: Nispacee, pp. 207–36

Brans, M., De Visscher, C. & Vancoppenolle, D. (2006), Administrative reform in Belgium: maintenance or modernisation?, *West European Politics*, 29(5): 979–98

Brinckman, B., Albers, I., Samyn, S. & Verschelden, W. (2008), *De zestien is voor u*, Tielt: Lannoo

Bursens, P. (2002), Belgium's adaptation to the EU. Does federalism constrain Europeanisation?, *Res Publica*, 44(4): 575–98

Bursens, P. & Geeraerts, K. (2006), EU environmental policy-making in Belgium: Who keeps the gate?, *Journal of European Integration*, 28(2): 150–79

Cantillon, B. & De Maesschalck, V. (2006), Social redistribution in federalised Belgium, *West European Politics*, 29(5): 1034–56

Chryssochoou, D.N. (1994), Democracy and symbiosis in the European Union: towards a confederal consociation, *West European Politics*, 17(4): 1–14

Coffé, H. (2005a), Do individual factors explain the different success of the two Belgian extreme right parties, *Acta Politica*, 40(1): 74–93

Coffé, H. (2005b), *Extreemrechts in Vlaanderen en Wallonië. Het verschil*, Roeselare: Roularta Books

Converse, P. & Dupeux, G. (1962), Politicization of the electorate in France and the United States, *Public Opinion Quarterly*, 26(1) (Spring): 1–23

Coolsaet, R. (2001), *België en zijn buitenlandse politiek, 1830–2000*, Leuven: Van Halewyck

Coolsaet, R. (2004), Trade and diplomacy: the Belgian case, *International Studies Perspectives*, 5(1): 61–65

Covell, M. (1993), Political conflict and constitutional engineering in Belgium, *The International Journal of the Sociology of Language*, 104: 65–86

Crisp (1971), Le FDF-RW, *Courrier Hebdomodaire du Crisp*, No. 516–517

Crombez, C. & Lebbe, J. (2006), Policy processes and positions for Convention and IGC: Belgium, in S. Hix & T. König (eds), *Preference formation and European Constitution building*, London: Routledge

D'Hoore, M. (1997), Le paradoxe libéral. Essay d'analyse de l'evolution du PRL (1979–1997), in P. Delwit & J.M. De Waele (eds), *Les partis politiques en Belgique*, Brussels: Editions de l'ULB, pp. 103–26

Dandoy, R. & Fournier, B. (2008), Démocratie locale: quelles perceptions des changements récents?, in B. Rihoux, J. Buelens & K. Deschouwer (eds), *Entre l'électeur et le quartier général. Les sections locales des partis et les élections communales de 2006*, Brussels: VUB Press, pp. 167–82

De Schaepdrijver, S. (1997), *De Groote Oorlog: het Koninkrijk België tijdens de Eerste Wereldoorlog*, Antwerp: Atlas

De Visscher, C. (2003), *La relation entre l'autorité publique et la haute administration*, Ghent: Academia Press

De Winter, L. (1988), Belgium: democracy or oligarchy, in M. Gallagher (ed.), *Candidate selection in comparative perspective. The secret garden of politics*, London: Sage, pp. 20–46

De Winter, L. (1996), Party encroachment on the executive and legislative branch in the Belgian polity, *Res Publica,* pp. 325–52

De Winter, L. (1997), Le CVP : entre gestion et conviction, in P. Delwit & J.M. De Waele (eds), *Les partis politiques en Belgique*, Brussels: Editions de l'ULB, pp. 65–82

De Winter, L. (1998a), Parliament and government in Belgium: prisoners of partitocracy, in P. Norton (ed.), *Parliaments and governments in Western Europe*, London: Frank Cass, pp. 97–122

De Winter, L. (1998b), The Volksunie and the dilemma between policy success and electoral survival in Flanders, in L. De Winter & H. Türsan, *Regionalist Parties in Western Europe*, London: Routledge, pp. 28–50

De Winter, L. (2002), Parties and government formation, portfolio allocation, and policy definition, in K.R. Luther & F. Müller-Rommel (eds), *Political parties in the new Europe. Political and analytical challenges*, Oxford University Press, pp. 171–206

De Winter, L. (2006a), In memoriam the Volksunie 1954–2001: Death by overdose of success, in L. De Winter, M. Gomez-Reion Cachafeiro and P. Lynch (eds), *Autonomist parties in Europe: Identity politics and the revival of the territorial cleavage*, Barcelona: ICPS

De Winter, L. (2006b), Multi-level party competition and coordination in Belgium, in C. Jeffery & D. Hough, *Devolution and electoral politics*, Manchester: Manchester University Press, pp. 76–95

De Winter, L. & Dumont, P. (2006a), Regeringsformatie, in E. Witte & A. Meynen (eds), *België na 1945*, Antwerp: Standaard Uitgeverij, pp. 289–329

De Winter, L. & Dumont, P. (2006b), Do Belgian parties undermine the democratic chain of delegation?, *West European Politics*, 29(5): 957–76

De Witte, L. (1999), *De moord op Lumumba*, Leuven (English translation as *The Assassination of Lumumba*, London 2001; French translation as *L'assassinat de Lumumba*, Paris 2000)

Dehaene, J.L. (2004), *De Europese uitdaging. Van uitbreiding tot integratie?* Leuven: Van Halewyck

Delwit, P. (1997), La voie étroite d'une refondation du parti socialiste, in P. Delwit & J.M. De Waele (eds), *Les partis politiques en Belgique*, Brussels: Editions de l'ULB, pp. 25–44

Delwit, P. & De Waele, J.M. (1997a), L'installation durable d'un jeune parti: Ecolo, in P. Delwit & J.M. De Waele (eds), *Les partis politiques en Belgique*, Brussels: Editions de l'ULB, pp. 155–72

Delwit, P. & De Waele, J.M. (1997b), Origines, évolutions et devenir des partis politiques en Belgique, in P. Delwit & J.M. De Waele (eds), *Les partis politiques en Belgique*, Brussels: Editions de l'ULB, pp. 7–24

Delwit, P. & Van Haute, E. (2008), Greens in a rainbow: the impact of participation in government of the green parties in Belgium, in K. Deschouwer (ed.), *New parties in government. In power for the first time*, London: Routledge, pp. 104–20

Depauw, S. (2002), *Rebellen in het parlement. Fractiecohesie in de Kamer van Volksvertegenwoordigers (1991–1995)*, Leuven: Universitaire Pers

Deschouwer, K. (1984), Continuïteit en contradictie: het FDF in de jaren tachtig, *Taal en Sociale Integratie*, 7: 105–30

Deschouwer, K. (1994a) The decline of consociationalism and the reluctant modernization of the Belgian mass parties, in R. Katz & P. Mair (eds), *How parties organize: adaptation and change in party organizations in Western democracies*, London: Sage, pp. 80–108

Deschouwer, K. (1994b), The termination of coalitions in Belgium, *Res Publica*, 36(1): 43–55

Deschouwer, K. (1997), Une fédération sans fédérations de partis, in S. Jaumain (ed.), *La réforme de l'Etat … et après? L'impact des débats constitutionnels en Belgique et au Canada*, Brussels: Editions de l'ULB, pp. 77–83

Deschouwer, K. (1998), De parlementaire onderzoekscommissies en de politiek, in L. Huyse, C. Fijnaut & R. Verstraete (eds), *Parlementaire onderzoekscommissies. Mogelijkheden, grenzen en risico's*, Leuven: Van Halewijck, pp. 12–35

Deschouwer, K. (1999), From consociationalism to federalism: how the Belgian parties won, in R. Luther & K. Deschouwer (eds), *Party elites in divided societies Political parties in consociational democracies*, London: Routledge, pp. 74–107

Deschouwer, K. (2000), Belgium's quasi-regional elections of June 1999, *Regional and Federal Studies*, 10(1): 125–32

Deschouwer, K. (2002), Falling apart together. The changing nature of Belgian consociationalism, 1961–2000, in J. Steiner & T. Ertman (eds), *Consociationalism and corporatism in Western Europe. Still the Politics of Accommodation?*, Special issue of *Acta Politica*, 37: 68–85

Deschouwer, K. (2005a), Kingdom of Belgium, in J. Kincaid & A. Tarr (eds) *Constitutional Origins, Structure, and Change in Federal Countries*, Montreal & Kingston: McGill-Queen's University Press, pp. 48–75

Deschouwer, K. (2005b), The unintended consequences of consociational federalism: the case of Belgium, in I. O'Flynn & D. Russell, *Power sharing. New challenges for divided societies*, London/Ann Arbor: Pluto Press, pp. 92–106

Deschouwer, K. (2006), And the peace goes on? Consociational democracy and Belgian politics in the 21st century, *West European Politics*, 29(5): 895–911

Deschouwer, K. (2007), Le VLD ou l'impasse structurelle du libéralisme en Flandre, in P. Delwit & J.M. De Waele (eds), *Les partis politiques en Belgique*, Brussels: Editions de l'ULB, pp. 127–38

Deschouwer, K. (2009a), Coalition formation and congruence in a multi-layered setting: Belgium 1995–2008, *Regional and Federal Studies* 19(1): 13–35

Deschouwer, K. (2009b), National electoral trends in decentralized states? The cases of Belgium and Spain, in W. Swenden & B. Maddens (eds), *Territorial party politics in Western Europe*, Basingstoke: Palgrave Macmillan

Deschouwer, K. (2009c), The rise and fall of the Belgian regionalist parties, *Regional and Federal Studies* (forthcoming)

Deschouwer, K. & Buelens, J. (2002), The Belgian Greens in government, in F. Müller-Rommel & T. Poguntke, *Green Parties in National Governments*, Special Issue of *Environmental Politics*, 11(1): 112–32 (also as book: Frank Cass, London)

Deschouwer, K. & Buelens J. (2007), Torn between two levels. Political parties and incongruent coalitions in Belgium, in Deschouwer, K. & Jans, M.T. (eds), *Politics beyond the state*, Brussels: VUB Press

Deschouwer, K. & De Winter, L. (1998), La corruption politique et le clientélisme: le spectre italien?, in M. Martiniello & M. Swyngedouw (eds), *Où va la Belgique? Les soubresauts d'une petite démocratie européenne*, Paris: L'Harmattan, pp. 139–52

Deschouwer, K. & Rihoux, J. (2008), Les sections locales des partis, de la hiérarchie à la stratarchie, in B. Rihoux, J. Buelens & K. Deschouwer (eds), *Entre l'électeur et le quartier général. Les sections locales des partis et les élections communales de 2006*, Brussels: VUB Press

Deschouwer, K. & Van Assche, M. (2008), Hard but hardly relevant. Party based Euroscepticism in Belgian politics, in P. Taggart & A. Szczerbiak (eds), *Opposing Europe? The comparative party politics of Euroscepticism*, Oxford: Oxford University Press, pp. 75–92

Deschouwer, K. & Van Parijs, P. (2007), Une circonscription fédérale pour tous les belges, *La Revue Nouvelle* (April)

Deschouwer, K. & Verdonck, M. (2003), Patterns and principles of fiscal and financial federalism in Belgium, *Regional and Federal Studies*, 13(4): 91–110

Deschouwer, K. & Wille, F. (2007), Het beschermde dorp. Nationale tendensen bij lokale verkiezingen in België, *Res Publica*, 49(1): 67–88

Destatte, P. (1997), *L'identité wallonne*, Charleroi: Institut Destrée

Dobbelaere, K. (1979), Professionalization and secularization in the Belgian Catholic pillar, *Japanese Journal of Religious Studies*, 6: 39–64

Dumont, P., De Winter, L. & Ackaert, J. (2008), La formation des coalitions communales: les pratiques anciennes en héritage, in B. Rihoux, J. Buelens & K. Deschouwer (eds), *Entre l'électeur et le quartier général. Les sections locales des partis et les élections communales de 2006*, Brussels: VUB Press, pp. 117–46

Dumoulin, M., Gérard, M., Van den Wijngaert, M. & Dujardin, V. (2006), *Nouvelle histoire de Belgique Volume II: 1905–1950*, Brussels: Complexe

Dumoulin, M., Dujardin, V. Destatte, P., Beyen, M. & Vanthemsche, G. (2007), *Nouvelle histoire de la Belgique: 1950 à nos jours*, Brussels: Complexe

Dupuis, P. & Humblet, J. (1998), *Un siècle de mouvement wallon (1890–1997)*, Gerpinnes: Quorum

Emerson, M. & Tocci, N. (2003), *Cyprus as lighthouse of the East Mediterranean: Shaping re-unification and EU accession together*, Brussels: CEPS

Erk, J. (2005), From Vlaams Blok to Vlaams Belang: The Belgian far-right renames itself, *West European Politics*, 28(3): 493–502

Eurobarometer surveys (ec.europa.eu/public opinion)

Eurostat (epp.eurostat.ec.europa.eu)

Ewans, M. (2002), *European atrocity, African catastrophe. Leopold II, the Congo Free State and its aftermath*, London: Routledge

Federal Public Service of Labour (2008), *Sociale verkiezingen 2008. Definitieve en goedgekeurde resultaten*, Brussels: Federale Overheidsdienst Werkgelegenheid, Arbeid en Sociaal Overleg (www.werk.belgie.be)

Fiers, S. (1998), *Partijvoorzitters in België, of 'Le parti c'est moi'*, Leuven: Afdeling Politologie

Fiers, S. (2001). Carrièrepatronen van Belgische parlementsleden in een multi-level omgeving (1979–99), *Res Publica*, 43(1): 171–92

Fiers, S. (2006), Evoluties in het parlementaire bestel, in E. Witte & A. Meynen (eds), *De geschiedenis van België na 1945*, Antwerp: Standaard Uitgeverij, pp. 263–88

Fiers, S. & Krouwel, A. (2005), The Low Countries: From prime ministers to president-minister, in T. Poguntke & P. Webb (eds), *The presidentialization of politics. A comparative study of modern democracies*, Oxford: Oxford University Press

Fiers, S. & Reynaert, H. (2006), *Wie zetelt? De gekozen politieke elite in Vlaanderen doorgelicht*, Leuven: Lannoo Campus

Fijnaut, C., Huyse, L. & Verstraete, R. (1998), *Parlementaire onderzoekscommissies. Mogelijkheden, grenzen en risico's*, Leuven: Van Halewyck

Flora, P., Kuhnle, S. & Urwin, D. (1999), *State formation, nation-building and mass politics in Europe. The theory of Stein Rokkan*, Oxford: Oxford University Press

Franck, C., Leclerq, H. & Vandevievere, C. (2003), Belgium: Europeanization and Belgian federalism, in W. Wessels, A. Maures & J. Mittag (eds), *Fifteen into one? The European Union and its member states*, Manchester: Manchester University Press, pp. 69–91

Frognier, A. & Aish, A.M. (1994) (eds), *Elections. La fêlure? Enquête sur le comportement électoral des Wallons et des Francophones*, Brussels: De Boeck

Frognier, A. & Aish, A.M. (1999) (eds), *Des élections en trompe-l'œil. Enquête sur le comportement électoral des Wallons et des Francophones*, Brussels: De Boeck

Gagnon, A.G., Guibernau, M. & Rocher, F. (2003), *The conditions of diversity in multinational democracies*, Montreal: The Institute for Research on Public Policy

Gallagher, M. (1975), Disproportionality in a proportional representation system: the Irish experience, *Political Studies*, 4: 501–13

Georges, Y. (1997), Les tribulations existentielles du parti social chrétien, in P. Delwit & J.M. De Waele (eds), *Les partis politiques en Belgique*, Brussels: Editions de l'ULB, pp. 83–102

Gerard, E. (1985), *De katholieke partij in crisis. Partijpolitiek leven in België (1918–1940)*, Leuven: Kritak

Gerard, E. (1995), Van katholieke partij naar CVP, in Dewachter W. et al. (eds), *Tussen staat en maatschappij 1945–1995*. *Christen-Democratie in België*, Tielt: Lannoo, pp. 13–27

Gerard-Libois, J. & Gotovitch, J. (1971), *L'an 40. La Belgique occupée*, Brussels: Crisp

Gondola, C.D. (2002), *The History of Congo*, Westport, CT: Greenwood Press

Govaert, S. (1997a), La Volksunie, in P. Delwit & J.M. De Waele (eds), *Les partis politiques en Belgique*, Brussels: Editions de l'ULB, pp. 185–96

Govaert, S. (1997b), Le Socialistische Partij, in P. Delwit & J.M. De Waele (eds), *Les partis politiques en Belgique*, Brussels: Editions de l'ULB, pp. 45–64

Govaert, S. (2002), La Volksunie. Du déclin à la disparition (1993–2001), *Courrier Hebdomadaire du CRISP*

Grodzins, M. (1966), *The American System: A New View of the Government of the United States*, New York: Rand McNally

Hasquin, H. (1999), *La Wallonie, son histoire*, Brussels: Pire

Hellemans, S. (1990), *De strijd om de moderniteit. Sociale bewegingen en verzuiling in Europa sinds 1800*, Leuven: Universitaire Pers

Henry, A. (1990), *Histoire des mots Wallons et Wallonie*, Institut Jules Destrée, Coll. «Notre histoire», Mont-sur-Marchienne

Heylen, W. & Van Hecke, S. (2008), *Regeringen die niet regeren. Het malgoverno van de Belgische politiek*, Leuven: Lannoo Campus

Hix, S. (2008), *What's wrong with the European Union and how to fix it*, Cambridge: Polity

Hochschild, A. (1998), *King Leopold's ghosts. A story of greed, terror and heroism in Colonial Africa*, New York: Houghton Mifflin

Hooghe, L. (2004), Belgium: Hollowing the center, in U. Amoretti & N. Bermeo (eds), *Federalism and territorial cleavages*, Baltimore: Johns Hopkins University Press, pp. 55–92

Hooghe, M. (1997), *Het witte ongenoegen. Hoop en illusie van een uniek experiment*, Groot-Bijgaarden: Scoop

Hooghe, M. & Pelleriaux, K. (1998), Compulsory voting in Belgium: An application of the Lijphart thesis. *Electoral Studies*, 17: 419–24.

Hooghe, M., Maddens, B. & Noppe, J. (2006), Why parties adapt: Electoral reform, party finance and party strategy in Belgium, *Electoral Studies*, 25: 351–68

Horowitz, D.L. (1985), *Ethnic groups in conflict*, Berkeley, CA: University of California Press

Horowitz, D.L. (2002), Constitutional design; proposals versus processes, in A. Reynolds (ed.), *The architecture of democracy. Constitutional design, conflict management, and democracy*, Oxford: Oxford University Press, pp. 15–36

Huyse, L. (1971), *Passiviteit, pacificatie en verzuildheid in de Belgische politiek*, Antwerp: Standaard Wetenschappelijke Uitgeverij

Huyse, L. (1981), Political conflict in bicultural Belgium, in A. Lijphart (ed.), *Conflict and coexistence in Belgium. The dynamics of a culturally divided society*, Berkeley, CA: Institute of International studies, University of California, pp. 107–26.

Huyse, L. (1986), *De gewapende vrede. Politiek in België na 1945*, Leuven: Kritak

Huyse, L. (1987), *De verzuiling voorbij*, Leuven: Kritak

Jans, M.T. (2001), Leveled domestic politics. Comparing institutional reform and ethnonational conflicts in Canada and Belgium (1960–1989). *Res Publica*, **43**(1): 37–58

Jans, M.T. & Tombeur, H. (2000), Living apart together. The Belgian intergovernmental cooperation in the domains of environment and economy, in D. Braun (ed.), *Public policy and federalism*, Aldershot: Ashgate, pp. 142–76

Janssens, R. (2001), *Taalgebruik in Brussel. Taalverhoudingen, taalverschuivingen en taalidentiteit in een meertalige stad*, Brussel: VUB Press

Jones, E. (2002), Consociationalism, corporatism and the fate of Belgium, *Acta Politica*, **37**: 86–103

Katz, R., Mair, P. et.al. (1992), The membership of political parties in European democracies, 1960–1990, *European Journal of Political Research*, **2**: 329–45

Keating, M., Loughlin, J. & Deschouwer, K. (2003), *Culture, institutions and developments: A study of eight European regions*, London: Edward Elgar

Kerremans, B. (2000), Determining a European policy in a multi-level setting: the case of specialized coordination in Belgium, *Regional and Federal Studies*, **10**(1): 36–61

Kerremans, B. & Beyers, J. (1996), The Belgian sub-national entities in the European Union: 'second' or 'third level players'?, *Journal of Regional and Federal Studies*, **6**(2): 41–55

Kerremans, B. & Beyers, J. (2001), The Belgian permanent representation in the European Union: Mailbox, messenger or representative, in. K. Hussein, A. Menon, G. Peters & V. Wright (eds), *National coordination in the EU: The EU level*, Oxford: Oxford University Press, pp. 191–210

Kesteloot, C. & Colignon, A. (1997), Le FDF : échec d'une expérience pluraliste, in P. Delwit & J.M. De Waele (eds), *Les partis politiques en Belgique*, Brussels: Editions de l'ULB, pp. 173–84

Kesteloot, C. (1998), The growth of the Walloon Movement, in Deprez K. & Vos, L (eds), *Nationalism in Belgium. Shifting identities, 1780–1995*, Basingstoke: Macmillan – now Palgrave Macmillan, pp. 139–52

Kesteloot, C. (2004), *Au nom de la Wallonie et de Bruxelles français. Les origines du FDF*, Brussels: Complexe/CEGES

Kozviridze, T. (2002), Europeanization of federal institutional relationships in Belgium, Germany and Austria, *Regional and Federal Studies*, **12**(3): 128–55

Kraus, P. (2008), *A union of diversity. Language, identity and polity-building in Europe*, Cambridge: Cambridge University Press

Lijphart A. (1969), Consociational democracy, *World Politics*, **21**(2): 207–25

Lijphart, A. (1977), *Democracy in plural societies. A comparative exploration*, New Haven, CT: Yale University Press

Lijphart, A. (1981a) (ed.), *Conflict and coexistence in Belgium. The dynamics of a culturally divided society*. Berkeley, CA: Institute of International Studies, University of California

Lijphart, A. (1981b), Introduction: the Belgian example of cultural coexistence in comparative perspective, in Lijphart A. (ed.), *Conflict and coexistence in Belgium. The dynamics of a culturally divided society*. Berkeley, CA: Institute of International Studies, University of Califorina pp. 1–12

Lijphart, A. (1999), *Patterns of democracy. Government forms and performance in thirty-six countries*. New Haven, CT: Yale University Press

Linder, W. (1994), *Swiss democracy. Possible solutions to conflict in multicultural societies*, Basingstoke: Macmillan – now Palgrave Macmillan

Lipset, S.M. & Rokkan, S. (1967), *Party systems and voter alignments*, New York: The Free Press

Lord, C. (2004), *A democratic audit of the European Union*, Basingstoke: Palgrave Macmillan

Lorwin, V. (1966), Belgium: Religion, class and language in national politics, in Dahl, R. (ed.), *Political oppositions in Western democracies*, New Haven, CT: Yale University Press, pp.147–87

Lorwin, V. (1974a), Segmented pluralism: Ideological cleavages and political cohesion in the smaller European democracies, in K. McRae (ed.) *Consociational democracy. Political accommodation in segmented societies,* Toronto: McClelland & Stewart, p. 34

Lorwin, V. (1974b), Belgium: Conflict and compromise, in K. Mc Rae (ed.), *Consociational democracy. Political accommodation in segmented societies*, Toronto: McClelland & Stewart, p. 179

Luther, K.R. & Müller, W. (1992), *Politics in Austria. Still a case of consociationalism?*, London: Routledge

Luyckx, T. (1985), *Politieke geschiedenis van België,* Antwerp: Kluwer

Luyten, D. (1995), *Sociaal-economisch overleg in België sedert 1918*, Brussels: VUB Press

Luyten, D. (2006), Corporatisme, neocorporatisme, competitief corporatisme: sociale regulering sinds 1945, in E. Witte & A. Meynen (eds), *De geschiedenis van België na 1945*, Antwerp: Standaard Uitgeverij, pp. 365–94

Mabille, X. (1986), *Histoire politique de la Belgique. Facteurs et acteurs de changement*, Brussels: Crisp

Maddens, B. & Weekers, K. (2006), De overheidsfinanciering van het Vlaams Blok/Belang, *Samenleving en Politiek*, 5: 49–56

Maddens, B., Beerten, R. & Billiet, J. (1998), The national consciousness of the Flemings and the Walloons. An empirical investigation, in Deprez, K. & Vos, L., *Nationalism in Belgium. Shifting identities, 1870–1995*, Basingstoke: Macmillan – now Palgrave Macmillan, pp. 198–208

Maddens, B., Weekers, K., Fiers, S. & Vanlangenakker, I. (2007), Op zoek naar een verklaring voor de persoonlijke score van de kandidaten bij lokale verkiezingen, *Res Publica*, **49**(1): 132–49

Maes, M. (1988), *De ledenaantallen van de politieke partijen in België*, Leuven: Afdeling Politologie, Katholieke Universiteit

Maesschalck, J., Hondeghem, A. & Pelgrims, C. (2002), De evolutie naar een nieuwe politieke cultuur in België: een beleidswetenschappelijke analyse, *Beleidswetenschap: kwartaalschrift voor beleidsonderzoek en beleidspraktijk*, **16**(4): 295–317

Mair, P. (2006), Party system change, in R. Katz & W. Crotty, *Handbook of party politics*, London: Sage, pp. 63–73

Mair, P. & van Biezen, I. (2007), Party membership in twenty European democracies, 1980–2000, *Party Politics*, **7**: 5–21

McRae, K. (1986), *Conflict and compromise in multilingual societies: Belgium*, Ontario, Canada: Wilfrid Laurier Press

Meier, P. (2000), From theory to practice and back again: Gender quota and the politics of presence in Belgium, in M. Saward (ed.), *Democratic innovation*. London: Routledge

Meier, P. (2004), The contagion effect of national gender quota on similar party measures in the Belgian electoral process, *Party Politics*, **10**(3): 583–600

Meier, P. (2005a), Le système électoral belge et les rapports de genre, in B. Marques Pereira and P. Meier (eds), *Genre et politique en Belgique et en Francophonie*, Louvain-la-Neuve: Academia-Bruylant

Meier, P. (2005b), The Belgian paradox: inclusion and exclusion of gender issues, in J. Lovenduski et al. (eds), *State feminism and political representation*. Cambridge: Cambridge University Press

Murphy, A.B. (1988), *The regional dynamics of language differentiation in Belgium, a study in cultural-political geography*, Chicago, IL: University of Chicago

Noppe, J. & Wauters, B. (2002), Het uiteenvallen van de Volksunie en het ontstaan van de N-VA en Spirit, *Res Publica*, pp. 397–471

Norman, D. (2003), *The accidental constitution. The story of the European Convention*, Brussels: EuroComment

Norris, P. (2008), *Driving democracy. Do power-sharing institutions work?*, Cambridge: Cambridge University Press

Nzongola-Ntalaja, G. (2002), *The Congo from Leopold to Kabila: A people's history*, London: Zed Books

O'Flynn, I. & Russell, D. (2005) (eds), *Power sharing. New challenges for divided societies*, London: Pluto

Paldam, M. (1986), The distribution of election results and the two explanations of the cost of ruling, *European Journal of Political Economy*, **2**(1): 5–24

Pedersen, M. (1979), The dynamics of European party systems: Changing patterns of electoral volatility, *European Journal of Political Research*, **7**: 1–26

Pelgrims, C. (2001), *Ministeriële kabinetsleden en hun loopbaan*, Bruges: Die Keure

Pelgrims, C. (2006), Personal advisors of minister: More than personal loyal agents?, in B. Connaughton, G. Sootla & G.B. Peters (eds), *Politicians and civil servants in the policymaking process*. Bratislava: Nispacee, pp. 69–90

Pelgrims, C. & Dereu, S. (2006), Ministeriële kabinetten in de Copernicushervorming. De terugkeer van iets dat nooit weg was, *Burger en beleid*, 3: 25–33

Pennings, P. & Keman, H. (2003), The Dutch parliamentary elections in 2002 and 2003: The rise and decline of the Fortuyn Movement, *Acta Politica*, 38(1): 51–68

Peters, B.G. (2006), Consociationalism, corruption and chocolate: Belgian exceptionalism, *West European Politics*, 29(5): 1079–92

Pharr, S. & Putnam, R. (2000), *Disaffected democracies. What's troubling the trilateral countries?* Princeton, NJ: Princeton University Press

Pilet, J.B. (2005), The adaptation of the electoral system to the etho-linguistic evolution of the Belgian consociationalism, *Ethnopolitics*, 4(4): 397–411

Pilet, J.B. (2007), *Changer pour gagner? Les réformes électorales en Belgique*, Brussels; Editions de l'ULB

Plavsic, W. (1989), *Mijnheer de eerste minister. Geschiedenis van het ambt sinds 1830. Biografieën van de Eerste Minister van 1944 tot nu*, Tielt: Lannoo

Poirier, J. (2002), Formal mechanisms of intergovernmental relations in Belgium, *Regional and Federal Studies*, 12(3): 24–25

Quévit, M. (1982), *La Wallonie: l'indispensable autonomie*, Paris: Éd. Entente

Quévit, M. (1988), *Les causes du déclin Wallon*, Brussels: Vie Ouvrière

Rae, D. (1968), A note on the fractionalization of some European party systems. *Comparative Political Studies*, 1(4) : 413–18

Rea, A. (1997), Le front national: force éléctorale et faiblesse organisationnelle, in P. Delwit & J.M. De Waele (eds), *Les partis politiques en Belgique*, Brussels: Editions de l'ULB, pp. 197–206

Reif, K.H. & Schmitt, M. (1980), Nine second order elections. A conceptual framework for the analysis of European elections results, *European Journal of Political Research*, 8(1): 3–44

Rihoux, B. (1997), Agalev 1970–1997: entre marginalité et pouvoir, in P. Delwit & J.M. De Waele (eds), *Les partis politiques en Belgique*, Brussels: Editions de l'ULB, pp. 139–54

Rihoux, B. & Walgrave, S. (1998), *L'année blanche. Un million de citoyens blancs*, Brussels: Éditions Vie Ouvrière

Rokkan, S. (1977), Towards a generalized concept of 'verzuiling'. A preliminary note, *Political Studies*, 25: 563–70

Sartori, G. (1976), *Parties and party systems*, Cambridge: Cambridge University Press

Schmitter, P. & Lehmbruch, G. (1979) (eds), *Trends toward corporatist intermediation*, London: Sage

Seiler, D. (1997), Un système consociatif exemplaire: la Belgique, *Revue Internationale de Politique Comparée*, 4(3): 601–24

Stengers, J. (1980), *Léopold III et le gouvernement: les deux politiques belges de 1940*, Gembloux: Duculot, 1980

Stepan, A. (1999), Federalism and democracy: Beyond the U.S. model, *Journal of Democracy*, **10**(4): 19–34

Swenden, W. (2002), Asymmetric federalism and coalition making in Belgium, *Publius: The Journal of Federalism*, **32**(3): 67–88

Swenden, W. & Jans, M.T. (2006), Will it stay or will it go? Federalism and the sustainability of Belgium, *West European Politics*, **29**(5): 877–94

Swyngedouw, M. (1992), National elections in Belgium: The breakthrough of the extreme right in Flanders, *Regional and Federal Studies*, **2**(3) (Autumn): 62–75

Swyngedouw, M. (2008), *Politieke kwesties en stemgedrag: een analyse op basis van het postelectorale verkiezingsonderzoek 2007*, Leuven: Centrum voor Sociologisch Onderzoek (CeSO)

Swyngedouw, M. & Billiet, J. (2002) (eds), *De kiezer heeft zijn redenen. 13 juni 1999 en de politieke opvattingen van de Vlamingen?*, Leuven: Acco

Swyngedouw, M., Billiet, J., Carton, A. & Beerten, R. (1993) (eds), *Kiezen is verliezen. Onderzoek naar de politieke opvattingen van Vlamingen*, Leuven: Acco

Swyngedouw, M., Billiet, J., Carton, A. & Beerten, R. (1998) (eds), *De (on) redelijke kiezer. Onderzoek naar de politieke opvattingen van Vlamingen. Verkiezingen van 21 mei 1995*, Leuven: Acco

T'Hart, P. & Pijnenburg, B. (1998), *Het Heizeldrama: Rampzalig organiseren en kritieke beslissingen*, Brussels: HD Samson

Tyssens, J. (1997) *De schoolkwestie in de jaren vijftig*, Brussels: VUB Press

Uyttendaele, M. & Martens, P. (2005), *Précis De Droit Constitutionnel Belge. Regards Sur Un Système Institutionnel Paradoxal*, Brussels: Bruylandt

Van Bunder, D. (1993), *De officiële inkomsten van de politieke partijen en hun parlementaire fracties*, Brussels: VUB, Vakgroep Politieke Wetenschappen

Van Dam, D. (1997) *Flandre, Wallonie, le rêve brisé, quelles identités culturelles et politiques en Flandre et en Wallonie?*, Ottignies: Quorum

Van Dam, D. (1998), Histoire du mouvement Wallon, in M. Martiniello & M. Swyngedouw (eds), *Où va la Belgique? Les soubresauts d'une petite démocratie européenne*, Paris: L'Harmattan, pp. 73–84

Van den Brande, A. (1963), Elements for a sociological analysis of the impact of the main conflicts on Belgian political life, *Res Publica*, **9**(3): 535–52

Van den Wijngaert, M. (1976), *Ontstaan en stichting van de CVP/PSC. De lange weg naar het Kerstprogramma*, Antwerp: De Nederlandse Boekhandel

Van Dyck R. (1992), *Federalisme en democratie: bescherming van taalminderheden in plurale samenlevingen. Taalminderheden in de besluitvorming in België, Canada en Zwitserland*, Brussels: Studiecentrum voor Federalisme

Van Dyck, R. & Buelens, J. (1998), Regonalist parties in French-speaking Belgium: The Rassemblement Wallon and the Front Démocratique des

Francophones, in L. De Winter & H. Türsan, *Regionalist parties in Western Europe*, London: Routledge, pp. 51–69

Van Haute, E. & Pilet, J.B. (2006), Regionalist parties in Belgium (VU, RW, FDF): victims of their own success?, *Regional and Federal Studies*, 16(3): 297–314

Van Velthoven, H. & Witte, E. (1998), *Taal en politiek. De Belgische casus in een historisch perspectief*, Brussels: VUB Press

Vancoppenolle, D. & Legrain, A. (2003), Le new public management en Belgique: comparaison des réformes en Flandre et en Wallonie, *Administration Publique*, 2: 112–28

Vande Lanotte, J., Bracke, S. & Goedertier, G. (2003), *België voor beginners. Wegwijs in het Belgisch labyrint*, Bruges: Die Keure

Vangroenweghe, D. (1985), *Rood rubber. Leopold II en zijn Kongo*, Brussels-Amsterdam (French translation: *Du sang sur les lianes. Léopold II et son Congo*, Brussels 1986)

Vanthemsche, G. (2006), België en Congo, in E. Witte & A. Meynen (eds), *België na 1945*, Antwerp: Standaard Uitgeverij, pp. 511–42

Vanthemsche, G. (2007), *Nouvelle histoire de la Belgique: La Belgique et le Congo: empreintes d'une colonie, 1885–1980*, Brussels: Complexe

Velaers, J. & Van Goethem, H. (1994), *Leopold III. Het Land. De Koning. De Oorlog*, Tielt: Lannoo

Verhofstadt, G. (2006), *The United States of Europe: Manifesto for a new Europe*, London: The Federal Trust for Education & Research

Versmessen, E. (1995), In the kingdom of paradoxes: the Belgian regional and national elections of May 1995, *Regional and Federal Studies*, 5(2): 239–46

Vos, L. (1998a), Le mouvement flamand: un aperçu historique, in M. Martiniello & M. Swyngedouw (eds), *Où va la Belgique? Les soubresauts d'une petite démocratie européenne*, Paris: L'Harmattan, pp. 59–72

Vos, L. (1998b), The Flemish national question, in Deprez, K. & Vos, L., *Nationalism in Belgium. Shifting identities, 1870–1995*, Basingstoke: Macmillan – now Palgrave Macmillan, pp. 83–95

Watts, R.L. (1999), *Comparing federal systems*. Montreal: McGill-Queen's University Press

Wauters, B. (2005), Divisions within an ethno-regional party: The Volksunie in Belgium, *Regional and Federal Studies*, 15(3): 329–52

Wauters, B. & Weekers, K. (2008), Het gebruik van de voorkeurstem bij de federale parlementsverkiezingen van 10 juni 2007, *Res Publica*, 50(2): 49–88

Weekers, K, Noppe, J. & Maddens, B. (2005), 35 jaar overheidsfinanciering van politieke partijen in België (1970–2004), *Tijdschrift voor Bestuurswetenschappen en Publiekrecht*, 7: 447–465

Weekers, K., Vanlangenakker, I., Maddens, B. & Fiers, S. (2007), Inteelt troef? Het profiel van kandidaten en verkozenen bij de verkiezingen van 10 juni, *Samenleving en Politiek*, 14(6): 3–11

Wils, L. (1998), The two Belgian revolutions, in Deprez, K. & Vos, L.,

Nationalism in Belgium. Shifting identities, 1870–1995, Basingstoke: Macmillan – now Palgrave Macmillan, pp. 33–41

Witte, E. (1988), Hertoginnedal 1963–1988. Ontstaan en evolutie van een taalcompromis, *Taal en Sociale Integratie*, **12**: 19–36

Witte, E. (1993), Language and territoriality. A summary of developments in Belgium, *International Journal on Minority and Group Rights*, **1**(3): 203–23

Witte, E. & Van Velthoven, H. (2000), *Language and Politics. The situation in Belgium in historical perspective*, Brussels: VUB Press

Witte, E., Craeybeckx , J. & Meynen, A. (2000), *Political history of Belgium from 1830 onwards*, Brussels: VUB University Press

Witte, E., Gubin, E., Nandrin, J.P. & Deneckere, G. (2005), *Nouvelle histoire de la Belgique: 1830–1905*, Brussels: Complexe

Zolberg, A. (1974), The making of Flemings and Walloons: Belgium 1830–1914, *The Journal of Interdisciplinary History,* 5(2): 179–236

Index